France, ... the ...rbo... British Institute ...y of Lill... d w...te ... various maga-... ...urning to ...g..., Ro...'d Bergan has ...d several biograph...s, includin... *Jean Renoir: ...ons of Paradise*, *Dus... Hoffman* ...d *Beyond the ...ange and Beyond...* (a four-part biograp... of ...onathan M...ler, Alan Benne..., Peter Cook and ...dley ...oore) and ...e is currently w...rking on a biogra...y of ...isenstein. A...ong his other bo...ks are *The United ...tists ...ry* and *Th... Great Theatres of London*. He is a...so a ...ular contrib...tor to the *Guardian*.

Also by Ronald Bergan

Jean Renoir: Projections of Paradise

Dustin Hoffman

Beyond the Fringe . . . and Beyond

The Great Theatres of London

The United Artists Story

The Foreign Film Guide *(with Robyn Karney)*

Glamorous Musicals

ANTHONY PERKINS

A HAUNTED LIFE

Ronald Bergan

A *Warner* Book

First published in Great Britain by
by Little, Brown and Company 1995
This edition published by Warner Books 1996

A CIP catalogue record for this book is available from the British Library.

ISBN 0 7515 0661 3

Printed in England by Clays Ltd, St Ives plc

Warner Books
A Division of
Little, Brown and Company (UK)
Brettenham House
Lancaster Place
London WC2E 7EN

CONTENTS

'You have conquered and I yield. Yet, henceforward art thou also dead – dead to the World, to Heaven, and to Hope! In me didst thou exist – and, in my death, see by this image, which is thine own, how utterly thou hast murdered thyself.'

from *William Wilson* by Edgar Allan Poe

ANTHONY PERKINS (THE RONALD GRANT ARCHIVE).

AUTHOR'S NOTE AND ACKNOWLEDGEMENTS

I have taken the liberty of calling Anthony Perkins by the diminutive 'Tony' throughout, which is the name most of his friends and colleagues knew him by. I feel that, having spent a great deal of time researching, writing about and attempting to understand, the subject of my biography, I am entitled to use this familiar form, even though I met him but once, and briefly.

A mutual friend took me to meet the star backstage at the Ethel Barrymore Theatre in New York in November 1979 on the second night of *Romantic Comedy*. While Tony was removing his make-up at his dressing table, we spoke to his reflection in the mirror. He was stripped to the waist, revealing the smooth-skinned svelte figure of a man half his age – he was forty-seven at the time – and what the actor William Chappell described as 'an Egyptian torso, unnaturally broad in the shoulder and small in the waist and so flat it is almost one-dimensional'. The mirror image asked us what we thought of the play, and his performance in particular, in a manner devoid of conceit or false modesty, as if his whole future lay in our replies. Because of the sincerity with which he imbued the question, my friend and I thought he was entitled to equal candour from us, rather than 'you were fabulous, darling' comments that are the commonplace of dressing-room talk. Fortunately, we had enjoyed his stylish, comic, performance and, with only minor reservations, the play. At our remarks, he flashed us the famous smile I had seen so often on screen, the smile that would convince anyone, as it did Norman Bates's victims, that he 'wouldn't even harm a fly'. Tony had that elusive attribute called charm, almost in its original supernatural sense of being able to ward off evil; ironic, considering the role with which he would always be identified. My short meeting with him put me in mind of the first lines of Joseph Heller's novel *Catch-22*, in the film of which Tony played the chaplain.

'It was love at first sight. The first time Yossarian saw the chaplain he fell madly in love with him.'

The following people were invaluable, in different ways, in helping me towards a familiarity with my subject, and in justifying my calling him Tony.

I am indebted to Robert Anderson, who went out of his way to talk to me about the production of *Tea and Sympathy*, and put me in touch with Teresa Wright, who took the trouble to telephone me from the USA; Brian Baxter and Patrick Duynslaeger, who recounted a couple of illuminating and amusing anecdotes; Noel Black, Claude Chabrol, Jules Dassin, Michael Ferguson, Nicolas Gessner, Curtis Harrington and Stanley Kramer, who provided me with insights into Tony's talent from a director's point of view, and Brian Sandler from the writer's; Ian Johnstone, who recalled his interview with Tony at the National Film Theatre in London; and John Kerr, the law's gain and the movies' loss, who gave me some extremely valuable material regarding Tony's boyhood.

Many thanks to Laura Kay Palmer, whose inestimable book,

Osgood and Anthony Perkins, acted as my compass throughout my journey, and who personally guided me through the intricacies of the Lincoln Center Library; Stephen Rebello, whose exemplary *Alfred Hitchcock and the Making of Psycho* I shamelessly plundered for information, and Frank Rose for his perceptive article, 'The Prodigal Son' in *Premiere* magazine, both of whom took time to speak to me; David Thompson, who generously made me video tapes of films I hadn't been able to see; Stephen Jenkins, from the BBC, who kindly arranged a couple of screenings for me; and Tom Vallance, who afforded me the chance to listen to Tony Perkins's recordings and a rare opportunity to see *Evening Primrose.*

I'm also exceedingly grateful to Ben Bagley, Alan Helms, Miles Kreuger, Christopher Makos and Dodson Rader for being so forthcoming about their personal knowledge of Tony. Finally, immense gratitude to Gilbert Adair, who first gave me the idea for the book, to Clive Hirschhorn for letting me use his library in the peace of the countryside, and to Robyn Karney, my editor, long-time friend and colleague, whose professionalism, expertise and consideration for the author, makes her a *rara avis* in the publishing world of today.

Ronald Bergan

Part I

A BOY'S BEST FRIEND IS HIS MOTHER

1

I AM NORMAN BATES

'*Well, a son is a poor substitute for a lover*' – Norman Bates in *Psycho* (1960).

Someone must have been telling lies about Anthony P., for without having done anything wrong he was arrested one fine morning. In fact, he had merely woken from one of his recurring nightmares of guilt and displacement.

Tony had arrived at the remote Bates Motel during a heavy rain storm and rung the buzzer, which echoed through the Gothic house on the hillside behind the motel. A light was on in one of the upper windows. From there, he heard an old woman's voice.

'You're a Mamma's Boy. That's what all your little playmates called you, and that's what you were. Were, are, and always will be!'

Norman Bates's ears pricked up at the signal that a customer had arrived at the motel. He turned his back on his mother, who was in one of her bad moods, walked into the hall, took his raincoat from the hanger, and went out into the darkness.

Tony was waiting outside the office.

'Looking for a room?' asked Norman, who could not see Tony clearly in the dark.

Tony drew out a knife and lunged at Norman, who managed to dodge the weapon, though he slipped in the mud beneath his feet. Tony pounced on Norman, and the two of them struggled in the mud for possession of the knife. Suddenly, Norman gave a cry of anguish as the blade sank into his heart.

When they came to arrest Tony, he protested his innocence on the grounds that, not only was Norman Bates a fictional character, but so was he. He sang them a Rodgers and Hart song he had recorded in 1978, 'I'm talking to my pal.'

Tony woke with a start. His mind was still in the dilapidated house on the hill near Fairvale, where thunder and lightning perpetually raged; his body was in his spacious and comfortable Hollywood hacienda under the eternal California sunshine. Norman Bates and Anthony Perkins had haunted each other for years, and each had vainly tried to kill the other. The problem was that they were ineluctably drawn to each other. Being both alike and opposites, they found it difficult to live apart.

On the surface, Anthony Perkins and Norman Bates had little in common. In Robert Bloch's 1959 novel, Bates was plump, balding, bespectacled and forty years old – the physical antithesis of the lean, lanky, and boyishly good-looking twenty-eight-year-old actor. Despite his reclusive nature, Tony was a cosmopolitan creature with a cultivated circle of friends, and had been acting professionally since his teens. Norman lived a sterile and isolated existence in which his only hobby was stuffing birds. Tony was bright, talented, gentle, generous and sardonically witty, some of which qualities rubbed off on Norman. Notwithstanding Tony's hidden traumas, there was no possibility of his becoming a matricidal or serial killer, or a necrophiliac.

But both Perkins and Bates were the only children of over-possessive mothers and absent fathers. Both Norman and Tony's fathers died when the boys were five years old. Both were tortured loners with a deep fear of women, and shared a crippling shyness and a fear of intimacy, which psychiatrists put down to their mother-smothered childhoods.

'She had to raise me all by herself after my father died. I was only five, and it must have been quite a strain for her,' Norman Bates tells Marion Crane (Janet Leigh), his potential murder victim in *Psycho.*

In the final minutes of the film, the psychiatrist Dr Richman (Simon Oakland) comments: 'Now he was already dangerously disturbed – had been ever since his father died. His mother was a clinging, demanding woman, and for years the two of them lived as if there was no one else in the world.'

Tony, though as harmless and hinged as Norman was harmful and unhinged, claimed to have suffered from the classic Oedipus complex symptoms, which his years in psychotherapy helped him confront. Using the language offered by his shrink sessions, Tony confessed: 'I loved my father but I also wanted him dead so I could have my mother to myself.'

This revelation was expounded, with variations, in several press interviews Tony gave in the late 1970s, when he was feeling more secure, enveloped as he was in a reassuring marriage. True or not, he had certainly begun to believe it.

'If he felt a strong attraction to any other woman, the mother side of him would go wild.'

The voice is Dr Richman's again, describing the motivations behind the homicidal actions of his patient Norman Bates, at the conclusion of *Psycho.*

Of Norman's mother, Tony once commented, 'She is so

undependable . . . she has moments of true affection and moments of love for Norman. He's not always on his guard about what betrayal or horror she's going to come up with next, because she suckers him into being tender and sweet with her.'

Janet Esselstyn Rane Perkins, Anthony Perkins's mother, known to her friends as Jane or Janey, has been described as a strong-willed, overbearing New England woman, who controlled every detail of her son's life. After her husband's premature death, she drew almost incestuously close to him. Yet Tony's description of Mrs Perkins makes her sound suspiciously like Mrs Bates. An interchange between role-playing and reality; a deliberate muddling of character and actor?

Accordingly to Tony's own testimony, his mother was constantly touching and caressing him, often stroking his thighs right up to his crotch.

'She didn't mean any harm, but she clearly channelled all the feelings she had had for my father onto me. We were more like lovers than mother and son.'

The confusion was compounded in an interview Tony gave Mim Udovitch in November 1990, at the time of the release of *Psycho IV*. He answers her question about Norman Bates by referring to himself.

'Do you think there was sexual abuse?'

'Yes. When I was a kid I had recurring nightmares of a clash of universes. They were cosmic nightmares. It was probably the clash between my fear of my father and my love for my mother.'

'You were frightened of your father?'

'Well, virtually all small children are frightened of their fathers. They fear their father's wrath should it be disclosed that the child loves the mother so much.'

'A boy's best friend is his mother.'

'She's not only his best friend, she's his most ardent lover.'

However, until his psychotherapy helped him to understand himself more fully, he had blocked this from his mind. Previously he had described his mother as a puritanical woman who had packed him off to boarding school and barely touched him at all. ('She was a product of her time. A product of sexual repression' – Norman Bates on his mother in *Psycho IV*).

No wonder he found it difficult to have a 'normal' relationship in adult life. Tony, whose main sexual drive, willy-nilly, was towards men, was appalled at the thought of having sex with a woman, until he was in his fortieth year.

'I saw women as beautiful predators,' he explained.

Joseph Stefano, who wrote the screenplay of *Psycho*, and was in psychoanalysis when he was hired by Alfred Hitchcock, knew almost nothing of Tony's family background. He had no idea that the elder Perkins had died of a heart attack when Tony was five; the same age as Norman at his father's death. (Likewise, Orson Welles did not realize that when he cast Tony in *The Trial*, the actor, at thirty, was exactly the age of Joseph K.) Nor was Stefano aware of Tony's relationship with his mother. Any similarities between the performer and the role were, as they say, purely coincidental.

Stefano was interested in how such intimacy with a formidable and overprotective mother could make Norman into a killer. So he wrote a scene between the adolescent Norman and Mrs Bates that was never intended to be shot. In the scene, which Stefano explained to Tony during the shoot, the boy and his mother are larking about on the floor. Suddenly she discovers that he has an erection, and her joy turns to hysterical anger. Screaming that he must forget he has such a disgusting part of the body, she pulls a dress over his head, smears his face with lipstick and locks him in a dark closet. (Stefano was eventually able to include this more explicit scene in the flashback to Norman Bates's adolescence in *Psycho IV*, Norman's last film appearance.)

Tony listened to Stefano silently. He must have been simultaneously attracted and repelled by what he heard. It certainly would have touched a nerve, because the complex and stifling mother-son bond had remained unvoiced except to a few very close friends. But the actor in him would have overridden any qualms or pain. How often does a part come along in which one can so easily find a point of reference? He was not to know then that Norman Bates would take over his public life and career to an eerie and finally detrimental degree. Paradoxically, Tony had to strive to 'live down' not a poor performance, but his greatest one.

'I couldn't believe that all the other films I had done previously had been forgotten, and that I was being narrowed into this one image that other people had of me.'

As much as Norman Bates literally 'identified' with his dead mother, Anthony Perkins believed he had become too closely connected with the deranged motel keeper. He fled to Europe to elude the other's shadow, but Norman was always dogging his footsteps in various guises. (Some years later, in Wales, was he the other Mr Perkins who mistakenly received a parcel of drugs meant for Tony, and called the police?) Finally, the actor came to terms with his alter ego by again confronting him directly after their first meeting – three times in the course of two decades.

'Face it, gang,' the actor told his friends. 'I *am* Norman Bates.'

Nevertheless, an extremely professional and experienced performer like Anthony Perkins realized that he was neither Norman Bates nor Joseph K. nor the many psychotic ghouls or even the sensitive young romantic heroes he played. Everyone knows that actors and their roles are disconnected and autonomous entities. Unlike biographies of authors, playwrights or film directors, biographies of film stars usually make a sharp differentiation between the life and the work. After all, don't actors only interpret the imaginings of directors and writers? Actors, with the complicity of audiences, generally know where fantasy ends and reality begins. Yet, in the case of Anthony Perkins, there was such an interplay and intersecting of the portrayals with his own life and personality, that the separation between the two worlds does not fall so easily into distinct blocks. It frequently seemed as if the roles he chose, whether consciously or not, reflected aspects of his emotive, imagined or absolute existence. Inevitably, therefore, there was a certain amount of blurring of the lines between the actor and the characters he embodied. In addition, everyone invents their lives to a certain degree and, due to the nature of their craft, actors are inclined to do so more than most. Now and again, the personality or personalities they have constructed are reinvented internally or by exterior events.

Was Norman Bates homosexual? According to Theodore Price in his sententious and simplistic book, *Hitchcock and Homosexuality*. 'No one says it straight out . . . [but] the not very manly mama's boy of the film, Tony Perkins, who might think that he wishes to go to bed with a girl (but never does and only looks), is a homosexual.'

This is the crossing of a psychological and ethical minefield, not only because the dogmatic statement suggests a link between homosexuality and murder, but because it denies the fact that Bates obviously gets a vicarious thrill from watching Marion Crane undress through his peephole. Indeed, when Dr Richman is expounding his theories to Lila Crane (Vera Miles), the victim's sister, he says,

'When he met your sister, he was touched by her – aroused by her. He wanted her. That set off the "jealous mother" and "mother killed the girl!"'

On Norman Bates's return to the screen many years later in *Psychos II, III* and *IV*, he became progressively more heterosexual with each film, finally marrying and becoming a father, thus mirroring Tony's own evolution: he had moved from a masturbating Master Bates to Mister Bates; from Norman Bates to Normal Bates.

Peter Biskind in *Seeing is Believing*, arrived at a more carefully considered conclusion than Theodore Price.

'By using Perkins for this role, Hitchcock could not help but make a comment on the kind of masculinity Perkins represented, after playing all those men who wore aprons in the 1950s. For Hitchcock, like everyone else, the handwriting was on the wall. Softness in men was a slippery slope. A few tears today might be a flood tomorrow. Suppose men were too sensitive – gay even? While *Rebel Without a Cause* came out for the Feminized Man, it was careful . . . to call a halt, and with Plato [Sal Mineo] we saw where feminization stopped and unhealthy homo-eroticism began.'

This may have some validity in that Hitchcock once said, 'Any profession that calls for a man to have to use paint and powder on his face to earn a living gives me evil thoughts.'

Tony Perkins's screen persona, as exemplified in the 1950s and early 1960s, was what Biskind calls the 'Feminized Man.' (In the 80s, he became 'The New Man.') A new generation of actors betokened a new masculinity – sensitive, vulnerable, unafraid to expose their most naked emotions. This 'Feminization' was unconnected with sexual predilection, because homosexual actors such as Rock Hudson, George Nader and Tab Hunter displayed traditional 'masculine' images, while heterosexuals like Warren Beatty, Marlon Brando, Paul Newman, John Derek, John Kerr and Robert Wagner exhibited 'feminine' qualities. There is some likelihood, however, that homosexuals like Tony

Perkins, Montgomery Clift, Sal Mineo, and the bisexual James Dean might have found it easier to get in touch with their feelings.

As a result of the moral climate in the 1950s, when Tony started out as a professional actor, gay stars were terrified of being exposed. This fear was particularly profound in Perkins because he was self-conscious, shy, and uneasy in the limelight. He was also afraid of being seen by the public in any way that might reflect badly upon him.

Tony's homosexuality was therefore complicated by a sense of guilt and a refusal to accept his nature. Predating Gay Pride, he was of the Gay Shame generation, extremely uncomfortable about his sexuality and prepared to undergo extensive psychotherapy in the hope that his desires could be altered. It was not, after all, until the 1970s that homosexuality was officially struck off the American Psychiatric Association's list of what are decreed to be aberrations.

Though it never changed his attraction to men, psychotherapy, at least, eliminated his aversion to having sex with a woman, and allowed him to make his first relatively mature commitment to another person. Tony finally attained the haven of contentment and stability he was seeking all his life, only to have it tragically invaded by the contemporary equivalent of the Black Death. Yet even at the funeral, his pal/foe hovered, and tabloid headlines shrieked: 'Norman Bates Dies Of AIDS'.

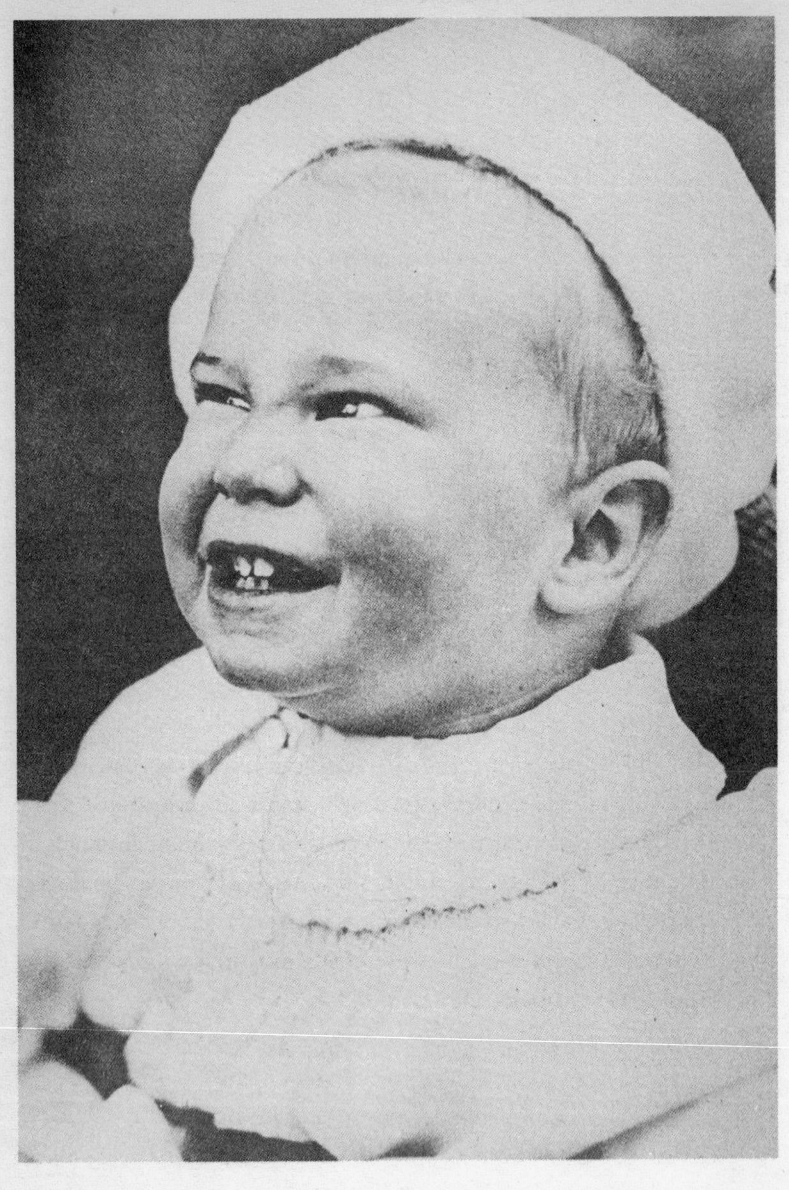

ANTHONY PERKINS AT TEN MONTHS OLD (*ANTHONY PERKINS STORY* MAGAZINE).

2

PRIVATE TRAPS

'*You know what I think? I think that we're all in our private traps – clamped in them*' – Norman Bates in *Psycho* (1960)

Leaving the memorial service for Osgood Perkins at the Little Church Around the Corner in New York, a few days after his father's death on 20 September, 1937, little Tony remained completely composed. ('I felt so sad, mainly because of how my mother looked. How she looked about always decided how I felt at any given moment. She looked so sorrowful all in black' – *Psycho IV*.) When an aunt consolingly caught his hand, he shook off her grasp, held his head high and walked out. Afterwards Tony and his mother took the train to Florida in an attempt to palliate their loss. That first night, as they started for the dining car, the five-year-old boy affectionately clutched his mother's arm and said, 'We're going to be alright, aren't we mother?'

She reassured him, but the widow had discovered that her husband had been under-insured, and left an estate of a mere $10,000.

A few days later, Tony, who was good at drawing with crayons and water-colours, sat painting left-handedly on the floor of the hotel suite, when he looked up at his mother and said with almost imperceptible sadness,

'Isn't it nice that Daddy taught me how to paint before he had to go away?'

Although Tony had spent most of his time with his mother while his father was away working, the boy remembered the first and last summer vacation they spent together on Fire Island, a few months before his father's death. They swam, fished, went sailing, and explored the island together. Father and son were beginning to get to know each other. Perkins Senior told his wife that he was relieved and happy to find Tony such an intelligent and imaginative boy. Unfortunately, even then his father had to slip back to New York to rehearse a play and do some radio programmes, leaving Tony to be looked after by friends. For Osgood Perkins was one of the most renowned actors on Broadway.

On 4 April 1932, Osgood Perkins was busy rehearsing for a new Broadway comedy, *Foreign Affairs*, when he heard the news that his wife had given birth to a son. He had become a father for the first time at forty-two, the exact same age as Tony would be when *his* first child was born. With either uncanny prescience or cock-eyed optimism, Osgood named the baby Anthony Perkins, deliberately giving him a seven-letter first name so that it would balance his last name on a theatre marquee.

It had taken Mrs Perkins almost ten years of marriage to persuade her reluctant husband that they should have a child. Like many children born comparatively late in a marriage, Tony was heavily pampered. At three-and-a-half, he was sent to a private nursery school, where he took a piano lesson every day, and learned French, which he picked up quickly. (This would stand him in good stead when embarking on an international career.)

In the afternoons he would come home and get out his paints. When he was bored with art, he would ask to be read to. Half an hour later he might decide to paste pictures in a scrap book or just go outside and play – sometimes with friends but more often alone. Restlessness was a trait noticed early on by his mother.

'I sometimes wonder how my son concentrates on a script and learns all of his lines. Then I think back – and I know the answer. Whenever Tony has become truly interested in something, he has followed it through all the way. But it must be his own interest, of his own choice – or there must be a good reason for applying himself. From babyhood, Tony had been very much the individual, and Osgood and I felt ourselves fortunate; even in the qualities about Tony that sometimes confused us. His intelligence and his imagination reached out in so many directions. As he grew the restlessness remained. The sudden impatience with the project of the moment. Even today [1958] when he isn't working, Tony will stroll aimlessly for hours, then rush home and listen to records, then swim or play on the xylophone or his guitar, then go to a movie or wander through a museum or just stay home and read.'

Shortly after his father died, Tony had a bout of scarlet fever and also contracted a mild tubercular infection from a maid, who later died of it. This resulted in his needing a good ten hours of sleep a night.

'I'm a wreck . . . When I'm tired, I stutter and my eyes cross. Even on the night *Look Homeward, Angel* opened on Broadway, I couldn't wait up for all the reviews.'

He would also find it virtually impossible to gain weight – at six-foot-two, he weighed a constant one hundred and sixty pounds.

John Kerr, the actor who had made his name on Broadway in *Tea and Sympathy* before going to Hollywood, went to the same school as Tony at East 67th Street in Manhattan – Miss Carden's private school – when they were around eight and nine respectively. Miss Carden encouraged the pupils to speak French.

When Tony was two, his parents had given him a small male Boston terrier, named Medor. John Kerr was impressed by the way Tony and his mother would address the dog in French, something which Kerr did not find at all pretentious. Medor lived to the age of twelve, and when he died Tony begged for another pet. His mother took him down to the pound and picked up a short-haired, part-terrier mongrel pup. Tony named him Skippy, and spent endless hours teaching him tricks. He was always inordinately fond of dogs, and throughout his life he had canine companions on which he generally bestowed far more affection than he reserved for most humans. During his early teens, besides baby-sitting for friends for extra pocket money, he would meet people walking their dogs in the street, and offer his services as a dog-walker. Thus he became one of the busiest dog-walkers in Manhattan.

'I like the sound of money jingling in my pocket,' he once told his mother.

Although Tony was a fairly solitary child, he seemed, to John Kerr, quite a happy one. Despite not having any great enthusiasm for sports, the very slender, long-legged gazelle-like youth was a fast runner.

'He was also a terrific mimic and always had a wonderfully wry sense of humour,' Kerr recalled.

Tony claimed to have had a chemistry set as a child, with which he prepared a red mixture which exploded. Following the explosion, his mother rushed into the room to investigate.

'When she saw the gory mess dripping from all sides, she screamed, then fainted. She thought that stuff on the wall was me.'

This story, true or false, told to a *Modern Screen* interviewer in

1957 when Tony was a twenty-four-year-old Hollywood pin-up boy, and long before he gained his gory reputation, reveals a blackly humorous streak.

Kerr would often visit the Perkins apartment. Kerr's mother, June Walker, had appeared in summer stock and on Broadway with Osgood in the early 1930s, and she and Jane Perkins were involved in the Women's Civilian Defense Corps during the war. The young Kerr always found Mrs Perkins, whom he recalls mostly in uniform at that period, a very intelligent and warm person.

Jane Wyatt, who had acted on stage with Osgood Perkins, remembers Jane Perkins as 'a very nice looking, warm and welcoming sort of person. I liked her very much. Jane didn't have time to come to rehearsals or hang around the theatre so I saw little of her. But they did have little after-the-theatre parties and I was invited. Tony was in a kiddie coop, and seemed a well-behaved baby, much indulged by his parents.'

How unlike the portrait of the monster mother and the feared father as painted by Tony himself! One wonders what sleeping serpents were stirred up in his mind by psychoanalysis later in his life.

Someone must have been telling lies about Anthony P., for without having done anything wrong he was packed off to boarding school one fine morning. It was this separation from his mother that caused him to suffer the first real trauma of his youth. Like many sensitive children, before and since, he felt that he had been sent there as a punishment and because his mother had stopped loving him. He found the situation difficult to come to terms with, particularly since he had always gone out of his way to gain her approval.

There was an element in most of his performances where one can see this need to ingratiate himself with audiences, no matter what kind of character he was playing. This usually manifested itself in a dazzling, heartfelt smile or a little-boy-lost look, acting devices which occasionally became strained, especially as he grew older. 'I can't stand to think that there's anybody anywhere who doesn't like me,' Tony once said. ('Since I've known you I've played the brilliant young lawyer, the bashful lover, the spoiled child – God knows what else. But it's all been for you, only for you. Don't you think that's love?' – *Goodbye Again.*) However, it is not difficult to imagine that these tricks seldom failed to work on a doting mother. If they were effective with her, why not with all those people sitting out there in the dark?

Although there can be no possible access to his private couch-talk files with his analyst Mildred Newman, many of her theories (which she no doubt expounded to Tony when applicable) can be gleaned from the slim best-selling book, *How To Be Your Own Best Friend*, a record of conversations with Newman and her husband Bernard Berkovitch.

'At five, we need our mother; we must please and pacify her to get the things we need. Our life literally depends on doing so. To accomplish our own thing as children, we must be able to manipulate adults. To get a candy bar or go to the movies, we must win them over. So it is appropriate in childhood, to look to others, to learn how to invoke their love, sympathy or understanding . . . The mistake lies in carrying this sense of helplessness, this need to placate others, into adulthood. What was once a fact has become a fantasy. As an adult, everything doesn't depend on pleasing others. What others once did for you, you can now do for yourself. When you're thirty you don't need your mother to love you the way she did when you were three. You don't need to feel about her as you did then. You don't have to fear her anger anymore . . .'

If there were events in Tony's life on which he drew in order to bring more authenticity to his portrayals – part of a technique encouraged by the Method school, strongly influential at the time he was making a name for himself – then his school experiences, either consciously or unconsciously, would have borne upon his interpretation of Tom Lee in *Tea and Sympathy* when he was twenty-two years old.

'I loathed school. At prep school they tell you, "We know you can do better", so I never did.'

Tony was twelve years old when he arrived at Brooks School in North Andover, Massachussetts, about a hundred miles from his home at Brookline, where he and his mother had moved, and where she ran the Boston Stage Door Canteen. He found the school 'all but completely buried me forever. I never had a happy hour in three years at *that* place. I had no friends. I spent all my time alone. I was someone that people could say they didn't like in order to get themselves accepted. For the first year and a half, I did not think that I could survive.'

Brooks School was modelled on an English public school, with the same kind of conformity and discipline behind the ivy-covered brick walls and on the hard playing fields. Tony spent most of his free time reading – Dickens became a favourite author, mainly because of his understanding of the sufferings of sensitive children in unsympathetic environments. In his self-dramatizing way, Tony saw himself as David Copperfield at Salem House, and as a pupil at Dotheboys Hall.

During his second year, he caught scarlet fever again and was delighted to be sent back to mother. But it was only a temporary reprieve and he was back again in the hated surroundings the following term. At least Brooks 'taught me not to run away from any issue. After my time there, I could face any eventuality with complete control.'

Yet, a number of reminiscences he penned some years later for *The Flamingo*, his Rollins College literary magazine, have the nostalgic glow of the Laurenceville School *Saturday Evening Post* stories of Owen Johnson, with elements of Kipling and Horatio Alger. To paraphrase Tolstoy, all happy recollections of schooldays resemble one another, but each unhappy recollection is unhappy in its own way.

In the autumn of 1952, Tony wrote, in *Brooks Revisited*:

'He visited his old rooms. The cubicle in Whitney and the room with two windows in Thorne House. Out of these the view remained unchanged; the Junior Varsity football field, a grove of pines, and then the slow hill to the lake. Back in the main buildings he walked through the study halls, found his old desk with his dates scratched deeply in the top . . . On the walls group pictures of yesterday's boys smiled out of dusty frames . . . Further down the hall in the library he found the books he had read as a boy. Their cards bore his name, a pencilled, disorganized scrawl. The lambent sun flickered in through the windows. It was late afternoon when he finally left . . . Gone, gone. The clatter of many shoes through the halls at noon bell. The shouts and smiles of friends of other years. And all the way down the darkening poplar-lined drive to the road, the pleas enticed him back, of familiar voices, long remembered, long forgotten.'

In another memoir, *Brooks Recalled*, he tells a story of the death on the football field of Bob Mauk, 'a favoured senior and house prefect at Old Whitney, the dormitory in which I lived . . .'

'That evening at bedtime there was no one to speed us along, to shut off the lights and read to us from John Buchan's *The Path of the King* . . . We felt quite alone, and, standing by our beds in the darkness, we whispered to each other over the walls, half expecting, and hoping too, that Mauk would rush out of his door and stand in a square of light and fiercely say that he'd count ten and anyone who wasn't in bed would translate Caesar's wars into French until he passed out over the book. But that long hall remained dark and silent and one by one we gave it up and returned to our beds and fell fitfully asleep.'

At fifteen Tony was sent to Browne and Nichols college prep school at Cambridge, Massachusetts, nearer home and where he seemed slightly happier. There he had the makings of a successful capitalist. He would trade a thermos bottle for a tennis racket, sell the racket and make enough money to buy two more thermos bottles. During the same period, he also ran a record shop, buying records cheap from schoolmates, then selling them at a profit. Yet in his adult life, although he made a comfortable living, and was neither a miser nor a spendthrift, he did not go into film production like many of his contemporaries.

'I've never really had the clout to form my own production company,' Tony remarked in the early 1980s. 'You have at least to have accumulated a bunch of box-office hits before you can put yourself in that position. I don't like inveigling myself in different departments. My career fell between two periods in film-making. Between the 30s and 40s when one was under contract, and the 70s and 80s where actors took more control. To be an actor waiting for the agent to ring is a disadvantageous thing. But it makes you so grateful when the phone does ring.'

From childhood, because of his mother's limited income (she first ran the Stage Door Canteen in Boston, and then did secretarial work for theatrical agencies) he learned to be practical with money, which took on a certain significance. This accounts for the many sub-standard roles he chose later in his career, which were based on dollars rather than artistic considerations.

At high school, Tony expressed his resentment of formality by refusing to study those subjects he considered useless for his purposes: science and mathematics. His teachers finally told him that failure in these examinations would mean failure to graduate. ('All the teachers were against me' – *Ten Day's Wonder.*) Because he knew that his mother would be disappointed in him if he failed, he studied ferociously with her all summer. When the tests came, he passed.

'His feelings for me were more important than his distaste for algebra,' she explained. 'That's where the real test of a person comes, and that's where Tony always passes. He will do anything if it means sparing the feelings of someone he really cares for.'

Nevertheless, those summer studies were a chore. He did not concentrate on them with one-tenth of the intensity he devoted to subjects he loved outside school: music, art, literature. Though he was later to play two sporting heroes on film (in *Fear Strikes Out* and *Tall Story*), he managed to avoid most sports.

'Whatever Tony did, he did completely,' remembered Henry Scammell, an ex-school friend. 'When he broke the rules, he broke them with a vengeance. When he read, he devoured his books. When he joined the drama society, he was not only the first to memorize his lines, he memorized the entire play in case he had to prompt someone else. I don't recall a single moment in which Tony doubted his ability to become a great actor.'

But Tony still hardly made a move without consulting his mother. She recalled a story that is revealing about her blind devotion and suffocating attitude towards him.

'I remember when we were living at Cambridge, Mass., and Tony was attending high school. He'd go out with the other boys in the evenings, but he would always phone me, saying where he was going and when he would be home. Once, he didn't call and he didn't show up all night. Naturally I was worried sick. Later, I learned what had happened. Tony and some of his pals had gone to a cafe a few miles out of town. The fellows sat around drinking Cokes and playing the jukebox. When Tony noticed it was getting late, he suggested they leave. But the others weren't ready to go. Tony ambled off by himself and, not having a car, thumbed a ride. The auto broke down and Tony tried to help the man fix it. Finally they phoned for a mechanic, but by the time the car was repaired and Tony had arrived within the city limits, it was early in the morning, and he went to a schoolfriend where he bunked for the night.

'"Mother, I didn't want to come in so late and wake you," he explained the next morning.'

This rather naive trust in her darling son – she failed to explain why he didn't ring her to tell her he would be late – may go some way towards understanding why he never wished her to discover, let alone accept, his unspoken longings. Hence his 'restlessness', reflected in his erratic career and peripatetic way of life. (In contrast, Norman Bates seldom strayed further than Fairvale, and stuck to only two tenuously related hobbies – taxidermy and homicide.) Until Tony and his family settled in the home he bought in Hollywood in 1977, when he was forty five, he had never remained in one place for very long. He had a horror of being hemmed in by literal or figurative walls.

One of his favourite songs, which he sang as a lullaby to his two sons when they were babies, was Cole Porter's 'Don't Fence Me In'. The lyrics about being free resound like an adjuration to all those ghosts and people – his father, mother, friends, critics, biographers and audiences, as well as society at large, who haunted him and attempted to categorize, constrain and circumscribe him.

3

I AM THY FATHER'S SPIRIT

'How'd I do, dad?' – Jim Piersall in *Fear Strikes Out* (1957).

In his early teens, Tony never dared say openly that he nursed the desire to be an actor like his father. He tried to cover it by displaying many different enthusiasms. However, when he was around ten years old, he came across a number of play-scripts of his father's in the apartment. When alone, he would read them aloud, taking all the parts.

'It didn't seem that difficult to make sense out of a line of dialogue on the page.'

Although these readings were solitary activities, his mother suspected a more than usual interest in the theatre and in performing. Harry Young, a friend of Jane's, was running a summer stock company at Brattleboro in Vermont. She approached him to ask whether Tony might play a few small parts. He agreed on the condition that she would also come and run the box-office. Naturally, this suited her because she would be able to keep an eye on her son. Up to this point Tony had never expressed any wish to

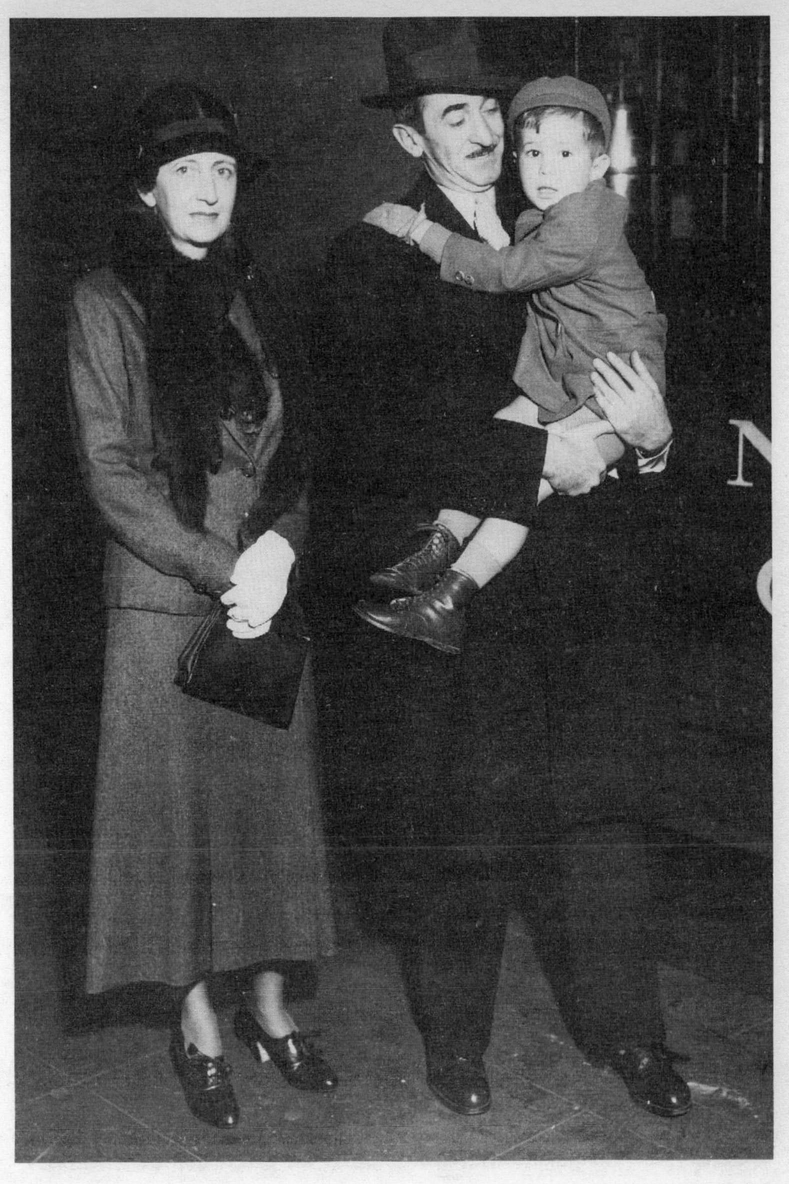

Osgood and Jane Perkins with four-year-old Tony (New York Public Library at Lincoln Center).

act, so she said nothing to him about her request to Harry Young.

'As with so many things he wants badly, he never gives a clue to show how much he does want them,' his mother remarked.

That summer of 1947, according to Mrs Perkins, she and Tony were driving up to the playhouse when she asked, 'Would you like to appear in some of the plays?'

'Well,' said Tony softly, looking away from her out of the window, 'I guess so.'

When they arrived Harry Young looked the tall fifteen-year-old over, and said that there happened to be parts for kids in the three plays they were putting on, and he would give Tony a chance.

Tony remembered his entry into the theatre rather differently.

'I got into acting perhaps because I was unconsciously into the idea of completing my father's career as well as beginning my own. Right after World War II, the summer theatres on the East Coast were starting up all over again. People were out of the habit of applying for work in them, particularly backstage and doing some of the scruffier stuff, and producers of summer theatres had to go round and give lectures to school kids and almost induce them to come and work for them. Nowadays, rich parents pay to have their kids taken on. I was one of those who heard one of these lectures and it seemed like twenty-five dollars a week was more than I could spend and a chance to play some parts and it seemed right up my alley.'

What Harry Young was actually hiring was a 'dirty boy', as summer stock apprentices were called. Tony was expected to sweep the stage, clean up paint buckets and help nail scenery together, but the job allowed him to make his professional acting debut. This took place on 30 June, 1947 at the Brattleboro Town Hall (now a police station) in *Junior Miss*, a comedy by Jerome Chodorov and Joseph Fields which had been filmed by twentieth Century-Fox in 1945. He played Haskell Cummings Jr, the escort of a young girl to her first formal party.

In *Kiss and Tell*, which had also been filmed previously as a vehicle for the adolescent Shirley Temple, Tony was the 'nasty kid brother' of the heroine, and in *George Washington Slept Here* by Moss Hart and George S. Kaufman, he played Raymond, the obnoxious nephew who creates havoc when dumped on a couple trying to restore a ramshackle house in the country.

These initial roles set the pattern for the next few years, during which he oscillated between playing swains in their late teens and brats in their early teens in warmed-over Broadway hits from past seasons.

Tony continued to gain experience in stock during the following three summers. In 1950, at the Robin Hood Theatre in Arden, Delaware, he had his most significant role, though there was nothing in it to make it seem so at the time. It was the small part of Fred Whitmarsh, the rather stiff young beau of the heroine of *Years Ago*, a semi-autobiographical play by Ruth Gordon. Three years later, due to his own efforts, he would make his screen debut in the role in the film version, retitled *The Actress*.

As befitted his background and personality, Tony took to acting with a certain ease, but it gave him a craving to do more. This was not satisfied by working in summer stock during every high school holiday, and it determined him to turn a vacation into a vocation.

After her husband's death, Jane Perkins made it a policy to mention Osgood to Tony almost every day, and there were photographs of him around the New York apartment. Despite being familiar with his father's looks through these photographs and stills, Tony was only able to assess his father's acting talent from the few of his films available.

He was only three and a half when he first saw his father act in a short-lived comedy on Broadway called *On Stage*, but from both actual memory and subsequent information, he recalled,

'He had a bit in that play where he played an author who was writing a play and found himself in the play that he was writing. And to test the presence of the study where he was doing the writing he crossed the stage feeling the presence of the fourth wall. And he did it so well – it was such an electric moment – that he was able to hold the audience's interest all the way from one side of the stage all the way to the other, walking very slowly, just feeling, holding onto the wall. It must have been a kind of triumph of almost pantomime rather than acting.'

The first role he had seen his father play, of which he had a clear recollection, was the slimy, spineless mobster Johnny Lovo in *Scarface*, the controversial Howard Hawks film. Although it was released concurrently with Tony's birth, he was taken by his mother to a re-showing some ten years later.

Johnny Lovo was based on Johnny Torrio, a major instigator of organized crime in the USA, a nasty hoodlum who got others to do his dirty work. Osgood was unafraid to paint a portrait of a vicious rat, without a semblance of charm, a quality that his son would later find hard to dispense with, however irredeemable the character.

'That guy is soft – I can see it in his face,' says Tony Carmonte (Paul Muni) of Lovo, who sports silk dressing-gowns and lives in a swanky apartment with his mistress Poppy (Karen Morley), a cool sexy blonde.

'She don't like anybody but me,' Lovo says with more self-delusion than self-satisfaction about Poppy, who very rapidly starts making eyes at Carmonte. Lovo realizes this later in a nightclub when he tries to light Poppy's cigarette but is beaten to it by Carmonte.

Osgood Perkins as Lovo has a longish pointed nose, a little

Adolphe Menjou moustache and greasy hair parted down the middle. His voice, which is thin, flat and nasal, rises to a falsetto when he gets excited or unnerved. When his time comes, and Tony Carmonte confronts him with a sub-machine gun, Johnny Lovo becomes a snivelling coward. He gulps and shakily pours himself a drink, pleading,

'Gimme a chance!'

It seems that Osgood – who once complained about having to play gangsters on the grounds that, 'I was born and brought up in Boston. Please let me speak English' – based his performance on a soldier who was in his regiment in World War I, according to St Louis Police Commissioner Dan Bartlett, who was in the same regiment. Bartlett, who was asked to preview the film for the purpose of determining whether, from a police angle, it should be censored, suddenly remembered the man during Osgood's death scene.

'With the prospect of death facing him, Johnny loses all of his suave manner, his face begins to twitch, the hands begin to work. The hands! The face! The twitching! Suddenly a picture flashed across my mind; a damp, foul-smelling dugout, half-lit by candles, a bunch of lieutenants grouped about a table listening while our betters are telling us what's to be done and what's in store for us. The thin face. The black eyebrows. The little moustache. The twitching muscles. The hands. It was the same guy!'

It is doubtful whether audiences today, unaware that Osgood Perkins was Tony's father, would discern a similarity between the two actors. Nevertheless, with that knowledge, points of comparision are easily made; 'the thin face . . . the twitching muscles', the somewhat dry and unwavering timbre of the voice, suddenly rising and falling with emotion, the long expressive hands. In fact, 'twitching' was the over-used adjective that critics applied to Tony's portrayals from *Friendly Persuasion* onwards.

Tony's introduction to his father on screen in *Scarface* might well have been disturbing, leaving an unpleasant taste in the boy's mouth, even though, at that young age, he was perfectly aware that it was only a performance. But, with eloquent concision, all he said to his mother on coming out of the cinema was, 'He was rather shorter than I expected him to be.'

However, the fascination with his father was so strong, that he went back to see *Scarface* a further dozen times.

Tony's own son, named Osgood, saw his father for the first time on screen when he was five years old. It was in *The Black Hole*, in which Tony dies a horrible death, disembowelled by the rotary blades of a robot. The experiences of the two children of seeing their fathers for the first time in films, in which they both expire brutally, differed in intensity. Osgood II was able to compare the film representation of his father with the man he knew in an everyday domestic setting at home. Tony had no such comparison. That chimerical 'twitching' hoodlum on the screen was the only animated image he had of his father for many years.

As Tony grew up and entered the same profession, he was continually reminded that he was Osgood's son, not only in that he was probably influenced to become an actor by his father's example, and met and worked with some of his father's colleagues, but in some of his methods.

'He was supposed to be famous for the way in which he used his hands for dramatic expression,' Tony explained in 1953. 'Whenever I do a reading of a play or a bit part for some of his old friends, they wait to see what I'll do with my hands. They stare at me, then say, "Osgood would never have done that!" or, "That's just the way he would make that gesture!" I'm just plain scared to death.'

Though Osgood became celebrated for his hands in later years, as a young amateur of fourteen he was a notorious arm-waver.

'My hands got on my director's nerves to such an extent at rehearsals that he made me rehearse with them tied!' Osgood once related. 'But when I got up before my audience – pouf! – there were the old hands gesturing again! So I decided that if those hands were just bound to act when I did, I had better train them!'

Tony's long 'artistic' hands were similarly trained to do his bidding. Nicolas Gessner, who directed Tony many years later in *Someone Behind The Door*, commented,

'For close-ups of hands, I usually insert my own, because it's an intricate and tricky operation. But obviously, I couldn't do it with Tony, because he had such very characteristic hands.'

As a pupil at Browne and Nichols prep school, Tony would only talk about his father to his two closest friends, Henry Scammell and Serge Bouterline, always adding that he was not going to be 'the son of anybody', but was going to be known as Anthony Perkins, solely on the merit of his own acting. Yet, some years later, when he saw the actor Paul Muni one day in Central Park, he went up to him and said, 'Hello, I'm Anthony Perkins. You knew my father.' He also hoped, when he put himself up for the film *East of Eden*, that the director Elia Kazan's acquaintanceship with Osgood would give him the edge on the other candidates.

Jane Perkins believed that when her son became an actor himself, he 'somehow, deep inside, must have made a silent vow not to let his father down.'

'I was fiercely, compulsively ambitious, and that kind of ambition is a tremendously uncreative impulse,' Tony admitted. 'It's a corrosive emotion. I've no doubt I felt deserted by my father's dying on me and my revenge was to become an even more successful actor than he had been.'

Undoubtedly Tony became a more universally famous actor than Osgood and more successful (in material terms). However, because he chose to take certain infelicitous paths, he was never fully convinced that he had become a better actor than his father. The 'revenge' on his father was mixed with a desire to provide Osgood with pleasure and pride in his son's achievements. But, as Tony, like Hamlet, discovered, it is exceptionally more difficult to gratify someone who is dead than someone who is alive.

4

OGGIE

'If it hadn't been for him . . . I wouldn't be where I am today' – Jim Piersall in *Fear Strikes Out* (1957)

The Theatre Hall of Fame is no more than a list carved into a marble wall in a corner of the Gershwin Theatre in Manhattan. But it is the only hall of fame Broadway has. The names inscribed there include George Abbott, George S. Kaufman, Moss Hart, Judith Anderson, Harold Clurman, Laurence Olivier, Lillian Gish, Katharine Hepburn, Maxwell Anderson, S. N. Behrman, Marc Connelly, Thornton Wilder, Helen Hayes, Ina Claire, Walter Huston, Noel Coward, Henry Fonda, Ruth Gordon, José Ferrer, Margaret Sullavan, Willie Howard, Jed Harris and Osgood Perkins. Because Osgood had only a fifteen-year career due to his relatively late start and premature death, the American Theatre Critics' Association had to waive the twenty-five-year-career eligibility criterion to induct him into the Hall of Fame in 1980.

Christen James Ridley Osgood Perkins was born in the affluent Boston suburb of West Newton on 16 May, 1892. His love for the theatre began at the age of eight, when his mother, Helen Virginia Anthony Perkins, took him to see *Ben-Hur*, with William Farnum as Ben-Hur and William S. Hart as Messala, at the Colonial Theatre in Boston.

'It was the beginning of a new life for me; the beginning of an entirely new me. From that moment on I was an actor. Nothing was real. If I laboured hard at mowing the lawn, I was a galley slave, chained to the oar. If I rode my bicycle swiftly down the country lane, the wind in my teeth, I was a conquering hero, driving a chariot drawn by white horses.'

His mother did not discourage him, and when Sarah Bernhardt appeared in *La Dame aux camélias* at the Boston Theatre in 1901, she paid ten dollars a seat to take Osgood. He was spellbound. It was 'The Divine Sarah' who decided him to become an actor, as well as instilling in him a love for the French language which he was to pass on to his son. Something else that Tony inherited from Osgood was musicality and a good singing voice.

Osgood, who had acted in a few church plays, had the chance to display his stage skills while at Harvard from 1910 to 1914. One of the Harvard Hasty Pudding productions in which he made an impact was *The Legend of Loravia*, a musical comedy. Billed as James Ripley Osgood Perkins, he gained fulsome notices. According to the *Harvard Crimson*, 'With the possible exception of [Robert] Benchley, J. R. O. Perkins is the best comic actor Harvard has had for years. He alone would make the show worth seeing.' The *Baltimore Sun* wrote: 'J. R. O. Perkins made a particular impression with his clever chatter and, in addition to his songs, gave two very funny monologues about baseball from the point of view, first, of an Englishman and then of an Italian.'

He was also elected Ivy Orator of the class of 1914. In the

Harvard Twenty-fifth Anniversary Class Report, a fellow classman (who could just as well have been describing Tony) wrote:

'I have a vivid recollection of him standing there in the stadium, delivering his oration on that hot afternoon of our graduation twenty-five years ago. Very slim, rather frightened, yet holding us with that magnetic personality which was later to dominate so many thousands of his admirers.'

After graduation Osgood, known to his friends as Oggie, drifted casually from one unsuitable job to another for eight years. While he was being trained to sell shoes in Russia, the First World War broke out. He volunteered, and became an ambulance driver in the Lafayette Esquadrille in France and later an officer in the American army. Back home at the end of hostilities, when a job with American Express failed, Osgood decided to pursue his boyhood ambition.

Fortunately, while vainly doing the rounds of New York casting offices, he met Frank Tuttle. The same age as Osgood, the thirty-year-old Tuttle, who had been at the rival university of Yale, and was assistant director of *Vanity Fair*, was forming a motion picture company with a few friends. He told Osgood that he needed an actor with the face of a villain to appear in the first film he was directing himself.

Thus Osgood made his professional acting debut on screen in the Film Guild production of *The Cradle Buster* (aka *Mama's Boy*), a circus melodrama released in 1922, the same year of his marriage to Janet Esselstyn Rane. It starred Glenn Hunter and Marguerite Courtot, with Osgood as the heavy, a pathologically jealous clown, called 'Cracked' Spooney.

There followed a further five undistinguished films (only two of which survive for viewing) directed by Frank Tuttle, most of them featuring Glenn Hunter as the clean-cut hero, and Osgood as the villain.

Osgood Perkins in *Scarface*, 1932 (Photofest).

Meanwhile, Osgood made his entrance on Broadway in George S. Kaufman and Marc Connelly's *Beggar on Horseback* in 1924. As Roland Young's hypochondriac brother-in-law, Osgood impressed powerful Broadway producer Jed Harris, who wrote:

'It was a grand show, with lots of good actors, but for me the best thing in it was the moment when . . . Osgood Perkins pointed his finger at another character in the play. I have never forgotten that gesture. It was malign, sardonic, contemptuous, weird and altogether funny. His forefinger seemed at least a foot long and I had the uncomfortable feeling that it was being poked into me. I looked up his name in the program and later discovered that it was his first part on the professional stage. Well, it was no effort to remember the name and I left the theatre with vague designs on this Mr Perkins.'

Harris, an astute spotter of talent, cast Perkins in his next Broadway production, *Weak Sisters*, the following year. Osgood commented that it was, 'My first minister role . . . I didn't feel so miscast. He was a cussed creature, a kind of fanatic – and it isn't hard for me to look like a fanatic when I cut off my moustache and comb my eyebrows heavenward.'

So successful was Osgood in the part, that he played 'dog-collar roles' in his next two Broadway productions. His son, who followed his father into the realms of evil, also had a line in curious clergymen, who grew progressively tortured – guileless and ineffectual in *Catch 22*; bizarrely bible-bashing in *The Life and Times of Judge Roy Bean*; lustily hitting the bottle in *For the Term of His Natural Life*, and a 'cussed creature' and 'fanatic' in *Crimes Of Passion.*

In order to shake off the 'religious' image, Osgood convinced Brock Pembleton to cast him as a gigolo in *Loose Ankles*, which ran for one-hundred-and-sixty eight performances at the Biltmore Theatre in 1926. From then on, Osgood's stage roles were more varied.

On film, however, his weasel looks and natty moustache usually had him cast as a nasty piece of work, and he had far less chance to shine. Nevertheless, Louise Brooks, opposite whom he played in *Love 'em and Leave 'em* (1926), once commented that Osgood was the best actor she ever worked with. In this picture, one of his few extant silent movies, he played an unctuous racetrack tout who tries to seduce Evelyn Brent. An intertitle explains the kind of man he is.

'Lem Woodruff is the man who spent six months curing halitosis only to find out he was unpopular anyhow.'

Tony saw *Love 'em and Leave 'em* for the first time over half-a-century later. He and his wife, Berry, turned up one evening at the Thalia, the famous re-run theatre in New York where it was showing. Berry went up to the box-office and announced, 'I'm Mrs Anthony Perkins. I would like two free tickets for tonight's show.' The manager, who was astonished by her cheapskate cheek, noticed Tony cowering behind her in embarrassment. What he felt about the film, or his father's performance is not recorded.

In 1928, on Broadway, Perkins Senior played his most famous and memorable stage role, that of Walter Burns in *The Front Page*. Burns, the shifty editor of the *Chicago Herald-Examiner* – a peach of a part for Osgood – spends the time desperately trying to hold onto his star reporter, Hildy Johnson, who insists on marrying, quitting the business and going into advertising. However, neither Ben Hecht nor Charles MacArthur, the authors, thought him right for the part, and Osgood himself had doubts, but producer Jed Harris insisted on hiring him.

'I read [*The Front Page*] on a train going up to Boston,' wrote Jed Harris. 'When I came to, the first thing I remembered was that long finger poking into me at the Broadhurst Theatre [in *Beggar on Horseback*] and Walter Burns was cast.'

Twelve years after *The Front Page* closed, Brooks Atkinson wrote that he could still see Osgood 'cutting through the uproar like a bright, sharp, penknife, and peeling off the layers of the plot as he went along.'

When Howard Hughes came to produce the film version in 1931, none of the acclaimed stage cast, including Lee Tracy (Hildy Johnson), Allen Jenkins, Joseph Calleia, Eduardo Ciannelli and Osgood Perkins, was considered. Both the director Lewis Milestone's suggestions for Hildy – James Cagney and Clark Gable – were rejected by Hughes. Instead, Hughes chose Pat O'Brien, on the mistaken understanding that he had played the role on Broadway. Osgood was passed over in favour of Louis Wolheim, but when Wolheim died of a stroke three weeks into production, Adolphe Menjou was signed. One can only speculate as to how Osgood's film career would have changed if he had been given the chance to repeat his most celebrated role on screen, just as one wonders what changes would have been wrought in Tony's career if he had not missed out on *Some Like It Hot* and *Lawrence of Arabia*, many years later.

After *The Front Page* closed in April 1929, Osgood resumed his film career with two musicals: *Mother's Boy* and *Syncopation* (both lost), before returning to Broadway in *Uncle Vanya* in 1930. Jed Harris felt that 'Osgood Perkins, even without the romantic beauty and distinguished style of Stanislavsky, who created the part, might make an interesting thing of Dr Astrov.' With Walter Connolly in the title role and Lillian Gish as Yelena, Osgood relished his first role in a drama classic. This was followed by his Sir Ralph Bloomfield Bonnington in Shaw's *The Doctor's Dilemma* in summer stock in Massachusetts.

Tarnished Lady (1931) was the first solo film made by George Cukor (who would direct Tony in *The Actress* twenty-two years later), and it also marked the sound-screen debut of stage star

Tallulah Bankhead. Osgood had the thankless role of the faithful friend of Bankhead, as a Park Avenue girl who marries for money, leaves her husband, and returns when he is ruined in the Wall Street crash.

According to Howard Hawks, he hired Osgood to portray the gangster Johnny Lovo in *Scarface*, his most widely seen screen role, when the director saw him playing a romantic lover on stage. 'I always had a theory that heavies had beady eyes, and Osgood certainly had them.' In contrast to Hawks's conventional reasoning, Alfred Hitchcock cast Tony against type in *Psycho*.

In the year of Tony's birth, Osgood was busier than ever. In *A Thousand Summers* on Broadway, he played a world-weary lover, losing his girlfriend to a young man many years her junior (Franchot Tone), the sort of part Tony Perkins would play in his twenties. Osgood then spent the summer at Westpoint Country Playhouse.

Prohibition was at its height, and Jane Wyatt, who was in the company before going to Hollywood, recalled Osgood making bathtub gin, because 'he loved his martini'. Wyatt recalled:

'He and Jane [Perkins] were so sweet and included me, a lonely ingenue, at their parties. I was also impressed when I saw their apartment in New York City. Instead of a headboard for their bed Oggie had painted a marvellous one on the wall. I thought that was most creative!'

After a run of commercial flops on Broadway, Osgood at last had a success with a play called *Goodbye Again*, which opened at the end of the busy year of 1932. Three decades later, when Tony was making the screen version of Françoise Sagan's novel *Aimez-Vous Brahms?*, he remembered the title of one of his father's hits, and suggested it for the film. The only thing the earlier *Goodbye Again* had in common with the later one, was the title. It was a tour-de-force for Osgood, who spent the entire third act in a hotel bed, during which time he had one hundred-and-eight pieces of business, including the balancing of a full breakfast tray on his fingers, and making the bed without leaving it. In the small part of the chauffeur was twenty-four-year-old James Stewart, newly graduated from Princeton.

In 1934, Osgood, the newly elected First Vice-President of Actors' Equity, made three films: the lavish *Madame Du Barry*, in which he played a wily Richelieu; *Kansas City Princess*, with Osgood as a French private eye, a stock funny foreigner; and *The President Vanishes*, a political melodrama which cast him as the President's secretary.

Osgood's two final films were *I Dream Too Much*, starring Lily Pons and Henry Fonda (a future co-star of Tony's), in which he was the opera impresario, and *Gold Diggers of 1937*. In the latter, despite looking rather old – he is grey-haired and has bags under his eyes – he proves what an elegant comic actor he could be. He plays a sly embezzler, continually rubbing his long hands with his long fingers, occasionally giving a not unfamiliar little sideways smile. In one scene, when his boss collapses, he whispers to his companion in crime, 'Don't give him any air.'

Gertrude Lawrence was taking the title role in *Susan and God* in the pre-Broadway tryout in Washington D.C. and Osgood was cast as her estranged alcoholic husband. After the opening night on 20 September 1937, Osgood said to his co-star, 'Thank God, we'll never have to go through that again.'

Gertrude Lawrence took it to mean that the first performance, always a strain, was over. But she never forgot his words.

'He said later that he had never been so nervous at a premiere in his life. He complained of heartburn, and said his throat was hurting him, and that he had pains in his arms. That was all the intimation we had that he was desperately ill.'

After the curtain calls, exhausted as usual by the performance,

Osgood walked slowly back to the hotel with his wife. He died of a heart attack in his room at the Willard Hotel early the next morning. He was forty-five years old. According to the obituary in the *New York Times*, his last words were, 'I like that role. I hope the play never closes.'

5

HELLO HOLLYWOOD ... AND GOODBYE

'It's a terrible thing, you know, to make a flop of the first job you've got in life' – Tom Lee in *Tea and Sympathy* (1954–1955)

While Tony was putting on the greasepaint in summer stock, he dreamed of enrolling in Harvard, his father's alma mater, where he could take theatre courses. Tony's boyhood friend John Kerr had already got into Harvard the year before, and was studying law. Curiously, when Kerr visited Tony in Cambridge, where he was in his final year at high school, ostensibly preparing for Harvard, Tony told him nothing of his college or his summer-stock acting, or of his ambitions. Obviously he was still reticent about admitting it to someone who had known him as a child – or to himself. He would first have to appease the theatrical deities into accepting his effrontery in wanting to emulate his father.

However, with his inconsistent work habits, Tony's grades were not high enough to meet Harvard's exacting standards. In fact he graduated twenty-fourth out of a class of twenty-five and was refused even the chance to take entrance exams.

'It's all right, Mother,' he said, believing he was covering up his disappointment. 'I'll go down to Rollins College in Florida. They have a very good drama department there.'

Thus, in 1950, aged eighteen, parting from his mother and beloved dog Skippy, Tony took up residence on the charming Spanish-style campus of Rollins College, on the shore of Lake Virginia in Winter Park, a suburb of Orlando, Florida. It was not Harvard, but the oldest college in the state did have a drama department of sufficient repute to attract Tony.

'When he went to college in Florida, his record in the fields he liked was excellent,' claimed a proud Mrs Perkins. 'One year, he walked off with all four twenty-four-dollar prizes for best stories in the quarterly literary magazine. And in his second and third years, he won scholarships as a history major. The scholarships meant a great deal to Tony, with his already well-developed sense of responsibility. He had helped to pay his own way through his freshman year.'

Praise for Tony's acting abilities was tempered in The Browne-Nichols Yearbook for 1950 which predicted that 'Ten years from now Tony Perkins will be seen in Hollywood as Roddy McDowall's stand-in.' Actually, a decade later, Tony would be merging into Norman Bates, and leaving behind the rather effete McDowall in terms of stardom.

'Perk', as he was called, acted in no less than eight college productions, including *The Importance of Being Earnest*, in which he played Algernon Moncrieff. The clear-sighted critic in the student magazine took him to task.

'Mr Perkins: *The Importance of Being Ernest* [sic] is a play; not an exercise in putting across the boyish personality.'

'When I was in college I just got through on charm,' Tony concluded. 'Charm and a loud voice and a pleasant face and an ability to make people laugh and the fact that I was good and tall.'

Tony as Algernon Montcrief in
The Importance of Being Earnest
at Rollins College in 1953 (Rollins College).

While appearing in *Squaring the Circle*, a satirical Soviet farce by Valentin Kataev, his last play for the Rollins College Players, he was dubbed by his fraternity brothers 'the poor man's Carleton Carpenter' for his gawky portrayals. At the time, Carpenter, now forgotten except by studious film buffs, was a gangling song-and-dance man at MGM, who sang 'Aba Daba Honeymoon' with Debbie Reynolds in *Two Weeks With Love*, but whose career was already fading fast in 1953. The critic in the local paper thought he was 'as excellent as Tony can be when the part fits his humorous interpretive style. He is constantly diverting and at ease. He is everything that he should be with the exception of a young Don Ameche.'

Tony was plainly not yet seen as himself. Roddy McDowall, Carleton Carpenter, Don Ameche – a strange assortment, though what they spelled was light entertainment. If he ever did make a career in films, then his charm and 'ability to make people laugh' would definitely thrust him into comedies and/or musicals.

Between acting at Rollins during the academic year, Tony continued playing in summer stock. In 1951 he was back at the Robin Hood Theatre in Delaware, where he acted with Barbara Rush, on the threshold of a Hollywood career and married at the time to Jeffrey Hunter, also just starting in films.

'Tony was about sixteen when we acted together. [He was nineteen.] He was tall, rangy and a mass of bones,' recalled Barbara Rush. 'I'd get bruises because his elbows and shoulders were so sharp. I could feel his ribs in a close embrace.'

In *Two Blind Mice*, by Samuel Spewack, Tony had a small part, while the lead was young John Drew Devereaux, another theatrical scion. He was the grandson of the actor John Drew, a member of the celebrated Barrymore family. These learning experiences reaffirmed Tony's belief that his only future lay on the stage.

'I went to college and everybody said they were going to be actors and I said I was going to be an actor. They said they were going to be stars, and I said I was going to be a star; they said it and I said it; they knew it and I knew it, but I really knew it.'

While at Rollins, Tony happened to chance upon an item in the *New York Times* which announced that MGM had bought Ruth Gordon's play *Years Ago*, in which he had made one of his first professional appearances.

Somehow the fact that he had already played the part of the would-be actress's young suitor, albeit before two hundred people every night in a small barn theatre in an obscure corner of Delaware, convinced him that he was qualified for the role; indeed, more qualified than any of the actors MGM had under contract. Absurd as this conceit was, it was translated into action.

'It was the power of self-confidence and a triumph of positive thinking that made me go to MGM to get the part,' said Tony, who, though socially shy, was not lacking in assurance when it came to his career.

The actor and director Kenneth MacKenna, who had worked with Osgood and was a great friend of the family, arranged, through his contacts, for Tony to get a summer job at the MGM studios. Tony then hitchhiked from Florida to Hollywood where he hoped to test for the role in *Years Ago*. At least he had managed to get into the studio, where he made himself as conspicous as possible. He even dated the daughter of Laurence Weintraub, the producer of the film he hoped to appear in.

'One day they were testing Margaret O'Brien and they needed the back of someone's head,' Tony asserted. 'They didn't know who to use. Then someone piped up and said, "How about that kid that's always hanging around here? We could use the back of his head!" They called me in and I stood in front of the camera, almost obliterating poor Margaret O'Brien's face and causing the director to say, "Please, move a little to the left." When he said this, I turned around and said, "Who me?" and I was in the test.'

In reality, Tony was asked to test with Margaret O'Brien, the former child star trying to make a comeback at the age of fifteen, and hoping for the principal role of the girl who wants to become an actress. In time-honoured fashion, Tony was given the 'don't call us, we'll call you' spiel, and he hitchhiked back to the East coast where he immediately joined the New England summer stock tour of *Theatre* by Somerset Maugham and Guy Bolton. In it, he played the seventeen-year-old son of Kay Francis, who had retired from the screen.

Meanwhile, he was still hoping for the call from Hollywood, despite his comment that 'having seen how big and important the MGM studio was and how many people they had under contract, it seemed to me no longer reasonable and logical that they would ever offer me the role.' As evidence of his great expectations, he turned down a part in the Rollins Players production of *The Gramercy Ghost* just in case he got the film role.

About six months after his screen test, Tony received a very courteous letter from MGM asking him to report for costume tests. 'I thought someone was kidding me. My part of the film was to be shot during the last part of December 1952 and the first part of January 1953, which happened to fall exactly during the Christmas vacation from college. So I speeded up my work, explained to my instructors – who really didn't believe me but thought that it was a hell of a good lie, no-one had ever come up with anything like that before – "Please, sir, can I have my final examinations a week early because I have to go to Hollywood to be in a movie." Since it was right before Christmas vacation, I headed out to Hollywood to make my first movie. And oh gawd, what an experience it was . . . I was so ambitious, nothing was going to stop me. I wanted to become a movie star and I would become one.'

Neither Margaret O'Brien nor Debbie Reynolds, who had been endlessly tested for the role, was cast as the young Ruth Gordon, whose sole ambition is to go on the stage. That privilege went to twenty-four-year-old English actress Jean Simmons. Tony was still, at twenty, young enough to be convincing as her spurned suitor Fred Whitmarsh, a role that was expanded slightly from the original play.

Teresa Wright, whose most famous role was in Hitchcock's *Shadow of a Doubt*, and who had just married writer Robert Anderson, on the point of completing a new play called *Tea and Sympathy*, played Jean Simmons's mother, though only ten years her senior. George Cukor, who had directed Osgood in *Tarnished Lady* a year before Tony was born, was the man responsible for getting a performance out of the novice screen actor. (Mary Wickes, in the cast, and Ruth Gordon, who wrote the screenplay, were further reminders of his father, who had acted with both of them.)

'Cukor would let me go through my scenes, praise everyone else involved and then . . . he would holler out, "Tony, you were terrible." I'd want to sink through the floor! "Now!" he would go on, "let's drop that Aw, shucks, Ma! school of acting, and try it this way." If you remember the scene when I'm talking to Jean in the parlour while her parents are preparing for bed, I started to play Fred for laughs as a sheepish, ill-at-ease young fellow the way I was directed in summer stock. Cukor straightened me out. To call him a good director is the understatement of the year. He's great!'

Cukor had already directed the star, Spencer Tracy, in four films and was a friend. Also part of the clique, from which Tony felt excluded, were Ruth Gordon and her husband Garson Kanin; and Katharine Hepburn, Tracy's lover, who had just flown in from New York where she had been appearing in Shaw's *The Millionairess* on Broadway. Though Teresa Wright recalled that the two youngest members of the cast got on very well – 'Off the set, Jean and Tony would sing together. They seemed to know all the show tunes' – Jean Simmons was then married to Stewart Granger, another British MGM contractee, and had little time to be sociable with the young actor outside working hours.

'But it didn't bother me,' Tony declared. 'I was too taken up with myself to care. I remember saying, "Good morning, Mr Tracy" every morning until one day Tracy said, "Good morning, good morning, good morning, good morning, good morning, good morning, good morning – now that should last you for a week.'

George Cukor, whose homosexuality was well-known among most people in the industry, would hold Sunday salons for his gay friends at his luxurious West Hollywood home, which had three guest houses on the estate. Invited were 'an ever-changing list of handsome young men for pool-side buffet parties that became famous throughout Hollywood as the time and place to meet the newest, most ravishing men in town.' On a few Sundays, Tony was an attractive addition to some of these sexually select gatherings. Cukor had a taste for young unknowns, and it was quite likely that he had seen Tony's test and liked his looks. But Tony, though enjoying the admiration of famous, older men, was not at ease in Hollywood, and he seldom would be.

'I wanted to get right out of there and do any acting that didn't involve films,' he later commented. After all, Osgood's fame rested on his stage work, and he was never treated fairly by Hollywood.

Set in the early 1920s, *The Actress* (as it was eventually called after the titles *Years Ago* and *Fame and Fortune* had been discarded), despite the budget restrictions, lovingly recreates the period and the theatrical productions of the time when Osgood was on the stage. Both Tracy, as the sea-dog father who opposes his daughter's ambitions, and Teresa Wright, as the mother who secretly supports her, gave likable performances. Tony played Jean Simmons's racoon-coated suitor with diffident charm and as a figure of fun (rather in the manner of Scotty Beckett in earlier folksy MGM comedies and musicals), delightfully dancing the Pink Lady Waltz with Simmons at a school prom. At the end of the film, when Simmons is leaving home to take up acting, Tony tells her not to carry her own suitcase, because 'You look like a suffragette.'

In such a minor role, however, few critics drew attention to him, though Bosley Crowther, in the *New York Times*, commented on the 'amusing gaucherie of Anthony Perkins in the role of a high-collared beau.'

'It was an adventure of brief duration in that I didn't exactly set Hollywood, or any other part of the world, on fire!' Tony recalled. '*The Actress* really didn't do anything for me. I had a small role but a role good enough for me to say when I saw it "Fellow, you just haven't got it yet. I'm sorry you can't stay in Hollywood with this kind of work, you've got to go back and learn more about self-confidence . . .'

The gentle film, despite generally favourable reviews, failed to draw audiences, and it would be three years before Tony was asked back to Hollywood.

6

TV AND SYMPATHY

'There's so much I don't understand' – Tom Lee in *Tea and Sympathy* (1954–1955)

With what he believed to be his ephemeral film career behind him, Tony returned to the stage (at Salt Creek Summer Theatre in Illinois) in *Family Portrait*, a curious play by Lenore Coffee and William Joyce Cowen about Christ's family. Judith Anderson starred as the Virgin Mary with Tony playing her youngest son Judah. (In 1960, Judith Anderson was one of the actresses Hitchcock teasingly told the press he was considering for the role of Mrs Bates.)

Although he was only one semester away from graduation from Rollins College, Tony decided to transfer to Columbia University. More resolute than ever to fulfil his father's dream of having his son's name up in lights outside a Broadway theatre, Tony considered that being in New York would afford him more professional acting opportunities in theatre and television.

Jane Perkins was on holiday in Europe when she received a letter from Tony explaining that the reason for the change was his desire to 'really get into the acting business.'

'I wondered how much attention his Columbia studies would get,' she reflected. 'Anyhow, I was delighted he had three-and-a-half years of college – more than I had expected. Just the same, I was worried about him. I'd been around the theatre long enough to be familiar with the problems of young people trying to break into show business: the insecurity, the disappointments, the small percentage of people who become "somebody" or even manage to make a decent living. I wondered how these would affect a shy and sensitive boy, in a world where these qualities take a constant beating. But I was too far away to do anything about it, and I don't think I'd have been able to in any case. Tony had made his decision.'

Before entering Columbia in September 1953, Tony went to New York in the summer and started knocking on doors. He had decided that television would be an easier medium in which to start, and he tried to get on almost every TV drama series on the air.

'In each letter I received, Tony tried to sound cheerful and optimistic, but I could detect his frustration,' continued Mrs Perkins. 'The truth was that all summer he hadn't been able to land even a small TV role. When I returned to New York, I was surprised to find Tony still determined to become a professional actor. It was a quiet kind of determination, a solid stubborness. No ranting, no rash promises. Just a set-jaw attitude and a firm, "I'll make it." I've seen that attitude since.'

Eventually, Tony did start to get parts on TV, many of them small ones. In *The Missing Years*, he played Mary Astor's teenage son, resentful of an absent father returning after twelve years away just as his mother is about to remarry. The role was the prototype for those in *The Lonely Man* and *Fear Strikes Out* – sullen juveniles with filial tribulations.

In *The Fugitive*, he played the title role of a young man hiding out in a French orphanage, unsure whether to give himself up or endanger the children.

Tony once commented that his television work consisted of a succession of 'family plays, in which I was the boy with hair falling down over his forehead.'

In July 1953, while in pursuit of an acting job, Tony put himself up for the role of Tom Lee in Robert Anderson's new play *Tea and Sympathy.* He was competing with James Dean, Steve McQueen and John Kerr and, though he had not yet appeared on the New York stage, was more seasoned in the theatre than any of the other three. Twenty-one-year-old Dean's only previous Broadway experience had been in *See the Jaguar*, which ran for six performances, though he had had bit parts in four movies previously. McQueen, nearly a year older, came from New York's radical Neighborhood Playhouse. John Kerr, who had graduated from Harvard, had already appeared on Broadway in an important part in the Mary Chase college comedy, *Bernadine*, the previous year.

Tony was confident that the director, Elia Kazan, who had acted with Osgood twice in 1932, would value him as his father's son, trusting to good theatrical stock. Kazan expressed his admiration for Osgood in his autobiography thus:

'He was the definition of the word "professional". There was no "take a minute" technique with him; in fact there was no emotion. Only skill. In every aspect of technical facility, he was peerless . . . I've never forgotten Mr Perkins. He stood for a whole other side of theatre art than the one I'd learned from Lee [Strasberg] and Harold [Clurman], and I thought it – and do now – immensely valuable . . . I believed I could take the kind of art Osgood Perkins exemplified – externally clear action, controlled every minute at every turn, with gestures spare yet eloquent –

and blend that with the kind of acting the Group was built on: intense and truly emotional, rooted in the subconscious, therefore often surprising and shocking in its revelations. I could bring these two opposite and often conflicting traditions together, as they should be brought together.'

However, the director's adulatory view of the father did not extend to the son. Although Tony also attempted to achieve this symbiosis of acting styles as he developed, Kazan had only his embryonic personality and career to assess in 1953. When both Robert Anderson and Elia Kazan opted for Kerr, with Tony as second choice, he was bitterly disappointed. The wound was even deeper, because his childhood friend had not only got the part and appeared on Broadway without the years of summer-stock apprenticeship that Tony had undergone but, like Osgood, he had graduated from Harvard. John Kerr seemed much more the son Osgood would have been proud of.

Robert Anderson explained that Kerr had the quality he was looking for.

'The very thing that has worked for Tony, particularly in the movies . . . a certain "differentness" we didn't want at the outset for Tom Lee. Jack Kerr once said to me that Tony "made" it in movies while Jack felt he really didn't, because of some edge . . . some specialness.'

In other words, Kerr gave out just the right 'straight' signals, so that, even if the other characters thought he might be 'queer', the audience knew him to be 'normal'.

Tea and Sympathy opened at the Ethel Barrymore Theatre on Broadway with John Kerr and Deborah Kerr (no relation) in the leads on 30 September, 1953. A little over six months later, when Kazan was attempting to cast the part of Cal Trask in the film of John Steinbeck's *East of Eden*, Tony decided to approach Kazan again, in the hope of getting the role. Up to then, he had failed to get any stage work in New York, and the few parts he had managed to obtain since *The Actress* were on TV, so he was anxious to impress Kazan. But this time, Tony was beaten by James Dean, another of the earlier candidates for Tom Lee. Luckily, Kazan was simultaneously seeking replacements for *Tea and Sympathy* to allow the Kerrs to go on tour.

When Tony went to see the director in his New York office about the role in *East of Eden*, he was, in his own words, 'paralyzed-trying-to-be-calm, a state of mind which has cost more actors more jobs than any other I can name, and to conceal this I was seated quite upright on a straight-backed chair, my hands clasped in front of me, and my legs straight out, heels on the floor. (I felt sort of braced and therefore secure in this position.) Kazan glanced at me briefly and started casually telling me a pleasantly racy little anecdote about himself and my father when they were youths together. The story came rather suddenly and startlingly to its conclusion and I remember my outstretched feet involuntarily sliding back under the chair and my face becoming deep red. Although I later read for him I have always felt that it was my naive and unsophisticated reaction to his story that won me the part [of Tom Lee] as much as anything.'

Kazan then asked Tony to audition for *Tea and Sympathy*, and he went along one morning to the Ethel Barrymore Theatre on West 47th Street. He described the experience in terms of Kafka's Joseph K.: 'The theatre was dark and – instantly thinking that I had come to the wrong theatre at the wrong time or on the wrong day or maybe all three – I groped my way through the darkness and there was Deborah Kerr sitting under this white light. At least twenty people were in front of her in the pitch black, but I could only hear their voices. They made me sit beside her on the sofa under the light and it was . . . it was like an initiation into some secret society, or like going to the crusades. And Kazan kept saying, "Stop acting and just read the lines." So I'd try not to act and I'd start reading again and he'd be more exasperated and he'd say, "Stop acting and just read it." And this happened a dozen times. And when we were through, John Kerr shook his head slowly and said, "You certainly rushed it."'

Nevertheless, Kerr told Kazan that, although he had never seen Tony act, he believed he had the right qualities for the role.

Tony was one month away from graduation when he was offered his first Broadway role. *Tea and Sympathy* might have cost him his college degree, but it launched his acting career in a big way.

Because Joan Fontaine, who was to take over from Deborah Kerr, had commitments in Los Angeles, Tony flew out to Hollywood in April 1954 to join her for rehearsals on the Warner Bros. backlot, under the direction of Kazan's friend Karl Malden. When they reached New York, Kazan put them through their paces with the rest of the company, and *Tea and Sympathy*, starring Joan Fontaine and the unknown Anthony Perkins, opened on 31 May.

'My hunch was justified when I saw him,' John Kerr remarked. 'He was excellent. I thought, however, that Joan Fontaine was not vulnerable enough. She was too tough, and you wondered why she hadn't left her husband earlier. Tony played it with more humour than I did. He was always able to find an element of humour in any part. That was his nature.'

Miles Kreuger, a drama student and friend of Tony's at the time, recalled that he was far better in the role than John Kerr, whom he thought, using Kerr's expression about Fontaine, 'not vulnerable enough.'

'Kerr was too sturdy for someone who is tormented by the problem of homosexuality. Tony portrayed Tom Lee as someone who was on the verge of being crushed by revelations of his sexuality.' In fact, Tom Lee, like Joseph K., begins to feel guilty for being something that he is not.

Robert Anderson's play is a sad and stinging study of a sensitive young man at a private boys' school in New England, taunted by his peers, because he would rather listen to classical music than play sports. They equate his sensitivity with homosexuality, and his father upbraids him for not acting more manly, and not being 'a regular fellow.' Of a dismissed teacher that Tom admired, the father says, 'He's a fairy, a homosexual.'

His room-mate is delegated to instruct the boy on how to be butch.

'I found myself self-conscious about things I've been doing for years . . . dressing, undressing,' explains Tom. 'I keep my eyes on the floor. Geez, if I even look at a guy that doesn't have any clothes on, I'm afraid someone's going to say something.'

Only Laura Reynolds, the housemaster's lonely wife, shows Tom understanding.

'A man knows a queer when he sees one,' her husband says.

'I bet he doesn't even know the meaning of the word . . . queer,' Laura replies.

'What do you think he is?'

'I think he's a nice sensitive kid who doesn't know the meaning of the word.'

When she threatens to leave him, her husband protests.

'And you're doing this . . . all because of this . . . this fairy?'

'This boy, Bill . . . this boy is more of a man than you are . . . Manliness is not all swagger and swearing and mountain climbing. Manliness is also tenderness, gentleness, consideration. You men think you can decide on who is a man, when only a woman can really know.'

She then accuses him of persecuting Tom for the thing he fears in himself.

Tom is goaded by his schoolmates into visiting the town whore to prove his manhood, but when he runs away from her in revulsion, he comes to the conclusion that he *is* 'queer' and attempts suicide. Finally, Laura offers herself to him to prove his sexual normality. As she brings the boy's hand to her open blouse, she says, 'Years from now – when you talk about this – and you will – be kind.'

Robert Anderson has explained that the chief meaning of the play was 'that we must understand and respect the differences in people. Along with this is the whole concept of what manliness is . . . I stump for essential manliness which is something internal, and consists of gentleness, consideration, and other qualities of that sort, and not just of brute strength. Another point, of course, is the tendency for any mass of individuals to gang up on anyone who differs from it . . . if there is nothing to persecute in the individual, they will invent something.'

Tea and Sympathy, however, has dated in regard to the small advances made by gay rights, and the slightly more sympathetic social perception of homosexuals in the years since. The play seems to suggest, perhaps unintentionally, that the shame was Tom being mistakenly accused of the horrible charge of being 'queer', and that the other characters' attitudes might have been justified if he really had been. Actually, Tom Lee is just slower than other boys at laying his first girl, which makes him think he might conceivably grow up to be 'different' all his life. At the end, a woman, old enough to be his mother, frustrated in her marriage, commits adultery with the boy in the rather pious belief that she is saving him from a fate worse than death. This is final proof that he is not homosexual. Curtain. Applause.

Initially, Tony's first Broadway appearance was an intimidating experience. First of all, he found Joan Fontaine a difficult woman to work with, and she gave him very little 'tea and sympathy.' One night after the show, he told his mother:

'I can't work with that woman! I can't! I won't!' To which she replied: 'Are you a boy or an actor?'

Mrs Perkins had originally discouraged him by saying when he got the role, 'You'll never be as good as John Kerr.'

Robert Anderson remembers that Tony 'always seemed to have a chip on his shoulder when I came around. Some tight-lipped challenge would come out as I visited his dressing room, like, "What are you doing around here?" etc. Because we (Kazan and I) gave the part originally to Jack Kerr, I'm afraid he carried over this "rejection" into his relationship with me.'

'I messed up the part for a few months, but the play had been running for a long time and nobody really noticed,' Tony declared. 'It was like throwing a kid into the water to teach him to swim – much better than studying acting. I tried out different things; I learned from the audience. It was easy to learn, when they began rattling programmes and yelling "Louder!" which they did . . . from playing Tom Lee over and over again, I learned how to be consistent in a performance and what people liked and what was effective.'

Despite all the tensions and the self-deprecation, Tony got good reviews. The *Variety* critic wrote: 'Young Perkins seems just about as good as his predecessor. The characterization may be slightly more contained than Kerr's but that appears to be merely a shading of personality, and no less effective in terms of the play. The performance is clear, direct, sensitive and very touching, and should establish Perkins as a highly promising juvenile. Incidentally, the young actor resembles his late father Osgood Perkins, not only in appearance, but also vocally and in various mannerisms, and he suggests something of the late star's crisp authority.'

For his performance, *Theatre World* acknowledged him as one of the Promising Personalities of the 1954–1955 season. Yet it was the original stage cast which was chosen by MGM producer

Pandro S. Berman for the bowdlerized film (the words 'homosexual' and 'queer' were replaced by 'sister boy') directed by Vincente Minnelli, after the play had closed on 18 June, 1955. In order to ensure that audiences were in no doubt as to the hero's heterosexual credentials, the film is told in flashback by Tom Lee, now a happily-married husband and father. Rather like Tony Perkins in the 1980s flashing back to the indiscretions of his youth.

Certainly, there were obvious reasons why Tony responded to the role of Tom Lee, not only because of his memories of being an outsider during his own schooldays, but because of the play's dialectic on what constitutes masculinity.

'During the time of *Tea and Sympathy* I was aware that Tony was gay,' recalled John Kerr. 'I think it was apparent to those that knew him, but he never seemed hung up about it.'

Having just turned twenty-two, Tony had already had several sexual experiences with men of around his own age, whom he had met in the theatre and at bars. Being unknown at the time just before *Tea and Sympathy*, he seemed not to suffer from any fear of exposure. But as soon as he started on the road to fame, he became more guarded in respect to his tastes and where he was seen.

One of the places he frequented during the long run of the play was Downey's, a typical Irish bar on 8th Avenue between 44th and 45th Streets. It was run by a tough Irishman called Jim Downey, had sawdust on the floor, and was full of Damon Runyon horse-racing characters. Gradually, however, the clientele consisted more and more of struggling actors, who knew that if they went in there for a beer they could also buy a very cheap hamburger. Downey's became an informal theatrical club.

Drama student Miles Kreuger used to visit Downey's in the mid-50s, where he met unknowns such as James Dean, Ben

Self-portrait circa 1954

(*Anthony Perkins Story* magazine).

Gazzara and Joanne Woodward, as well as the up-and-coming Tony Perkins, who had just taken over from John Kerr in *Tea and Sympathy.* Tony and Miles became close friends, lovers being too strong a word for so casual a sexual relationship.

'We shared a common interest in the theatre. He was fascinated by the fact that I seemed to be his only friend who knew that his father was Osgood Perkins. He was delighted by that, because he was very proud of his father.'

Many a time, Tony saved Miles a seat in the front row of the theatre, and they would go out together afterwards, often to Downey's.

'I would sit in the front row, right in the centre, and he would wink at me from the stage. Although he was very serious about his profession, he always had an impish sense of humour,' Kreuger recalled.

As Miles and Tony were built almost exactly alike – both were over six foot, were in their early twenties and had shocks of black hair that used to hang down over one eye, Tony asked Miles to stand in the stage alley after the show, so that all of his young fans would see Miles in the shadows and think it was Tony. The star would then escape, and meet Miles at Downey's.

At the time, Tony was sharing a small brownstone house at 127 West 56th Street, just behind the New York City Center, with a photographer called Helen Merrill. He paid her fifty-five dollars a month for what had been her daughter's room, a small den, accessible only through Helen's bedroom, so no hanky panky could go on without her knowledge. His hot water was shut off at midnight. To reach this groundfloor nest, he had to squeeze through a door under a stairwell, pick his way through darkness down a narrow passage and stumble through the doorway with beads across it. His small, windowless living room had a series of self-portraits on the walls; his bedroom, which he decorated himself, had a sky-blue ceiling painted with stars, white walls, white bed, white sideboard and a white hardbacked chair. Later, he placed stills from his movies on the wall. To satisfy his desire to see his name in lights (before it actually happened), Helen strung twinkling Christmas-tree lights above his bed that spelled out his name.

Like siblings, Helen Merrill and Tony shared a childish private language, giving nicknames to most of their acquaintances such as 'Mr Winker' to the butcher, because he winked at her.

According to Alan Helms, who became a close friend of Tony's a few years later, 'He cared for Helen very much. They had a very close relationship and she exercised some kind of influence over him. I never discovered what its nature was. I guessed Helen served as a kind of mother to him. I found her very daunting, in personality and intellectually.'

'She ruled his life,' commented Paul Jasmin, a friend and one of the voices of Mrs Bates in *Psycho.* 'No-one contacted him without speaking to her first. Even his agent had trouble getting through.'

'A stern looking woman of Germanic bearing,' was how journalist Frank Rose described her. 'Formidable, forbidding, daunting' were similar epithets used by some acquaintances of Jane Perkins, and by extension, Mrs Bates. So, just like Norman Bates in *Psycho II*, Tony had two mothers, his real one and his adopted one.

Though Tony now had a separate New York apartment from his mother, he saw or called her every day. She lived a few blocks away and, when he visited her, they would watch the television Tony had given her. They particularly enjoyed the *Andy Williams Show* together.

Mrs Perkins explained why Tony lived apart from her. 'I have a small apartment in New York, and naturally I could arrange to have my son stay with me when he's in town. But Tony sees it differently. "I'd be getting phone calls, coming in all the hours of the day and night," he says, "and you wouldn't get any rest." And that's why Tony keeps his own tiny place in New York and I keep

TONY THE PIN-UP BOY OF FAN MAGAZINES IN THE LATE 1950s (PHOTOFEST).

mine. Even this arrangement sometimes worries him. "You don't mind, do you Mother?" he'll ask.'

Helen allowed Tony to keep a little dog called Fluffy, which he adored. Fluffy was supposed to be white, but because of the polluted New York air his coat had a yellowish tint.

'Oh, I can't keep him white. I can't keep him white!' Tony would complain. (He later swapped Fluffy for a Siamese cat called Pansy.)

On most evenings, Miles Kreuger and Tony walked the dog, then went to a quiet restaurant.

'When we were together, we were always alone. I never knew him within a larger social context.'

Tony made few friends, preferring to stay in his room and read or paint – mainly self-portraits. When he got bored, he would walk over to Fifth Avenue and see if people recognized him.

Despite the success of his Broadway debut, almost a year passed before Tony was offered another choice role. However, he was kept busy in half a dozen TV dramas during the run of *Tea and Sympathy* and after. The parts ranged from a cop, who looks young enough to infiltrate the ranks of high-school drug users in *The Case of the Narcotics Racket*; Mr West Wind in an Oriental allegory called *Mr Blue Ocean*, in which he competed with Boris Karloff for the hand of Susan Strasberg (the seventeen-year-old daughter of Lee and Paula Strasberg of the Actors Studio); and as the son of a returning convict (Brian Donlevy), who protects his mother (Glenda Farrell) from her husband's brutality in *Home is the Hero*. The 51-year-old Farrell, whose film career was virtually over, had played some sparky scenes opposite Osgood in *Gold Diggers of 1937*, almost twenty years previously.

In *The Silent Gun*, Tony had his first Western role. Accompanied by Lloyd Bridges, he was offered a foretaste of *The Lonely*

Man and *The Tin Star*, in which a father-son relationship engenders deeper mutual comprehension. In contrast, he portrayed a social climber in love with the spoiled Piper Laurie (a Hollywood old hand at twenty-four) in *Winter Dreams*, based on an F. Scott Fitzgerald story.

All of these plays were broadcast live. Tony explained the hazards of such an enterprise:

'On live TV you'd get just a little bit of rehearsal and they'd sketch out how it would be. It was the most perilous kind of work you could take as an actor, because anybody could freeze and they did. You would turn to the veteran actor who was knocking back jokes right until air time and you would see nothing more than the stare of someone whom you knew was permanently afflicted with having suffered through this experience. Shaking, you shout, "You've got to go on. This is nationwide." This was routine. This gave you the courage to face anything. There's never been anything like that before or since, at least in the USA. There was incredible tension surrounding these live 90-minute shows. They stopped for commercials, but after them you were right back on. Away from the paprika and onto you. There was no time for reflection.'

The last TV drama Tony would appear in before screen stardom was *Joey*, broadcast in March 1956. A year later, it was one of the projects mooted for a film, when Tony was put on contract to Paramount. In it, he played a slow-witted dishwasher with an over-protective mother (Ruth White) – shades of *Psycho II* – who gets interested in an ex-stripper (Kim Stanley).

Joey was significant only in that it marked the beginning of Tony's professional singing career – although he had sung 'Plaisir d'amour', accompanying himself on the guitar, in *Tea and Sympathy* – an aspect of his work often ignored and forgotten by the public at large. Here, he crooned a song called 'A Little Love Goes A

Long, Long Way', with sweetness and charm. He recorded it at the same time as he sang 'Thee I Love', the theme song from the film *Friendly Persuasion*, on a 45rpm. Although the latter could not compete in any sense with the hit version put out by clean-living Pat Boone, as sung on the soundtrack, it revealed Tony's sincere and tender, albeit untrained, tenor voice. This can be appraised in the many discs he made over the years.

'I'm very adaptable,' Tony claimed. 'I never thought of myself as a singer, but if they wanted to pay me to sing, I'd sing. If President Eisenhower called me up and said they'd been looking through the records and I was the perfect guy to go to the moon, I'd go to the moon.'

In her usual laudatory tone, his mother commented:

'He had always sung for his own enjoyment, but he didn't talk about doing it professionally. With his customary reticence, he held back because he wasn't sure he could do it well enough. Without telling anybody he continued to sing for himself and by himself. When he made his first album, everybody at the recording session was amazed to discover how much his voice had strengthened and how much command of the music he had acquired.'

Tony continued to record throughout his life, although in a 1972 interview with his future wife, he said, 'I made quite a few records. Talk about second-rate art!'

Working in live television drama between 1954 and 1956 brought Tony into contact with Eli Wallach and Kim Stanley, members of the Actors Studio, as were Karl Malden and Elia Kazan with whom he had worked on *Tea and Sympathy*. The Actors Studio had been formed by a group of stage actors and directors in 1948 to advance the acting technique known as the 'Method'. Influenced by the teachings of Konstantin Stanislavsky, the Method stressed a more instinctive approach to acting, enabling the performers to arrive at their interpretation of a role through seeking equivalent emotions in their own experiences.

While appearing together in *Joey*, Kim Stanley told Tony that 'acting is like playing the piano or the guitar; no matter how good you are, you're never as good as you can be – you never realize the full potentialities of your instrument, which is yourself.'

The actor who more than any other typified the Method School was Marlon Brando. Others such as Rod Steiger, Montgomery Clift, Joanne Woodward, Paul Newman and James Dean benefited from his example. Despite having never taken an acting lesson in his life, and though he came from a different tradition, Tony would become associated with the above. With all the proselytizers for the Method around him, Tony was bound to be converted.

'I believe in Method acting, but I've always been afraid to audition for the Actors Studio. They might say no,' he admitted in 1961. He did, however, become a member two years later.

At the time of his emergence, the Method was becoming the most caricatured of acting styles with its mumbling delivery, shrugging of shoulders, fidgeting and scratching. But Tony profited from the popularity of the new stars among the growing youth audience, who identified with their anti-conformist attitudes and adolescent rebellion and despair. The self-conscious young Perkins was now about to ride on the new wave towards immeasurable stardom, for which he was ill prepared.

Part II

FATHERS AND SONS

7

THOU SWELL!

'*Mother, I hate fighting . . . but thee knows thee must fight*' – Josh Birdwell in *Friendly Persuasion* (1956)

While Tony was appearing in *Tea and Sympathy*, William Wyler, one of the most lauded of American film directors, made one of his routine trips to New York to spot actors to take back to Hollywood. In those days, whenever there was a part that producers did not want to cast out of Players Guide, they would get onto trains or planes with tickets to all the Broadway shows.

Wyler was looking for a young actor to play the part of Gary Cooper's son in *Mr Birdwell Goes to Battle* (later re-titled *Friendly Persuasion*), an adaptation from the Jessamyn West book of short stories about a Quaker family in Civil War Indiana. Wyler saw Tony in the Robert Anderson play and asked to meet him. Tony's agent suggested he see Wyler even though he had already agreed to appear in a new John Van Druten play due for Broadway the following season.

'It was a most ironic thing because the people who were putting

Anthony Perkins with Maria, Gary and Rocky Cooper at the opening of *Friendly Persuasion*, 1956 (Photofest).

the play together said, "We'll sign you to do it, but if we don't like you at the end of two weeks we'll be able fire you . . . it's the two-week clause." Well, I felt that wasn't right, and I guess I had a high opinion of myself and we were wrestling over this point when William Wyler came to town. Although I was convinced I would finally end up doing the play, I did go up for the interview with Wyler.'

When Tony arrived at the St Regis Hotel for the meeting, he was told by Wyler's assistant that the director was hard of hearing and he had better speak up if he wanted to get any results. Subsequently, Tony learned that the assistant only told that to the candidates he thought might be good in the parts, which was his way of indicating to Wyler those he felt were most suitable.

In the hotel room, while Tony answered the director's questions in a loud voice, Wyler peered at him with a cigar in his mouth. As Tony left, Wyler offered him a script and asked if he would like to come back and read for him. Although Tony's hopes were up, he believed Wyler was reading a good many actors for the part and that his chances were very slim.

When Tony returned for a reading, Wyler was sitting in his dressing-gown eating scrambled eggs and bacon. He looked up.

'Oh yes, I remember you, how do you see this scene?'

Tony explained how he thought he would like to play it.

'Alright,' Wyler said as he was pouring his coffee, 'Read it.'

Tony read the scene, while Wyler sat there eating his toast.

'Would you like a cup of coffee?'

'Yes, please.'

'Well, I'd like you to do the part.'

Thrilled as he was, Tony was placed in a dilemma. Because he never dreamed he would be offered the film, he had, more or less, committed himself to the Van Druten play. The people who were handling it were now all too eager to forget about the two-week clause that had originally kept him from signing their contract.

He was now faced with the problem of accepting a part in which he knew he could shine on stage, where he felt his talents lay, or taking a risk and returning to film acting, something for which his earlier experience had given him little taste.

'I think it was the most agonising decision I've made in my entire career. Finally, I opted to do the picture, which really turned out so well. Ironically, the play closed out of town and never reached New York.

'It was in *Friendly Persuasion* . . . that I realized what acting could be. When I watched Phyllis Love and Mark Richman [who play his sister and her suitor], I saw the difference for the first time. When I worked in *The Actress*, I didn't learn. In all the time I played in *Tea and Sympathy* I didn't learn. But I saw Phyllis Love on the set . . . making copious notes and then I heard her asking the director all kinds of questions like, "What time of day is it supposed to be?" So I started to wonder what I was really doing and I'd say, "What time of day is it supposed to be?" Then the lights went on and I was learning about Method acting. I began to rely less on intuition and to study the architecture of the role. It's easy, as a young actor, to depend on your intuition, which often leads to an inaccurate motivation for the character you're portraying. I began to get a reputation as a director-botherer.'

Most of all, however, as he later admitted, he learned from Gary Cooper.

'He was a man to watch. If you wanted to learn something about motion picture acting and how to get your little bits of business in there, no-one was more adept than he. It's true that he looked up for microphones. He waited until the mike swung his way. He would time the beginning of the line to the arrival of the microphone.'

Tony got the notion that as Cooper's son he should have the same mannerisms as his 'father'. He shadowed Coop incessantly, studying his every move. He even dated Maria Cooper, the actor's eighteen-year-old daughter. But the veteran macho star was less impressed by Tony.

'That boy should get out on a ranch and meet some real people. Do him good,' he remarked.

The bashful and lanky Tony passes easily for Cooper's son in the movie, and John Kerr remembered Tony doing a brilliant imitation of Gary Cooper. Kerr, who had wanted the role himself, but whose agent advised against it, had already made his screen debut in *The Cobweb*, and had just completed shooting *Tea and Sympathy*. Thereafter, he appeared in a couple of stinkers at MGM, which did his career no good. Meanwhile, *Friendly Persuasion* launched Tony as a film actor, and the wounds of his envy of John Kerr were healed.

Because Wyler had the habit of contenting himself with only four or five takes, Tony considered him rather casual and unthorough, reckoning he could have afforded endless takes, as even directors of B-films sometimes required at least ten. The rookie movie actor, therefore, developed a system by which he would get Wyler into a corner and show him four versions of every scene so that when the time came to actually shoot, the director could pick one that he wanted. Tony knew that everyone else in the film would be asked for at least four versions of their close-ups and he thought he could bypass that.

'Wyler was a practical man, but he just didn't know what he wanted,' Tony recalled. 'He was happy to get a little encouragement from somebody who was able to say, "Look I can do it this way or that way." I always brought him four, because I thought, after having brought him four for the first few days, if I started bringing him in three he would think I was a less serious actor.'

For many years afterwards, Tony would offer directors a variety of possible interpretations to choose from. On *Friendly*

Persuasion, he also learned how 'not to take my work home with me but not even as far as lunch.'

'We were doing an intense scene at the dining room table. It was tremendously charged with tearful and agonised emotions. We had shot the master and the next shot was my choker. And it was all there. Then the assistant director called, "Lunch, one hour", before Wyler had a chance to do it, but even he went along with it. And he came up to me and said, "I'm sorry about that, kid. Grab a little nap and we'll pick that up later. Sorry we had to interrupt your scene, but you know unions", and he went off with his cigar. I wanted to keep the emotion of the scene going, but I was really hungry and I really craved a cheeseburger and a couple of malted milks. But I resisted. Yet as I started up towards my dressing-room, I thought, I'm in the movies now and I'll have to get used to these interruptions. So I went and had the cheeseburger and the double malts, and went right back into the scene and I faced it and was able to get through it and do it well, I think.'

Friendly Persuasion tells the story of the Birdwells, a peaceful Indiana family of 'theeing' and 'thouing' Quakers whose sanctuary is disturbed by the coming Civil War in 1862. Gary Cooper is the patriarch married to Dorothy McGuire. Josh (Tony Perkins), their teenage son, listens to a Union Officer make a plea for young men to take up the cause. Although morally opposed to war, he wonders if he is hiding behind religion to mask a cowardly streak.

Sitting in the Friends' Meeting House – resembling a Modigliani portrait with his long neck and a large Quaker hat seemingly too big for his head – he is asked by a recruiting officer, 'Are you afraid to fight?'

'I don't know', he replies in all sincerity, and visibly flinches as a member of the congregation shouts in his ear that a Quaker can never consider killing another man.

Later, at the fair, he attempts to contain his excitement when his friend is involved in a wrestling match. His boyish vulnerability and indoctrinated passivity is shown when he gets shaken up by some hooligans.

In a superbly played comic scene, Tony is surrounded by the three man-starved daughters of a widow (Marjorie Main), who refuse to let the boy out of their sight or give him space to move. He gesticulates desperately to his father and tries to move away. When one of them approaches him, he meticulously does up every button on his jacket.

When the news breaks that the Southern band, known as Morgan's Raiders, is approaching, he is determined to join the local militia and take up arms to defend the territory. His mother is shocked, and he hangs his head and glares down on the ground. However, his father says, 'We can't keep him tied to your apron strings all the time.'

Then, in a speech delivered with splendidly restrained passion, Tony exclaims, 'Mother, I hate fighting. I don't want to die. I don't know if I could kill anyone if I tried. But I have to try so long as other people have to.'

She tucks him into bed and holds his hands.

'I have to do what's right,' he murmurs.

While waiting for the 'rebs' to attack, the boy (like Henry, the youth in *The Red Badge of Courage*) is afraid, holding his gun tightly. When the battle comes, he shoots a man while fighting back his tears – he is going against all his upbringing. As he lies wounded, he clutches at the man he has killed.

The father goes into the war zone, finds his son and brings the wounded boy home. Josh has convinced himself and others that he is a brave man.

Friendly Persuasion gave most film audiences a first sight of Tony – not many would have remembered him from *The Actress* three years before – and their responses to the attractive, impressionable youth were favourable. Although the part of Josh Birdwell called for a deeply sensitive characterisation, Tony successfully avoided the conventional mannerisms which were becoming awkward, almost brash, trademarks of young actors. What may have seemed Method mannerisms then, now seem natural and subtle. He does often tuck his hands in his arm pits and even wraps them round his neck at one point, and his delivery contains a few hesitations, but he is not out of key with the rest of the cast, or with the period. Perhaps it was to his advantage that, at that stage in his career, he had not been to the Actors Studio.

Most of the reviews he received were affirmative. The *New York Times* commented that 'a great deal of admiration must go to Anthony Perkins as Josh. He makes the older son of the Birdwells a handsome, intense and chivalrous lad.'

'I had previously made one film . . . I was given a second chance,' Tony declared. 'Because if you perform in a rather good supporting role in Los Angeles and you don't really do it well and you don't really come off well, you may not ever get any second chance. So I was tremendously grateful to that film and to Wyler for giving me that chance, because I came back in an entirely different kind of role. It was so different from the first film that they had the nerve to say "Introducing Anthony Perkins", which really wasn't the case.'

A movie magazine at the time, noting the forthcoming film, wrote: 'Does the public really want to see new faces? Wyler believes yes. He has signed three young players from the New York stage. Making their screen debuts [sic] are Anthony Perkins, Phyllis Love and Mark Richman.'

The trailer for the film did its best to tag Tony as a 'second James Dean', a claim put about for practically any good-looking newcomer at that time, with the usual disregard for actor and role.

'They call me another James Dean or a young Gregory Peck,'

Tony stated in the late 1950s. 'Just about the only star I haven't been compared to is Lassie.'

It was during the making of *Friendly Persuasion*, in September 1955, that James Dean was killed. Tony was visiting the eccentric Finnish-born actress Maila Nurmi (who played Vampira) at her house on Larrabee Avenue when the phone rang. It was a friend, who broke the news.

'You must be joking,' exclaimed Maila, who looked up to see that one of the pins holding up a photograph that Dean had given her of himself had dropped on the floor. The picture was swaying back and forth like a pendulum. Tony, already pencilled in by producers to be the beautiful and brooding Dean's successor, restored the photo to its position, and left.

Friendly Persuasion was an enormously successful film, but it carried a repugnant undertow. The screenplay had been written years earlier by Michael Wilson for Frank Capra. When Wyler decided to revive the project he needed extensive rewrites. He therefore brought in Robert Wyler and the book's author, Jessamyn West, to change half the script's structure and about ninety percent of the dialogue. Nevertheless, Wilson was awarded sole writer's credit. But Allied Artists shamefully chose to deny it 'to a writer revealed to be a member of the Communist party or one who refused to answer charges of Communist affiliation.' (Wilson had evoked the Fifth Amendment when called as a witness in 1951 to the House Committee of UnAmerican Activities.) Thus, *Friendly Persuasion* was released without any screenwriter credit at all.

As a consequence of the HUAC's blacklisting and its abiding influence on the Hollywood community, the winner of the 1956 Oscar for Best Motion Picture Story was one 'Robert Rich', the scenarist of *The Brave One*. 'Rich' was not present at the RKO Pantages Theatre to collect his prize, which was picked up by Jesse

Lasky Jr. To the Academy's mortification, however, it subsequently transpired that 'Robert Rich' was the pseudonym of Dalton Trumbo, a blacklisted author and one of the 'Hollywood Ten.'

Tony was among the nominees for Best Supporting Actor, for his second screen role, the others being Don Murray (really a co-starring role) in *Bus Stop*; Mickey Rooney in *The Bold and the Brave*; Robert Stack in *Written on the Wind*, and Anthony Quinn as Gaugin in *Lust for Life*. When it came to the announcement, Tony remembered hearing. 'And the winner is Anthony . . . Quinn.'

Friendly Persuasion led to a contract with Paramount Pictures, and Hollywood stardom. Like Charlie Chaplin caught in the huge machine in *Modern Times*, Tony was suddenly plunged into the Hollywood processing apparatus operated by producers, agents, lawyers and PR people. But Charlie passes through the wheels of the machine only to emerge safely at the other end. Tony, on the other hand, returned to earth after regrooming, interviews and publicity stills aplenty, bruised and dizzy from the experience. Despite, or because of, the exaggerated curiosity and extravagant flattery that Hollywood stars arouse, nagging doubts lingered in his mind.

'The one thing I can never be comprehensive or articulate about is what it [stardom] has done to me. I may wake up screaming. What is all this? Why has it happened to me? I am not good-looking or experienced or what you'd call a "build". It's not nepotism nor have I spent years as an actor. Yet here I am . . . I'm shocked, at times, at my lack of qualifications . . . I'm afraid to start studying [acting] now, just as some actors are afraid of analysis – they fear it will change them. I'm really on treacherous ground.'

Many of his contemporaries managed to take movie celebrity in their stride, and appreciate the material benefits it brought. Tony, while enjoying some of the fuss made over him – after all nobody

usand years older than you.'
tells him,'Jacob is a man, that's something you're not.'
you teach me,' he replies.
rther on, she is saying,'You're not a man, you're a boy.'
refuses to break in a horse, his father lassoes him.
you like any wild horse. I'll break you or kill you. I'll
n of you.'
e's told by his father's friend,'You're not a man, you're a

Riley proves his manhood by capturing a wild white
nd helps his father in the climactic gunfight, in which
In the perfunctory ending, it cuts away from any dis-
f as he reaches out over the dead body.
beat, taut, psychological Western was one of the more
films directed by studio hack Henry Levin. Having
m Phyllis Love in his previous film not to just accept
director tells you to do without motivation, he and
in, whom Tony described as 'an absolute slave to the
. . finished off Henry Levin, the director, with our

male leads speak in a rather portentous monotone, and
llen and solemn throughout until they are reconciled.
s it more affecting when Palance smiles, and paternal
s up his face for the first time when his son calls him 'Pa'.
ic wrote of Tony's role as 'a hesitant, watchful, obstinate
kid, played so brilliantly at times by Anthony Perkins,
titudinizing at other times – particularly in the open-
- seems almost to be a schizophrenic parody of the Meth-
from which he obviously comes.'
r reviewer thought Palance and Perkins 'out-smould-
other as father and son. Of the two actors specializing

becomes an actor in order to retain their anonymity – already had a highly developed degree of scepticism. This enabled him to treat, more readily, those two imposters, Triumph and Disaster, just the same.

8

STRIKE THE FATHER DEAD

'No, I'm not running away, father. Yesterday I was, but today I'm not. Today I know exactly where I'm going and what I have to do, and then I'll be back' – Abel in *Green Mansions* (1959)

A cowboy walks up to a handsome young man, who is leaning on a bar counter, alone. The older man stares at the boy. The boy, plainly under the influence, says, 'You looking for somethin'?'

'Can I buy you a drink?' the man asks.

The boy smiles sideways. 'Oh, anybody can buy me a drink!', he replies, pushing his glass along the counter for the barman to fill.

The man continues to fix the boy in his gaze. Two drinks are poured. With a smile, the boy lifts the glass to his lips and slurs, 'Well, who are you?'

The man answers in a deep voice that seems to come from the grave. 'I'm your father.'

The glass stops at the boy's lips, then languidly, describing an arc with his arm, he splashes his drink into the man's face. The boy

scowls and blinks, takes his hat o
the saloon in a hunched manner, l

This is the opening sequence of
Tony made under his new contrac
could be seen as the start of a tri
has to prove his manhood to his fa
The plot has the son, Riley Wade,
ex-bandit father, Jacob Wade (Jack
for fourteen years. As neither of t
set out for the ranch of Jacob's girl
the boy takes with him on the jour
whom he believes his father betraye
'I look like her, don't I? . . . Eve
remember you killed my mother.'
Thus, in this minor Western, in a
what was to become Tony's scarlet
Prynne's, his was a capital M for
first of his many mother-fixated ch
apotheosis in Norman Bates.
Every time anyone mentions Rile
lent response.
'You mention my mother in this ho
tells one of his father's ex-cronies.
When he learns the unpleasant tru
serted his father and not vice versa), T
his arms.
'You're a l-l-liar,' he protests in angu
has been told.
As long as he remains a Momma's B
hood. Confronting Ada, a real wom
man like Jacob, Riley says, 'You're n

my age.'
'I'm a th
Later, sh
'Suppos
A reel f
When h
'I'll brea
make a ma
Again,
boy.'
Finally,
mustang,
Jacob dies
play of gri
This of
interestin
learned fr
what the
Elaine Ai
Method .
questions
Both th
both are
This mak
pride ligh
One cr
mixed-up
that his a
ing scene
od Schoo
Anoth
ered each

in suppressed emotion, Perkins won by a twitch.'

Curiously, Levin forced Tony, as a left-hander, to learn to switch to the right hand, especially when pulling a gun, because it was the received wisdom that anything done in a left-handed manner distracts the audience. There is still a residue of superstition and a prejudice towards left-handedness, which is considered perverse or 'sinister'. Arthur Penn's first film, the Western *The Left-handed Gun*, made a year after *The Lonely Man*, involved Paul Newman as a crazy mixed-up Billy the Kid, in which there were homosexual undertones.

Tony's left-handedness would become an issue again in his next film, *Fear Strikes Out*, and in the shower scene from *Psycho.* When Tony was around five years old, his mother (right-handed like Mrs Bates) tried to train the boy to switch. Unfortunately, after arduously attempting to write or paint with his right hand, Tony would begin to stammer. Mrs Perkins was advised to let the child develop in the way that felt natural to him. If only society were as tolerant towards other harmless deviations from the norm, Tony, among myriads of others, would have led a more contented life.

The father-son theme (the imitator of the father, the imaginary father etc) was popular in the mid-1950s viz. *Rebel Without a Cause*, *East of Eden*, *The Young Stranger* and *The Rack*, with James Dean, James MacArthur and Paul Newman, respectively, achingly trying to gain a father's love. In *Fear Strikes Out*, Tony's second Paramount picture, the link between father and son is stretched to breaking point. In this biopic, he impersonated Jim Piersall, outfielder of the Boston Red Sox, who suffered an emotional collapse. (A year previously, Tony's close friend, Tab Hunter had starred in *The Jim Piersall Story* on CBS)

For many Americans, sport forms a bond that ties sons to

KARL MALDEN AND ANTHONY PERKINS IN *FEAR STRIKES OUT*, 1957 (PHOTOFEST).

fathers. (Philip Roth gives a poignant description of Portnoy's father playing baseball in *Portnoy's Complaint.*) The tie between nine-year-old Jim Piersall and his dad is strengthened by their shared love of baseball. Dad Piersall (Karl Malden), never having got beyond minor league status in his youth, is determined to live out his own life through his son. Every day after school he coaches young Jim.

'We're going for the big leagues, boy,' he mutters.

Jim is a highly-strung lad, always striving to please his father. At seventeen, his all-round talents help his high-school team to win the championship.

'How'd I do, dad?' he asks with the flush of victory on his face.

'Not bad, son. But you weren't on your toes all the time, and you know it.'

Jim is signed by the Red Sox and sent to the Scranton team for training. His father tells him that next year it has to be Boston. His batting wins Scranton the pennant, but the pressure on him is great. When he finally gets to play for the Red Sox, it is as shortstop, a position he has never filled. The fear of failure is so strong that the strain of the past years takes its toll and he goes berserk, attacking his team-mates and trying to climb the high wire fence. (A powerfully directed moment.) He wakes up in a straitjacket. The real irony of Piersall's dilemma is brought out in what he says of his father to the psychiatrist at the hospital.

'If it hadn't been for him standing behind me, pushing me and driving me, I wouldn't be where I am today.'

When he realizes that it is his father's monomania that has driven him to the edge of madness, he reaches the road to recovery and success.

Hollywood has always been rather simple about complexes, but the film avoids glib psychological theorizing while still making the reasons for Piersall's breakdown perfectly clear. Obviously there were contributory causes inherent in Piersall's nature, but for dramatic purposes the paternal cause eliminates the others.

In effect, Piersall suffered from what is called the Laius complex. Laius, the father of Oedipus, tried to kill his son at birth, but the boy grew up and killed his father instead. The Freudian expression, 'Strike the father dead' (with its hint of baseball) is essential before the son can be a man in his own right.

The director Robert Mulligan made effective use of the visual motif of fences and wire bars that separate father from son. It was an auspicious film, being thirty-two-year-old Mulligan's first movie as director, Alan Pakula's first production, and Tony's first starring role. *Fear Strikes Out* also happens to be one of the most interesting of sporting biopics.

Prior to filming, Mulligan, whose background was in live television, had the cast give a staged performance of the whole film for the Paramount brass. This innovative procedure gave Mulligan the chance to have a dress rehearsal, so to speak, and the executives a taste of what the film would be like.

'Tony went through the scenes showing the actual breakdown for three days and three nights. And because Tony doesn't spare himself when he acts, he was in a state of nervous exhaustion the entire time,' Mulligan explained. 'I felt like a monster; my wife thought I was one. After she watched the shooting, she wouldn't speak to me the next day . . . Once . . . Tony gripped a bat and swung it with such violence I was afraid he really had cracked up. Often, I had to run down to him and take him out of the scene for a few moments so he could cry it out. Tony lived his role, and his tortures were real.'

This recalls an incident during the filming of *The Lonely Man*, when a fist fight between Robert Middleton and Tony ('living the part') had to be stopped. 'I thought the crazy kid was trying to kill me!' Middleton gasped.

Tony, who usually lost weight under the strain of film work in the 1950s, was hospitalized after the shooting of *Fear Strikes Out.*

As a child, Tony was considered too sensitive to play baseball. Whenever his mother encouraged him to join a team because his father enjoyed the game (Osgood had achieved some glory on the Harvard team), he would retort, 'You're out on the field, and you miss catching a ball, and everybody's mad at you. Not me!'.

Nevertheless, Tony's portrayal of a professional baseball player, on the field, was fairly convincing, though he failed to persuade Paramount to reverse the film so he could appear right-handed while pitching but batting with his left. Determination and ambition shines from his eyes as he works to achieve the success which will please his father. When departing for camp by train, he stretches his hand out to get some warmth from his father, who fails to offer it. When in distress, he tenses his whole body, hunching his coat-hanger shoulders. But the edgy, angular performance is not without moments of tenderness and wit, and after the breakdown he retains a certain stillness, proving that the playing of a mentally disturbed man can be done with subtlety.

'I don't understand the things I do,' he exclaims in desperation to the psychiatrist, while drumming his fingers on the wall, a similar gesture to the one he uses in *Psycho.* Another anticipation of the later film is his attachment to his mother – 'We made a pretty good team me and my mom' – though she is almost effaced by the father.

Some commentators were disturbed by the subversion of the rigid codes of masculinity that usually underpinned sports stories. Tony's portrayal supported Peter Biskind's theories of incipient 'feminization' of many male protagonists in the 50s, and the changing of attitudes.

'There's a feminized man inside him [Tony Perkins and/or Jim

Piersall] waiting to be born. He's shy, awkward and speaks with a slight stutter. On his first date with his wife-to-be, he does the cooking and the dishes, and yes, ties on an apron. Tony's having trouble making the Red Sox because he can't hit, he doesn't have enough "power", which is to say, he has to struggle against feelings of effeminacy.'

In order to publicize the film, both Tony and Jim Piersall appeared on *The Ed Sullivan Show.* Among the other guests were Lena Horne, Bill Haley's Comets and Heidi, a trick dog. The latter, at least, was more at home jumping through hoops for a TV audience than Tony would ever be.

However, though he constantly complained about having to roll over and have his tummy rubbed for publicity, Tony, according to Alan Pakula, would 'get a big kick out of publicity. When a story appeared about him anywhere, he used to run to the front office showing it off to anybody who'd pay attention.'

'He loves being important. His life is occupied with success,' claimed Paramount costume designer Dorothy Jeakins.

'You can go to school to learn anything in the world – except what happens to you when you become a movie star,' Tony commented at the time. 'It's the most disconcerting experience imaginable. Half of you thinks you're not worthy, you don't deserve it. The other half thinks this is what you were meant to be.'

There is a possibility that Tony, like Woody Allen, was gripped by Anhedonia, a psychological reaction to events which causes the sufferer to be unable to enjoy anything, even the most pleasurable experiences, without feelings of anxiety.

Henry Fonda followed Gary Cooper, Jack Palance and Karl Malden in the line of fathers and father-figures who took Tony under their wings in the early part of his film career.

The Tin Star was shot in the autumn of 1956, after Fonda had just married for the third time. (His daughter Jane was then a rebellious eighteen-year-old student at Vassar.) Tony found the older actor in meditative mood, and the usually reticent Fonda told Tony the story of his life during the daily drive out to the Paramount ranch which they shared.

'It was one hour out and one hour back for three weeks,' Tony recalled. 'He paced the story to last, picking it up every morning where he'd stopped the day before.'

Fifty-two-year-old Fonda, in films almost as long as Tony had lived, was impressed by the young actor's dedication. He also saw a lot of his earlier self in Tony – gangling, and embarrassed by the opposite sex. The difference being that the women-shy personae of Fonda, Gary Cooper and James Stewart did not reflect their real-life attitudes. Tony had little problem expressing his own insecurity with women on screen, though he was yet to have a real love scene. In *The Tin Star*, Tony is given a grumpy girlfriend (Mary Webster), with whom he has only a minimal relationship beyond her criticism of his job. He does not even get to kiss her.

He first appears practising drawing his guns (unlike in *The Lonely Man*, he is permitted to be left-handed), clumsily dropping one when Fonda enters.

'I'm just getting the feel of these guns,' he says with embarrassment, an emotion of which he was already a past master.

'Where's the sheriff?' Fonda asks, before noticing the tin star on Tony's coat.

As the green sheriff, Tony merely looks petulant when the heavy (Neville Brand) kills a half-breed. He gulps and then approaches the man tentatively. The villain is seen from behind, ready to draw, an angle which makes him look far larger than Tony standing before him.

'I just want your guns, that's all,' Tony pleads, his voice reaching the high Osgood range. Fonda saves the day by shooting the man's gun from his hand, after which Tony approaches Fonda hesitantingly.

'I'd l. . . l. . . like to talk to you about. . . Is it true you used to be a sheriff like me?'

'Not like you.'

'I'm only temporary.'

'More temporary than you think.'

In the saloon with Fonda, he orders whisky, while the older man drinks beer.

'I'd get laughed at if I had beer.'

'Nobody's laughing at me,' says Fonda as he takes a sip of beer from his glass. 'Stop acting so mean and surly all the time. You think it makes you look older and tougher.'

Tony eventually turns one of his broad smiles on his mentor. Fonda is a bounty hunter, who has ridden into town. He had been a sheriff himself but resigned the post through bitterness. Handing over a lucrative corpse to the sheriff, he learns that he will have to wait for the money to come through, so he spends the time schooling the novice in marksmanship and cool-headedness.

'A gun's only a tool, you can master a gun if you have the knack. It's harder to learn men.'

The inexperienced, foolhardy and idealistic young sheriff believes in giving law-breakers a fair trial, but in the unruly West many consider this a weakness. The issue is whether the sheriff will modify his principles under the hard-bitten tuition of the bounty hunter.

At the climax, Tony faces a lynch mob and the same villain with more self-confidence. This time, he sets his jaw with determination, and is photographed from behind making him seem larger. With his slightly stooped walk, the guns at his side weighing him down, he comes up to the man and slaps his face. The

Anthony Perkins and Henry Fonda in *The Tin Star*, 1957 (Photofest).

maturation of Tony's character seemed as inevitable as the showdown.

Compared with the five classic films of the genre, starring James Stewart, which he had directed between 1950 and 1954, *The Tin Star* was one of Anthony Mann's minor Westerns. Although the movie creates some tension and pathos, especially in the relationship between Fonda and Betsy Palmer, as a widow with a half-Indian son, the total effect is more modest than intended. The two male leads give muted, interior performances; the unshaven, balding, seasoned adult and the smooth-faced stripling make an odd couple. The supreme confidence of Fonda, as character and actor, contrasts with Tony's gaucheness and slight stiffness, again a callow youth who has to earn his manhood. His instruction in sheriff-ship from Fonda echoes the lessons that Tom Lee takes from his room-mate on how to be masculine in *Tea and Sympathy*.

Betsy Palmer, like Elaine Aikin in *The Lonely Man*, was from the Actors Studio, and a devotee of the Stanislavsky, method of which Tony had only a superficial knowledge. Palmer, who had been a girlfriend of James Dean's, was eager to tell Tony as much as she could about the Method.

In *The Tin Star* Tony is not a rebel – with or without a cause – but a fine and upstanding member of the community, a clean-cut youth doing his job. Unlike some of his contemporaries, Tony was seldom the crazy mixed-up kid of the 50s, but someone who yearns to be part of society. It was Henry Fonda, and Jack Palance in the earlier Western, and Gary Cooper in *Friendly Persuasion*, who were the non-conformists.

There was a narrow choice for young actors in Hollywood at the time, with youth itself so often treated as a Problem, along with drug addiction, alcoholism and crime. Until the school of James Dean, most movies and advertisements showed what fun it was to be a teenager, the majority of whom had lovable and understanding parents. Ironically, for someone who made a name as a tortured young man, Tony's comic gifts, too often submerged, might have blossomed in the more innocent pre-Freudian days.

9

BUT WHEN I BECAME A MAN

'I'm Six Foot Two. I Have to Start Some Time' – Cornelius Hackel in *The Matchmaker* (1958)

Eugene O'Neill's tragedy, *Desire Under the Elms* (derived from Euripides' *Hippolytus* – the same source as *Phaedra* and *Medea*), had been a great success on the stage in 1924, but censorship had kept it off the screen since. Taking advantage of a more indulgent attitude to heterosexual sex in Hollywood in the late 1950s, Paramount decided to film it as a vehicle for their new foreign contractee, Sophia Loren.

The Italian sexpot, at twenty-three two years Tony's junior, was embarking on her second film in the USA, after having been given a great publicity build-up for her first English-speaking film, *Boy On a Dolphin*, opposite Alan Ladd.

'Sex appeal is 50 per cent of what you've got, and 50 per cent of what people think you have . . . The figure Heaven has seen fit to give me I owe to spaghetti,' Loren explained.

It was Sophia Loren in *Desire Under the Elms* who transformed

Anthony Perkins from boy into boy-man on screen. After having played a number of immature youths, whose only experience of the opposite sex was of an innocent kind with rather insipid heroines, Tony was given the chance to grow up and tangle with a sensuous woman. The fact that she also happened to be Latin added spice to the prospect. When he was asked how he felt about doing an erotic scene for the first time on screen, Tony said he found it easy because Loren had 'such a sense of humour about herself and the scenes, that one couldn't help enjoying them.'

In order to accommodate Loren's nationality, the character was changed from Abbie to Anna, an Italian woman. In the play she is described by O'Neill as 'thirty-five, buxom, full of vitality. Her round face is pretty but marred by its rather gross sensuality. There is strength and obstinacy in her jaw, a hard determination in her eyes and about her whole personality the same unsettled, untamed, desperate quality.'

According to the playwright, Eben, her stepson, Tony's role, is 'twenty-five, tall and sinewy. His face is well-formed, good-looking, but its expression is resentful and defensive. His defiant, dark eyes remind one of a wild animal's in captivity. Each day is a cage in which he finds himself trapped but inwardly unsubdued. There is a fierce repressed vitality about him. He has black hair, moustache, a thin curly trace of beard. He is dressed in rough farm clothes.'

The mighty Burl Ives played Ephraim Cabot, the unbending and miserly septuagenarian Puritan farmer, who makes his three sons work their fingers to the bone on his farm, which the youngest son, Eben, claims as his own, because it had been his dead mother's property. Ephraim is the prototype of the primal father, hard, all-powerful, ruthless. Eben is a brooding neurotic who violently hates his father for driving his 'maw' into an early grave.

The action takes place in 1850 on a small New Hampshire 'sixty

Sophia Loren and Anthony Perkins in *Desire Under the Elms*, 1958 (Photofest).

acres of dirt' farm and concerns Eben Cabot's struggle to regain what he believes to be his rightful heritage: the Cabot farm. He is frustrated in this by his father's third marriage to an Italian girl. When Ephraim comes back with his young wife, fifty years his junior (Loren had recently married producer Carlo Ponti twenty-four years her senior), Eben, afraid for his inheritance, looks at her with a mixture of intense interest and distaste.

Tony starts off the film looking a little older, stronger and sterner than he had on screen before, with the help of a five o'clock shadow from the make-up department. Yet his father derides him for being 'soft like your maw'. It was inevitable that no matter how rugged the disguise, Tony would be seen as unmanly.

Later, while stripped to the waist and chopping wood – Tony is no longer the skinny youth but a well-built man – Anna starts to flirt with him. All he can do is flash his eyes and claim he detests her, but that night, lying on his bed (bare-chested again), he tries to block his ears to shut out her laughter, his desires, and the fact that she is with his hoary, horny father. It is only a matter of time before she enters his room, while her husband is away.

'Ever since I came here you've been fighting nature. Trying to tell yourself, I'm not pretty to you. Nature will beat you.'

It does. A hackneyed thunderstorm underlines the seduction scene, as they kiss.

'I hate the sight of you,' he says.

'But you kissed me back. Your lips were hot.'

When he resists her again, the refrain from *The Lonely Man* comes back.

'You're not a man.'

But he soon proves he is one with the first genuinely erotic kiss audiences had seen him give, although tame by European standards then and restrained by those of today. Even when they are in the hayloft together, all the couple do is talk and cuddle a little. Passion turns into romance, and he opens up, smiling broadly and lovingly as he watches her run down the hill or serve breakfast. His five o'clock shadow disappears and Tony looks baby-smooth again.

When Anna bears him a son, Ephraim mistakenly believes it to be his own. Ephraim taunts Eben with the new heir to the Cabot farm, and Eben thereupon turns on Anna, convinced that their whole affair has been engineered by her to secure the farm for herself and her son. Eben stands by the cot staring at the child, with barely any expression on his face, almost as if Tony had full confidence in the director to make something of it. After all, the Russian film-maker Lev Kuleshov's famous experiment intercut the same unaltered close-up of the face of an actor with three different scenes, so that it seemed he was expressing hunger, fear and pleasure in turn. The Kuleshov effect not only proved the power of editing but , unwittingly, how easily an actor's performance can be manipulated by the director. But Delbert Mann was no Kuleshov, nor even a William Wyler or a Robert Mulligan, the two directors who had got the best performances out of Tony so far.

Anna kills her baby in a desperate attempt to prove her love for Eben. Eben is horrified when he finds out and collapses onto the ground, crying while holding his face – much easier to act extreme emotion that way, though Tony could display it if he had to.

Eben goes to fetch the sheriff, but later, overcome with remorse, he decides that as he shares the guilt, so must he share the punishment. He and Anna are led off to justice leaving Ephraim alone on the farm.

Everybody seems to regard the farm as something special, although it is no more than a small artificial sound stage on the Paramount lot around which echoes the actors' voices. O'Neill's enormous elms 'brooding oppressively over the house like exhausted women' have become two delicate, rather beautiful trees in the prettified set. Although the film has the look of a superior TV studio drama, its airlessness is applicable to the foggy atmosphere of the farm, where, as Ives says, 'There is something dark in the corners of this house prowling.'

Though it is stolidly and sometimes awkwardly directed by Delbert Mann ('a charming guy', according to Tony), the film allowed all three stars equal opportunity to shine through the murky tale. The *New York Times* thought Tony was 'suitably passion-charged. He lashes and lowers with wild resentments' and Loren 'throbs poignantly in the toils of love.'

However, Tony disliked the film and his role, though it did not prevent him from playing a similar one in *Phaedra* a few years later. He found it ironic and inappropriate that a play about the need and lust for property was not even shot on the Paramount lot but on a sound stage. After seeing the film, he commented,

'I couldn't sit through the damn thing. It was nothing but talk, talk, talk, talk, talk, talk, talk. When you make a moving picture it's supposed to move.'

As most of it was O'Neill's talk, and it was all in the script when he accepted the part, he did not have much cause for complaint, even if it does contain lines like 'By God A'mighty she's purty, and I don't give a damn how many sins she's sinned afore mine or who she's sinned 'em with , my sin's as purty as any one of them.'

Tony also found fault with Sophia Loren.

'Somebody told her she should get her face in the camera in every scene. I didn't like my part anyway, and all you could see of me, even in my scenes, would be the back of my head and my ear. By the next picture, five years later [*Five Miles to Midnight*], she realized that this wasn't what made her a big star – which she is. She reformed.'

This is not apparent on watching the film; it may only have seemed so to Tony on the set. Nor is Tony's claim visible to the naked eye that he was trying to do an impression of Laurence Olivier in *Wuthering Heights* 'with an added nasty streak.' As Heathcliff is intrinsically a nastier character than Eben, it shows a misunderstanding of the Emily Bronte character.

Tony was not comfortable in tragic drama, where there was virtually no room for his inherently mischievous, quirky and black humour which he could exercise in a thriller (*Psycho*) or an allegory (*The Trial*) or soap opera (*Goodbye Again*), and in the disappointingly few genuine comedies he made.

It was around the time of *Desire Under the Elms* that Tony gained a reputation for being a 'spoilt brat', a rebel without cause, and a difficult person to work with, much of which was exploited by the Paramount publicity department. By behaving as he did, Tony allowed them to use the 'revolting' image to sell him to the teenage followers. In the late 50s, people were more easily shocked or, rather, it was easier to produce the pleasurable frisson of outrage in audiences.

Don Hartman, the *Desire Under the Elms* producer, stated, 'I thought the other actors and Delbert Mann would go mad. Why, Perkins would ask, is the character I'm playing doing this, saying that? What is he thinking?'

Always a defiantly casual dresser, Tony was given to strolling around Los Angeles in bare feet, or turning up at a posh press lunch in jeans, sneakers with holes in them, and an old shirt. Once he proceeded to set about eating spaghetti with his hands.

On *The Lonely Man*, Tony was lunching with other cast members when one of the grips sat down at the table. Tony told him abruptly, 'Scram! This is the star's table.'

Later, when a crew member climbed into the rented car that was to take Tony and others into town, Tony shouted, 'This is the star's car! Bail out!'

The man then had to wait a full thirty minutes until the same car made the return trip.

An actor colleague said, 'Everything about him is immature. He's like a twelve-year-old. Everything he does is an extreme act. He has a small malicious streak in him. He has no friends. He wants to be accepted. He probably feels if he could be a movie star he would be accepted. But this is a false premise. When he grows up he'll have everything he needs for this profession. Right now he's like a beautiful dust jacket of a book with nothing between the covers. I think he ought to meet a good psychiatrist.'

One day, lunching at the studio canteen with Paramount story editor D. A. Doran and other studio brass, Tony scanned the menu and asked why he could not have a sandwich named after him.

'I've got the greatest combination,' he said, 'Chicken and grilled cheese.'

When Doran and the others agreed to try it, Tony laughed. 'You will? My God, I wouldn't be caught dead eating it.'

Nevertheless the Tony Perkins Special was put on the Paramount menu.

Many other anecdotes attesting to Tony's misbehaviour were rife in the late 50s. But in the opinion of Jules Dassin, who directed Tony in *Phaedra*, 'The brat stories are bullshit.'

'It's become a bore . . . to be Tony who tries to abide by one rule after another,' the star himself commented.

'Mustn't do this, mustn't go there, mustn't bite his fingernails. Every other day I'd like to be someone else. I'd like to be short and fair – maybe a pre-med student at New York University born in Pittsburgh of a wealthy family.'

But if Tony's brattish behaviour could be put down to overcompensating for his intrinsic lack of confidence, his ego must have expanded somewhat under the fuss that was being made of him. A Paramount executive stated: 'Tony represents the studio's lifesaver. We invested fifteen million bucks in this kid, and figured he'd better click or we'd all be out looking for jobs. Well, he's clicked.'

The producer Don Hartman told *Newsweek*, 'Perkins seems the only young man about Hollywood today who has an excellent chance for long-term stardom. He has that indefinable quality that seems to leap from the screen in a personality all its own. Veterans like Cooper, Cary Grant, Spencer Tracy and Gable have it. Of course, they are fine actors, too, but there have been a hell of a lot of fine actors who didn't last five years. Each of the lasting big ones has maintained his own individuality, that special personal appeal necessary to longevity. And the audiences getting older right along with them, have continued to pay to see that individuality.'

'Mr Perkins was no Garrick. He would have been the first to toss back his head and laugh at such a suggestion. His would have been a sardonic laugh; an inner chuckle too large to be quite self-contained . . . Primarily he is likely to be remembered as a comedian; as the player of our day who could most tellingly deliver the dryest, most deflating lines our most irreverent dramatists were able to concoct.'

If, as he was equipped to do, Tony had followed in his father's light footsteps, the sketch above of Osgood Perkins, by John Mason Brown in 1938, could quite easily have fitted him.

Certain descriptions of Tony by his friends and colleagues keep returning – 'he had a wonderfully wry sense of humour', 'he was always able to find an element of humour in any part. That was his nature.'

Although Tony was known for his comic gifts in college productions and in summer stock, he had had little opportunity to display them on film. Perhaps if *The Actress* had not been a dead-end at MGM, he might have been able to explore that vein of his talent at that studio. Up to now, apart from a few flashes, Tony had to glower most of the time in overheated dramas like 'Perspire Under The Arms', as one wit called the O'Neill film. But behind the solemn mask there was always a grinning one waiting to be exposed. So it was fortunate that Don Hartman, the producer of *Desire Under the Elms*, cast him in *The Matchmaker*. (It was Hartman's last production before his death in 1958.)

It was to have been one of the first films Tony signed to do for Paramount back in December 1956, along with being slated to play the Richard Dix role in a remake of *Cimarron*. (This was eventually taken by Glenn Ford in a dull MGM movie in 1961.)

Like *Desire Under the Elms*, the film version of Thornton Wilder's comedy *The Matchmaker* (derived from the play by Nestroy, who based it on *A Day Well Spent* by John Oxenford, which later became *Hello Dolly*!) was closer to a TV production of a theatrical event, without the liberty and freshness of a film. Yet, in a way, it enabled Tony to demonstrate a sustained performance rather as he would on a stage. The *New York Times* critic pointed out that his 'loose-limbed, youthful delineation of the country bumpkin who finds adventure and romance in New York, strongly indicates that he is equally at home in farce as he is in serious drama.'

'*The Matchmaker* was a sad story,' Tony recalled. 'We were scheduled to make a colour film and all the sets and the lighting plots had been designed to accommodate colour. But at the last moment, Paramount, which was having a bit of a failure with VistaVision – it was too expensive to run – decided to economize by shooting it in black and white. It was a very murky film and that perhaps contributed to the fact that it seems a little dour. It should be a light-hearted romp, instead it looks rather Russian.'

Russian in Tony's lexicon obviously stood for gloomy. Perhaps if it did look Russian, it might have been more filmic. For want of colour, the picture needed at least an Ernst Lubitsch or Billy Wilder to make it really work. Instead, it got former Broadway director Joseph Anthony. Although it was a little too slow and the timing was often off, it was nonetheless a buoyant affair, played by a glittering cast which included Shirley Booth (Dolly Levi), Shirley MacLaine (Irene Molloy), Robert Morse (Barnaby Tucker) and Paul Ford (Horace Vandergelder).

John Michael Hayes' script tackled the form of the play head on, keeping the concept of three acts – Vandergelder's shop, Irene Molloy's hat shop, and the Harmonia Gardens restaurant – linked by a minimum of new material; while the director allowed the actors to address the camera in soliloquies and asides. At one point, Shirley Booth in the title role turns to the audience and says, 'Life is never quite interesting enough, somehow. You people who come to the movies know that.'

One of Tony's asides has him bursting with enthusiam as he expostulates: 'A fine woman is the finest work of God. Women are so different from men.'

Despite having reached a kind of manhood in *Desire Under the Elms*, he now, at twenty-five, regressed to adolescence again, albeit a carefree one. The plot actually revolves around Tony's character of Cornelius Hackel, a repressed, overworked young store-clerk, determined to have one great day out in New York city and not return to Yonkers until he has kissed a girl.

'I'm six foot two-inches tall! I have to start some time!' he exclaims.

Tony's stuttering delivery, often used in dramas to convey inner torment, is comically effective here, as when his penny-pinching boss, Horace Vandergelder, announces he is going to get married.

'She has my sym . . . my congratulations,' he stammers.

'Is there a m-m-m? Maybe a fiance?' he asks Shirley MacLaine, whom he fancies, long before Norman Bates mumbling 'b-b-b' in *Psycho II*, because he is unable to say the disconcerting word 'bathroom'.

MacLaine as Irene Molloy has put it about that Cornelius is 'the wittiest, the gayest, richest and most charming man in New York,' the as yet unmerited reputation that he is determined to live up to. There is poetry in the gauche way he attempts to put his arms around her corseted waist, and looks at her intensely before jerking away as she talks.

'If I tell you the truth would you let me put my arms around you?'

He then flashes his smile, that charm weapon which he uses far too frequently here, as if relieved to be working in a comedy. A better director might have told him how much more effective it is when used sparingly.

As the farcical elements of the plot thicken at the Harmonia Gardens, where all the characters come into contact, Tony is forced to get into drag, offering audiences a foretaste of Norman Bates's cross-dressing proclivities.

'Madam, you need a shave,' says Dolly dancing with the tall Tony.

Instead of letting go, as an actor more secure in his sexuality might have done, Tony checks any effeminacy, despite using a falsetto in the manner of an adolescent boy's breaking voice.

Shirley MacLaine gave *Newsweek* some behind-the-scenes tittle-tattle just before the film opened.

'Whenever Tony and I had a close-up . . . he would say, just before a take, "Wait a minute, there's something on your nose. Oh, make-up! Well, never mind. It probably won't show." Or else, during a shot photographed over his shoulder, he would stand there making funny faces at me. I mean it's one thing to be amateurish on his own time. When he interferes professionally, it's another

Anthony Perkins and Shirley MacLaine in *The Matchmaker*, 1958 (Photofest).

matter. I got mad at him . . . But he has a flair for comedy – for anything, as a matter of fact. He has a sense of humour and what seems to be the courage to do idiotic things. Or maybe he's just terribly ignorant.'

It was the twenty-three-year-old MacLaine's fifth film, and Tony's seventh. She would only make a breakthrough the following year in *Some Came Running*. Tony claimed to have learned a great many tricks from the veteran Shirley Booth, whose penultimate picture this was, before she returned to the stage.

At the finale of *The Matchmaker*, Tony, at his sunniest, delivers the last moral directly to the audience:

'The test of an adventure is when you're in the middle of it, you say to yourself, oh, gosh now I've got myself into an awful mess. I wish I were sitting quietly at home. Yet, it is a sign that something's wrong with you when you're sitting quietly at home wishing you were out having an adventure. So I hope that in your lives you have just the right amount of sitting at home and just the right amount of adventure.'

Although Tony believed in this philosophy in his own life, there were certain adventures he would rather have avoided. Around the time he was making *The Matchmaker*, he met a 19-year-old songwriter called Gwen Davis at a Hollywood party. She became madly infatuated with him, and he found it convenient to date her a number of times. However, she started getting anonymous calls in the middle of the night, telling her that the object of her love was at the beach with another man. Davis channelled her passions into a novel called *Naked in Babylon* (published in 1960), a steamy story of a gorgeous movie star and a tender young woman, who discovers in the last chapter that her idol is a homosexual. Davis naively sent Tony the manuscript. He called her from Paramount sounding hurt and lost.

'I have a friend who writes me songs and poems and sends me funny telegrams in French,' she recalls him saying, 'and I was so excited when she told me she was writing a novel. Then I took it to the studio and read the ending – have you ever been put inside a Waring Blender?'

She changed the ending of the story for his sake, though she knew it to be true.

10

LOOK ABROAD AND HOMEWARD, ANGEL

'I want to find the world. Where is the world?' – Eugene Gant in *Look Homeward Angel* (1957)

In 1957, Tony was given the chance to work abroad for the first time, an offer made by Columbia Pictures at a salary of $125,000. They would distribute the Italian-made film, to be shot in Technirama at Cinecittà in Rome and in Thailand. Having made five films for Paramount in the space of a couple of years, Tony had almost fulfilled his contractual obligations, though he still owed the studio one picture. If he had not, he might never have made *Psycho* two years later.

Richard Conte, Jo Van Fleet and Nehemiah Persoff were among the other Americans who joined Tony in the cast, which also featured two Italian stars, Alida Valli and Silvana Mangano. The film, based on the French writer Marguerite Duras' 1953 novel, *Barrage Contre le Pacifique*, was produced by Dino de Laurentiis, Mangano's husband, and directed by Frenchman René Clément. With an utter disregard for authenticity, the Italian-accented

Mangano played Tony's sister, while her mother (Van Fleet) and brother are plainly American, although the family is supposed to be French. When this international mélange was released in the USA a year later in 1958, it was called *This Angry Age* (presumably to attract the youth market), and later it cropped up under the documentary-sounding title of *The Sea Wall*.

Shooting began in January 1957 on Pechburi in the Indian Ocean, three-hundred miles south of Bangkok. For his first foreign location, on his first trip outside the United States, Tony could not have asked for anything more exotic. A typhoon interrupted the filming a few weeks later, losing the production time and money, but work soon resumed.

René Clément, who had originally conceived Tony's role for James Dean (killed eighteen months earlier), spoke neither English nor Italian, so, as Tony recalled, he 'would have a lengthy hand-throwing conversation with the interpreter . . . Many words, and I'd wonder what it was all about. Then, the interpreter would tell me, "He wants you to go over there." '

One is led to ask why the actor needed an interpreter at all. Is this the Tony Perkins who spoke French as a child, even using it to converse with his dog? Is this the Tony Perkins whose command of the French language was as good as his mother had boasted about? It was only later, when he worked and lived in France, that his schoolboy French progressed to college boy level.

The formidable Jo Van Fleet (who had played James Dean's mother in *East of Eden*) was Madame Dufresne, a French widow in Indo-China, struggling to keep her rice plantation going despite her children's waning interest in it. Both her son and daughter want her to sell up and move back to Bangkok.

The film obliquely suggests an incestuous relationship between brother and sister, but the nearest they get to intimacy is their sensuous dancing of a number called The Crawl – Tony in shorts,

Mangano in tight slacks.

When big-city businessman Nehemiah Persoff says, 'Would you and your charming family join me for dinner?', Van Fleet replies, 'Get one thing straight. We are not a charming family.' How right she is!

Tony lies on his bed listening to rock 'n' roll records, while dreaming of city lights and lovely women. When a storm destroys the sea wall, and renders the land almost worthless, he leaves for the capital, because he cannot cope with all the pressure put on him by his domineering mother. Once there he goes to the cinema, where he is bored by a lousy film called *Flesh and Blood.* He scowls out of the screen at us, the audience, as if to say, 'We're all in the same boat.' Luckily, he meets a bored older woman (Alida Valli), with whom he has a brief fling.

At the end, the matriarch dies, Mangano ends up with Richard Conte, a government agent sent to get them off the land, and Tony goes back to the plantation to rebuild the wall after the flood.

Tony's performance captured the moods, the snarls and the whimpers of adolescence, and his explosive joy on his first evening in the big city as he tests his new-found freedom, reveals his ability to shift emotional gear smoothly. He also got to sing a song entitled, 'One Kiss From Heaven'.

The film, which caught the rich hues of the tropics in Technirama, and was only Tony's second film in colour, suffered from its hybrid parentage and over-melodramatic moments, but was absorbing enough as a study of a colonial family. *Time* commented: 'Anthony Perkins, a skilful young man who has gained his craft so easily that he may be in danger of losing his art, does the best work of his brief screen career.' However, another critic thought Tony 'is getting very good at playing James Stewart. He should now try Henry Fonda.' This echoed Sam Goldwyn's earlier comment, after seeing *Tea and Sympathy*: 'The kid's alright, but he's seen too many Jimmy Stewart movies.'

To Tony, these comments 'rolled off my back', justifiably, because he was finding his own style. He described *This Angry Age* as 'Rose Tattoo in the Orient', a witticism which bears little relation to the Tennessee Williams play and film. It was closer to being 'Glass Menagerie in the Orient', with its forceful mother and rebellious son.

Just after Tony had completed the picture in Italy, his mother wrote: 'When things are really upsetting him, Tony seldom tells me. It seems he doesn't think anybody else should carry his burdens. While he's making a picture abroad he writes to me oftener than most young men would who are as busy as he is. Mostly, he isn't much of a correspondent. If he writes a lot then I begin to suspect that he's unhappy or lonesome or homesick. I'd never hear this directly from him. In letters, Tony always skims over troubles, serenely thinking, I suppose, that I can't read between the lines. When he was working in Italy, he wrote that it was a little difficult getting used to the Latin routine. The Italians, he said, began shooting their scenes after lunch and worked until late at night. Well, this isn't for Tony. He's always one to rise early in the morning, full of energy and ideas. Even as a youngster he had a dozen things that just had to be done before he went to school; walk the dog, play a record he'd bought the day before, try a new magic trick or think up new ways to earn money.'

At the time of the release of *La Diga sul Pacifico* (the Italian title), Tony publicized the film by pretending to date Silvana Mangano's younger sister, Natascia. Despite going along with the publicity needs of the studios, he disliked the whole process.

Since *Friendly Persuasion*, and the release of his first Paramount pictures, Tony's youthful face stared out regularly from movie fan magazines. Although, like James Dean, he attracted

Above: Anthony Perkins, Tab Hunter and Natalie Wood in 1956 (Photofest). Top: Tab Hunter (Photofest).

a homosexual following, he was sold as a teenage girl's delight. There were often studio-orchestrated demonstrations by young girls screaming and pursuing him, but there were also many spontaneously gathered crowds of fans, noisily proclaiming their infatuation for him.

'When I see a group [of girls] that looks aggressive, I whistle or chew on one corner of my face which throws the face out of focus.'

The articles that appeared in these fanzines had titles such as *Why Tony Perkins Is Girl Shy* (because he's too concerned with his career, and hates small talk), *Has Tony Lost His Heart* (yes, when posing with Natascia Mangano in Rome), *Tony Perkins – Could You Be His Bride* (only if you put his career first), *The Teenage Dates I Dig The Most* (she must be feminine enough to be a good listener), *Why Tony Perkins Won't Take Girls Home To Mother* (because it is tantamount to a proposal), *You'd Take Him Home To Mother* (he is so clean-cut and charming), *Tony Perkins Tells Why Hollywood Girls Leave Me Cold* (because they can't hold up their end of the conversation), *Now Hear This, Girls! Tony Perkins Is In Marrying Mood* (because he is now grown up), *Would Tony Date You Twice* (only if you are socially mature).

For Tony, this was as nightmarish as for Joseph K. in *The Trial*, hounded by a group of young girls pursuing him up a tenement staircase as he makes his way towards the painter's studio. There, they yell and leer at him through wooden slats. When he leaves the *atelier*, he is chased by the screaming girls through tunnels.

'Goddesses of the hunt in full cry,' says the painter.

At the same time, Tony was having a relationship with another Hollywood 'dreamboat' of the 1950s that girls wanted to date, and whom they would be pleased to take home to mother – Tab Hunter.

'He had a face that was so handsome that it didn't look real,' George Abbott, the director of *Damn Yankees*, once said of Hunter.

Tab Hunter, an All-American blond pin-up boy, was only a year older than Tony but had made it in films a few years earlier. However, their careers were congruent in some ways. They were both launched as paradigms of clean-cut American youth, for whom teenage girls craved; both made films with Sophia Loren at Paramount; both dated Gary Cooper's daughter, and other young women, for publicity purposes; and both turned their backs on Hollywood to work abroad. They even played a couple of the same roles – in the musical *Damn Yankees*, Hunter on screen, Tony on stage, and as baseball hero Jim Piersall, Hunter on TV, Tony in the movies.

Tab had to live for many years with the story that pursued him since he started out in films. In October 1950, aged nineteen, he had been arrested with others after a gay pyjama party in Beverly Hills, an incident that was reported in the tabloid press. He claimed in public that he was there out of naivety, and had no idea what kind of party it was. He survived to become a star, despite the persistent rumours.

He had just the sort of bronzed Californian beach boy beauty that excited Tony. However, the latter took pains to make sure nobody knew of their frequent trysts. Tab was relatively more daring and open about his sexual conquests, and could be fairly outspoken at Hollywood parties. Yet, such was the homophobia in Hollywood – a microcosm of prevalent views in America as a whole – that the revelation of such a liaison would have been like a large boulder pitched at the glass facade of the dream factory, shattering the entire edifice.

Despite being uneasy, for different though related reasons, in both his private and public life, Tony's return to the stage was a particularly happy one, in which an ideal conjunction was found between character and actor. *Look Homeward, Angel*, skilfully adapted by Ketti Frings from Thomas Wolfe's first novel, opened on

28 November, 1957 at the Ethel Barrymore Theatre, scene of his Broadway debut in *Tea and Sympathy.*

It was at her house on the dunes in Truro, Cape Cod, a couple of years before, during one of their summer vacations, that Helen Merrill claimed to have introduced Tony to the novel. Although he is quoted as saying, 'I was a kid in high school when I first started to read Wolfe, and right away I identified myself with Gene.'

Whenever it was that he became acquainted with the novel – *Look Homeward, Angel* is one of those homegrown classics that most American schoolchildren read – he felt a special affinity for the character of Eugene Gant.

'It's a character I can identify with, but I wouldn't emulate. Wolfe was bent on self-destruction – he was an agonized man, fruitlessly searching for things he never wanted to find. He used to walk up and down the streets looking in windows for "it", but if he found it he would have nothing much to write about. Within reason I hope I'm different and mature enough to know what I'm searching for and to not be afraid of it when I find it.'

Tony, always a seeker, was not yet mature enough to know what he was seeking, but he did know a good role when he found one. Indeed, one of the reasons he had signed with Paramount in 1956 was because the studio owned the rights of *Look Homeward, Angel*, though, for contractual reasons, it has yet to be made into a film.

The play tells of a family in 1890s North Carolina dominated by a grasping, narrow-minded, materialistic mother who drives her tormented sculptor husband to drink, one son, Ben, to a premature death, and the younger son to leave her so that he may be 'unbeaten and beloved'.

Wolfe describes Eugene as 'seventeen, tall, awkward, with a craving for knowledge and love.' As Tony was seventeen going on twenty-five, it was easy to get into the part with the distancing effect of the stage. The last scene of the play, when Eugene decides to leave home, vibrates with Tony's own close relationship with his mother, and adds another bead to the thematic string of his career.

Mother: That's all right, I know your mind's made up and I'm not complaining! It seems all I've ever been fit for around here is to cook and sew. That's all the use any of you have ever had for me.

Eugene: Mama, don't think you can work on my feelings here at the last moment.

Mother: I hate to see you go, son.

Eugene: Goodbye, Mamma.

Mother: Try to be happy, child, try to be a little more happy.

Eugene: MAMA. (They cling) Goodbye . . . Goodbye . . . Goodbye . . . Mama

Mother: Poor child . . . poor child . . . poor child. We must try to love one another.

Epilogue:

Eugene: Then I'll search for an end to hunger, and the happy land; There is no happy land. There is no end to hunger. Ben help me . . . I want to find the world. Where is the world?

Ben: The world is nowhere, no-one Gene. You are your world.

Tony was reunited with Jo Van Fleet (his mother in *This Angry Age*), who played Eliza Gant, the money-grubbing boarding-house mother. At the last moment, she substituted for Bette Davis, who had suffered a heavy fall just before rehearsals. Davis had not been on stage since 1952, and her parts in films had dwindled. While Van Fleet and Welsh actor Hugh Griffith, as the father, tried to upstage one another, Tony, who remained in the production for seven months, quietly stole the laurels, and won a nomination for the aptly-named Tony Award.

In a *Newsweek* special called 'Shooting Star' on 3 March 1958, the writer thought Tony 'possibly the most gifted dramatic actor under thirty in the country. Notable among his precocious gifts is an ability to play young men at the brink of maturity without delivering either of dramaturgy's current stereotypes – the comical puppy or the darkling member of the "beat generation". Perkins' young men actually possess dignity and a certain elevation of spirit . . .'

Tony had a passion for working in the theatre, not only because of his desire to match Osgood's reputation, but because it gave him the opportunity to develop a role and allow a performance to grow. However, his love for it did not extend beyond the commercial.

In an interview which Tony gave the *New York Post* during the run of *Look Homeward, Angel*, he said: 'Shakespeare? It just doesn't make any sense to me. I don't understand it from one word to the next. If I had to act it – Good God! All the sentences are backwards for God's sake! How the hell are you supposed to make any sense of that? You can't act it, it's all you can do to say it.'

A pity when one considers the kind of Romeo he might have played when young, and Iago when older. If the above can be taken as an indication of a twenty-five-year-old actor's views, they had not changed substantially over fourteen years later.

'Intellectual and exploratory cerebral theatre doesn't interest me. The mind exercises of Pinter, Beckett and Albee doesn't turn me on. I'd rather read those kind of plays. What I like to act in are plays with a sense of theatre built into them.'

Grover Dale (left), Debbie Reynolds and Gus Trikonis in *The Unsinkable Molly Brown*, 1964 (Photofest).

While Tony was appearing in *Look Homeward, Angel*, he met Grover Dale, the tall, good-looking choreographer and lithe dancer, who had eye-catching parts on Broadway in *Li'l Abner* and *West Side Story*, and would be the lead dancer in Tony's first Broadway musical, *Greenwillow*, two years later.

It was with Grover Dale that Tony had his longest relationship before his marriage, although their discomfiture in being part of the homosexual demi-monde never allowed them to call it more than friendship. In fact, even when they shared a house some years later, lanky look-alikes Grover and Tony would often arrive at parties separately, sometimes even enacting a farce in which the host introduced them to each other as if they were strangers. Naturally, many of the guests were perfectly aware of the charade, and there was much sniggering behind hands.

As a self-imposed restraint on his sexual activities, Tony retained his room at Helen Merrill's, while also renting a small, spartan apartment a block away on 56th street. There, when the situation arose, he could take Grover or a casual pickup.

For Tony, and a number of other actors at that period, there was always an underlying fear that homosexuality, if exposed, might threaten their careers. Perhaps, if his ambition had been restricted to the New York stage, Tony would have been less anxious. But further tempting offers were coming to him from Hollywood, and he knew that revelations of his sexual leanings might abort them. Slim, gentle and highly-strung actors like Tony were already suspect.

Hollywood in the 1950s was a conservative place. It liked to present an image of America as a country where men were men and women were women, which meant that large-breasted women and wide-chested men were attracted to one another. Since the beginning of movies, Hollywood had groomed its stars to appeal to opposite-sex audiences, and a star's life was controlled by the studio whose job it was to create the fantasy of healthy sexuality. Hollywood lived by the eleventh commandment: 'Thou Shalt Not Be Found Out.'

Just as *Variety* was about to break a story on Rock Hudson's homosexuality, his manager stepped in to save it with a sacrificial lamb, his assistant Phyllis Gates. Hudson was unhappily married to her for a year. Women like Gates were known as 'beards', because they provided gay men with that emblem of spurious virility. Beards or walkers (the male equivalent), important players in the Hollywood game, are either unknown, in which case they can be paid handsome fees, or they have a high profile and therefore benefit from such a marriage themselves.

Yet, then as now, there were many homosexuals in Hollywood holding important positions in the film industry, but they remained a closet community. They gathered at private parties, such as those held by gay directors George Cukor and Mitchell Leisen, or well-known agents such as Henry Willson, who represented many homosexual actors, including Rock Hudson. James Dean once commented, 'You know I've had my cock sucked by some big names in Hollywood and I think it's pretty funny because I wanted more than anything to just get some little part.'

Apart from exposure, there were other spectres on Tony's horizon. In the very week that *Look Homeward, Angel* opened on Broadway, a fifty-one-year-old simpleton called Ed Gein (rhymes with mean) was arrested in Plainfield, Wisconsin. Gein had tortured, disembowelled, decapitated and skinned at least ten women. The author Robert Bloch read about the case in the newspapers, and Norman Bates was born.

11

TALL STORIES

'They have turned lying into a universal principal' – Joseph K. in *The Trial* (1962)

It had been the dream of Hollywood for over twenty years to film *Green Mansions*, the 1904 South American fantasy by the distinguished naturalist W. H. Hudson. RKO had first bought the novel as a vehicle for Dolores Del Rio, then dropped it. After MGM had obtained the rights in 1953, Vincente Minnelli began work on it, with Edmund Purdom and Pier Angeli cast, but it also fell through. Minnelli went on instead to make another airy-fairy romance, *Brigadoon*, and the property was left on the shelf for four years until picked up and given to Mel Ferrer, who was looking for a screenplay in which to direct his wife, Audrey Hepburn.

Rima the Bird Girl seemed perfect casting for Hepburn's fragile beauty. In her two previous films, the twenty-eight-year-old star had been romatically co-starred with fifty-nine-year-old Fred Astaire (*Funny Face*) and fifty-seven-year-old Gary Cooper (*Love in the Afternoon*), both old enough to be her father, a point many critics prudishly seized upon. It was, therefore, a relief for Hepburn to be playing opposite Tony, three years her junior, and almost as gazelle-like as she.

He portrayed Abel, a young man in hiding after a political uprising in which his father has been killed. He discovers Rima in the jungles of Venezuela and falls in love with her, after she has saved his life when he is bitten by a snake. She then communicates with her dead mother (not the monopoly of Norman Bates) in the sort of dialogue with which the film was handicapped.

'Oh, mother, hear me. It's about this young man in the forest.'

Talk of gold in the area catches Abel's ear as he searches for money to avenge his father's murder. Rima, who communes with nature, is seen by the Indians as an evil spirit, and the chief's son Kua-Ko (Henry Silva) wants to kill her. She is presumably burnt alive when the Indians trap her atop a tall, hollow tree which is set on fire, but Abel is comforted by a vision (or reality?) of his beloved Rima at the end.

Although the producers 'gratefully acknowledge the co-operation of the government officials of British Guiana, Venezuela and Colombia, who made it possible to photograph scenes of this picture in the actual locales of the story', most of it was filmed in a studio jungle on a sound stage at MGM. None of the principals went to South America, only their stand-ins had that pleasure. In fact, it was so synthetic a jungle, and the rock pools so plainly man-made, that it would not have been surprising if Esther Williams had surfaced in one of them. (As the screenplay was by Dorothy Kingsley, who wrote most of the Hollywood Mermaid's films, it seemed even more likely.)

'They sent two doubles to Brazil for Audrey Hepburn and me,' Tony divulged to Rex Reed. 'Mine was bitten by a poisonous insect as he stepped off the plane and he was replaced by an assistant director. The whole thing was shot on Stage 24 at MGM. They even imported a South American tribe to Culver City to live on the backlot, that's how realistic that film was. Did you see it? It was pretty horrible.'

With so many things against him, including a dud script, Mel Ferrer used what assets he had by concentrating on the alluringly fresh faces of the two young stars – a colt and a filly romping through the artificial undergrowth.

It was only Tony's third film in colour, and one sees for the first time, as he bathes in a stream under a waterfall, how smooth his skin was. As Alan Helms, a lover of his explained. 'Tony had the smoothest skin I've ever known. I was amazed at it, and I asked him what he used on it. He replied that he never used soap, except on the face if he had to, and then it was a special Spanish brand.'

Opposite the simpering and fey Audrey Hepburn, Tony seems almost three dimensional. However, he can do precious little with a hero who starts off as a passionate avenger only to be lulled into becoming a lovesick nature boy.

'I came here with hate and anger, seeking revenge, instead I found love . . . . your dear [deer?] eyes looking into mine.'

It was, however, the closest Tony ever came to portraying a real manly hero on screen, the sort of adventurer that Stewart Granger was playing at the time. It also gave him a chance to handle a knife (Norman Bates's favoured weapon) for something other than a culinary purpose. Tony's big scene comes when, knowing a tribe of Indians admire courage, he stands facing them all day in the sun, without food or water, telling them his story to delay their killing him. With caked lips and cracked voice, he finally wins them over.

'The sun's going down , and I've outlasted the sun , I've outlasted the flies and I've even outlasted your foul odour.'

Neither audiences nor critics survived the foul odour of the movie. Tony described his performance (unfairly) as 'almost like a zombie', while the reviewer in *Time* depicted him 'clumping

Anthony Perkins pre-Norman Bates (Photofest).

through the greenery as gingerly and gracelessly as an agonized boy scout bound for a merit badge in campcraft.'

At one stage, Tony holds up the non-action by playing a guitar and singing in a rather strained manner an anachronistic song. Although MGM had persuaded the Brazilian composer Heitor Villa-Lobos to write 'the special music' for the first and only time for film (he died a year later), most of the score was composed by Bronislau Kaper, who also wrote the 'Song of Green Mansions'.

As Bosley Crowther wrote in the *New York Times*: 'They have plucked a guitar out of nowhere and given it to Anthony Perkins to strum while he croons "Song of Green Mansions". He has the right air of youthful wonder and incredulity. Except for the obvious embarrassment with the guitar, the boy is good.'

Tony's encounter with Rima the Bird Girl, and various other feathered denizens of the forest, calls to mind the importance of ornithological images in his early career. Aside from having played Josh Birdwell in *Friendly Persuasion*, and reacting to birds singing and the Reverend Birdsong in the musical *Greenwillow*, the bird-like Norman Bates's hobby was stuffing birds. Stuffed birds of prey hover as he converses with Marion *Crane* from *Phoenix*, who 'eats like a bird'.

'I think only birds look well stuffed because – well, because they're kinda passive to begin with.'

Green Mansions was a particular disappointment for Tony in that he had already committed himself to it when Billy Wilder offered him the Tony Curtis role in *Some Like It Hot*, which might have changed the course of his career entirely. Instead of being known as Mrs Bates, he might have been remembered as Josephine. Instead of trading on a reputation for crackpot thrillers, he might have become an exponent of screwball comedies. There would also have been a direct link to his father, as Tony would have worked with George Raft, taking off the coin-spinning gangster character he created in *Scarface*. Coincidentally, the character played by Joe E. Brown in *Some Like It Hot* was called Osgood.

Related or not, it was a short while after *Green Mansions* that Tony expressed a desire 'to do something about my inner life, so that I wouldn't virtually vanish into my own smallness and meagreness of spirit.' This malaise eventually led him towards the couch and many years of psychotherapy.

After not going to South America to make *Green Mansions*, Tony was asked to go to the other end of the world to make a film about the end of the world. Stanley Kramer, who produced and directed *On The Beach*, insisted on shooting the whole picture in Australia where Neville Shute's bestselling apocalyptic novel was set.

Leaving the winter of the Northern hemisphere for the summer of the antipodes, Tony joined Gregory Peck, Ava Gardner, Fred Astaire and newcomer Donna Anderson on location in Melbourne. The State of Victoria was in the midst of a heat wave at the time, which may account for some of the sluggishness of the film. Ava Gardner, who liked a drink or two, complained about the licensing laws which resulted in glasses being snatched from restaurant tables at nine p.m. Fortunately, Gregory Peck and his wife Veronique had not only rented a huge Victorian house, but had brought their own French chef with them. The Pecks entertained Ava, Kramer, Astaire and Tony regularly after a hard day's shoot, and there was plenty of booze to satisfy them all. Of Tony, Ava commented, 'Perkins was shy about everything except attacking his plate.'

The billboards claimed *On The Beach* to be 'The Biggest Story Of Our Time!' Although the picture earned over five million dollars, it failed to live up to its claim or to its theme – nuclear annihilation. Not that Neville Shute's novel had managed much better, but at least the reader was spared 'Waltzing Matilda' blaring forth from the soundtrack at regular intervals as a reminder that the location was Australia.

The futurist setting was Melbourne in 1964 after an atomic war in the northern hemisphere. Five people's lives are spotlighted among the population waiting for the radioactive drift to reach them: American submarine captain Gregory Peck (busily moving his eyebrows); nervous, hard-drinking Ava Gardner; conscience-stricken nuclear physicist Fred Astaire, and young couple Tony Perkins and Donna Anderson, with the responsibility of a baby to look after. Aside from a slight sense of urgency from the latter couple, most of the characters behave as if the war is little more than an irksome interruption to a cocktail party. Ava Gardner's only regret is that she had never been to the Rue de Rivoli to buy a pair of gloves because she knew the French for gloves. In this version the world ends not with a bang but a whimper. At least Tony is there at the finish.

Stanley Kramer said he cast Tony, whom he described as 'a loner who went off by himself,' because, 'I looked at Tony's previous work and thought he'd be right. He had an inner sensitivity, which his homosexuality might have helped. I wanted him to show a tenderness from the beginning.'

Only the liberal Kramer's prior knowledge of Tony's sexual leanings could have made him express the received opinion that homosexual actors find the portrayal of sensitivity more forthcoming than their heterosexual counterparts; a conclusion comparable to 'all blacks have natural rhythm.'

Tony first appears in a white T-shirt preparing the baby's bottle. He tests the temperature of the milk, and has a safety pin in his mouth. He then brings his young wife (Donna Anderson) tea in bed. The perfect 'feminized' husband and father. His naval hat on a hook reveals him to be a lieutenant in the Australian navy.

The role of Peter Holmes, that of a straight-as-a-die married man with a child, was an unusual one for Tony. He makes him charming and solicitous, but Kramer does not permit him to be sexy, although he looks attractive in his white uniform and knee-length shorts.

Watching Peck and Gardner kissing on a sailing boat through binoculars, Astaire remarks, 'It's like looking at a French movie.'

When the same couple start to wrestle on the beach, Donna Anderson turns to Tony and says. 'You never wrestle with me any more.'

'I thought you were everything I dreamed about,' he coos at his wife, recalling their first meeting.

'I thought you were so underfed,' she replies, which is another attempt by film-makers to draw attention to the fact that Tony was not built like Rock Hudson.

Donna Anderson was extremely inexperienced and Tony helped her get through every scene, which, in a sense, echoed their relationship in the film. Astaire, in his first non-musical role, also had cause to be grateful to Tony.

'He was terribly, terribly nice to me,' commented the great screen dancer. 'He knew that I was concerned about playing my first serious part, and I used to talk to him about that. I had several scenes to play with him, and he'd give me sort of signs of encouragement when he was off screen. I really appreciated it.'

Assuming the conscience of the film, Astaire, while under the influence, declares: 'The war started when we believed we could defend ourselves with weapons we couldn't possibly use without committing suicide.'

Astaire played an Englishman, but he can only muster a trace of stage Irish from time to time. Ava Gardner, also supposed to be Australian, makes not the slightest attempt to sound like one. 'Fair dinkum' Aussies were reduced to supporting parts, one of whom plays a secretary called Hosgood, a name which when pronounced sounded like an in-joke. Tony made a good shot at an

Australian accent, most often pitching the timbre correctly and getting the vowels right – carefully saying 'patty' for 'party'

'I didn't want too many accents, but Tony came by it easily. I said if he wanted to do it Australian then okay, let's hear it. It was very light and did not distract,' Kramer remarked.

Tony is especially effective in the emotional moments, the only ones that ring true among the soap operatics. Towards the end, the population is issued with suicide pills to avoid the suffering that radiation will bring, its effects sounding now rather like AIDS.

'How can you tell the woman you love that she has to kill herself and her baby?' Tony asks Astaire.

Yet, he has to explain to her why she and the child must take the pills.

'You get weaker and weaker.'

'This pill cures it?' she asks.

'No, it ends it.'

'There is still time – brothers!' is the Salvation Army slogan written on a banner in the last image of the film, a judicious warning to the audiences of 1959, at the height of the Cold War. However, the message was that though nuclear war was bad for the health, it was good for the box office. It did no harm to Tony's career either.

While a relative novice at film acting, Tony had gained experience by working with Henry Fonda in *The Tin Star*. Now, on his return from Australia early in 1959, at the age of twenty-eight and already a veteran of ten movies, he became the mentor of Fonda's twenty-three-year-old daughter Jane, making her screen debut in a film whose working title was *The Way the Ball Bounces*. She had been at the Actors Studio and had just appeared on Broadway for the first time in *There Was a Little Girl*, winning the New

York Drama Critics Circle Award

Fonda Sr was pleased Jane was working with Tony, whose dedication had impressed him, and who also saw a lot of himself in the young actor. In his earlier days, he had himself had a line (which Gary Cooper and James Stewart also exploited in their youth) of gangly young men who are tongue-tied in the face of the opposite sex.

Originally, Joshua Logan, the director and producer of what was finally called *Tall Story*, wanted twenty-three-year-old Warren Beatty, who had just made an impact on Broadway in William Inge's *A Loss of Roses*, but he decided that he could not take a risk on two film debutantes. Tony, a client of Logan's agent, was a known name, still looked young enough to play a college boy, and was tall enough to convince as a basketball hero.

'Although Tony was delightful as the basketball player, I was sorry again later not to have used Warren, as I would have avoided one mistake,' recalled Joshua Logan. 'During the filming of the picture Tony came to me and asked if he could go privately with Jane to work out the love scenes with her alone. He would take the responsibility for the direction, but, of course, I could change anything later that I didn't like. He was so eager and enthusiastic that I said yes. They worked very hard, devotedly in fact, on their intimate scenes. When they showed them to me they were strangely slow and full of pregnant pauses, but apart from that quite attractive, so I filmed them as rehearsed. Unfortunately, when cut into the picture they were endless and, I think, hurt the picture almost more than the charm of the two people helped it.'

When they started working together, Tony cued Jane for her close-ups by just reading the lines flat, without feeling. With essentially nothing to react to, Jane could not work up the requisite emotions. On the third day of shooting, she went up to him and

Jane Fonda and Anthony Perkins
in *Tall Story*, 1960 (Photfest).

threatened to deliver her lines in the same lifeless manner when the time came for *his* close-ups. From then on Tony read all his cue lines to Jane with gusto.

On Logan's directing of Fonda, Tony commented: 'In a way it was touching. Josh crouched over the camera, having her do take after take in the style he had developed when directing Marilyn Monroe in *Bus Stop.* He coaxed a performance out of her.'

The plot of *Tall Story* concerned tall girl Fonda arriving at Custer College, the home of one of America's top basketball teams, in search of a tall man to marry. Her quarry is the college's star, Tony, who, by applying scientific theory to the game, is able to score with ease. Fonda becomes cheerleader, attends all the same courses as Tony and sits next to him at lectures. She soon gets him to propose. Because of his new responsibilities, he accepts a large bribe offered him by crooked gamblers to throw a match against a visiting Russian team. When he fails a mid-term ethics exam and becomes ineligible for the team, he tells all. Ray Walston, the professor who failed him, permits him to take an oral exam just before the game. ('Plato, Schmato, throw the boy an easy question').

Tony rushes to the basketball court to find the Russians leading by a huge margin. Quickly changing into his sports gear, he enters the game and pulls off a dramatic last-minute victory. Another blow struck for the USA in the Cold War!

Custer College can only be found in tired campus comedies such as this, but Tony gave credible performances on court (long-legged and athletic) and off (unaffected boyish appeal), and got to sing 'Cuddle Up A Little Closer' with his co-star. Jane Fonda, with false eyelashes and falsies, was quite pleasing in an irritating role, though miscast as a girl with only marriage on her mind. Even a clairvoyant would have had difficulties predicting superstardom. The *New York Times* commented: 'Gangly Mr Perkins jounces around convincingly enough. Near Miss Fonda, he generally gapes and freezes, and who can blame him?'

Fonda had to adjust to the ballyhoo which goes with movies. For example, Tony and Jane were asked to neck on a couch for publicity stills.

'Jane turned pale,' recalled Tony. 'It was her first encounter with one of the absurdities of this business, and it was as if she said to herself, "My God, is this what being an actress means?"'

There was also a rumour going around (possibly started by a desperate PR person) that she had attempted to seduce Tony when he entered her dressing-room and found her rehearsing her lines in the nude. Many years later, Tony repudiated this.

'Jane Fonda wasn't naked in the dressing room repeating her lines. What's the sense of that? In any film, or in the theatre or touring company, have you ever seen anyone rehearse in the nude? I don't care if it's a Xmas pageant, I don't care what it is.'

During the filming, Tony introduced Jane to a handsome twenty-three-year-old actor-dancer called Timothy Everett. Dark and fresh-faced, he was considered to have 'James-Dean-like qualities,' though he looked more like Sal Mineo. He had been at the Actors Studio, and seemed on the verge of stardom after appearing as the young Jewish boy in William Inge's *The Dark at the Top of the Stairs* on Broadway and just completing a small role in Otto Preminger's *Exodus*. Everett and Jane became inseparable.

'Timmy was a troubled guy. He was aggressive, antagonistic, soulful. He didn't leave anything out,' remarked Tony.

What Tony failed to say about Everett, was that he was a tormented homosexual like himself, and with whom he had gone to bed. Tim and Jane broke up after a short while, though Tony saw him from time to time over the years. Everett, who had played the juvenile lead in the film version of *The Music Man*, found his career petering out. He died aged thirty-nine in March 1977 from a heart attack brought about by drug abuse.

There were obvious dangers lurking for Tony in the world in which he moved. But on the eve of the 60s, he had not yet succumbed to the attraction of drugs. His fame, which was now unquestionable, was having the same effect as drugs would have on him, both detrimental and exhilarating. He told the *New York World Telegram and Sun*, 'I like . . . walking past Lindy's . . . You can see them inside pointing at you and exclaiming but you can't hear them and they can't get at you. You're absolutely immune. You can do anything. Make faces or rude gestures.'

It was just after he had completed the filming of *Tall Story* that his agent phoned to tell him of an offer of a role in a forthcoming Alfred Hitchcock movie.

Part III

PSYCHO THERAPY

12

HOT AND COLD RUNNING BLOOD

'We all go a little mad sometimes. Haven't you?' – Norman Bates in *Psycho* (1960)

Anthony Perkins, being an inveterate player of intellectual games, might have found stimulation in a game called 'What if . . .' in which participants invent alternative histories for people on the lines of what would have happened to them if they had not made certain choices. What if Tony had not been offered the role of Norman Bates in *Psycho*? What if he had turned it down when it did come his way? But as Shakespeare's Brutus knew, 'there is a tide in the affairs of men, which, taken at the flood, leads on to fortune.' Tony's taking of the tide, that led to his fortune and the merging with Norman Bates, came about due to a series of chance incidents.

Paramount was lukewarm about the project when Alfred Hitchcock first brought it to them. *Vertigo* had just flopped, and they were not prepared to lay out money for a potboiler about a knife-happy madman who dresses up as his mother. Finally, the studio gave in.

'Well you're not going to get the budget you're used to having for this sort of thing,' Hitchcock was told. This meant no Technicolor, no Jimmy Stewart, no Cary Grant. Hitchcock said,'All right, I'll make do.'

What Paramount did not know was that Hitchcock was thinking along different lines anyway. He had recently complained that stars' salaries had become astronomical.

'The minute you put a star into a role you've already compromised because it may not be perfect casting.'

Not wishing to repeat himself, Hitchcock was looking around for a smaller scale screenplay that could be shot cheaply, rather like one of his television stories extended to feature length.

Influenced by the success of Henri-Georges Clouzot's *Les Diaboliques*, a gruesome black-and-white French thriller, Hitchcock was suddenly heard to dismiss his recent films as 'glossy Technicolor baubles.' What also interested him about the film by Clouzot, who was being touted as 'the French Hitchcock', was the way in which *Les Diaboliques* had been marketed. In France, nobody was allowed into theatres after the start of the picture, and there were cautionary titles at the end: 'Don't be diabolical yourself. Don't spoil the ending for your friends by telling them what you've just seen. On their behalf – Thank You!'

It was a technique that Hitchcock would adopt on the release of *Psycho*.

'The manager of this theatre has been instructed, at the risk of his life, not to admit any person after the picture starts. By the way, after you see *Psycho*, don't give away the ending – signed Alfred Hitchcock.'

Joseph Stefano, who had been under contract to Twentieth Century-Fox, was hired to adapt the Robert Bloch novel. When he met the director to discuss the script of *Psycho*, he confessed to having a problem about the assignment: he disliked the character of Norman Bates.

'I really couldn't get involved with a man in his forties who's a drunk and peeps through holes. The other problem was that there was this other horrendous murder of a stranger I didn't care about either. I just kept talking to him in the vein, "I wish I knew this girl," "I wish Norman were somebody else." '

As to the writer's qualms about the central male character, Hitchcock pacified Stefano with the question, 'How would you feel if Norman were played by Anthony Perkins?'

'I said, "Now you're talking." I suddenly saw a tender young man you could feel incredibly sorry for. I could really rope in an audience with someone like him,' the writer recalled.

Hitchcock's motives in suggesting Tony were not wholly connected with aesthetic considerations. He knew that Tony owed Paramount a film under an old contract and could be hired for $40,000. (The same amount that Janet Leigh's character steals from her employers.) This was in stark contrast to the $450,000 plus ten per cent of the gross over eight million that Cary Grant had obtained to star in *North By Northwest.*

Coincidentally, when at Fox, Stefano had been hired to adapt a J. R. Salamanca novel, *The Lost Country*, as a vehicle for Tony, but it never happened. It was made a couple of years later as *Wild in The Country*, starring Elvis Presley with a script by Clifford Odets.

Naturally, Tony jumped at the chance to work with Hitchcock, believing that it would give his film career a much-needed shot in the arm. In fact, he accepted before he had even read the script. Hitchcock was happy to cast Tony, whom he had seen in *Fear Strikes Out*, 'one of my first talking films.'

'He always cast from seeing the actors in other films. He couldn't subject any of them to the ritual reading, or even the meeting in his office was too tender for him to contemplate,' Tony remarked.

ALFRED HITCHCOCK DIRECTING VERA MILES, JOHN GAVIN AND ANTHONY PERKINS IN *PSYCHO*, 1960 (PHOTOFEST).

'He never auditioned, he never screen-tested actors for major roles or even minor roles. He chose them always from other performances, which I think is rather a unique quality. I've never known another director to have the confidence in himself to do that. By the time I was in his office, I'd already got the part. So the getting of the job step was one I didn't have a chance to strive for.'

The only doubt Tony had in accepting the role of a transvestite schizophrenic knife-killer, was that he might lose many of the young girl fans who mobbed him whenever he stepped from his powder-blue T-bird, a car his agent recommended he buy as contiguous with his screen image.

'I asked the question "Was it a wise thing to rush into in the 60s?" Probably less so than in the 80s, when it seems to be people get away with anything . . . Hitchcock agreed it would be a gamble. He had no idea of the real possible success of the picture, but he suggested I give it a try anyway.'

Shooting began on 11 November, 1959 at the Revue Studios, the TV branch at Universal that Paramount had rented for Hitchcock. Unlike Janet Leigh, on whom Hitchcock lavished considerable preparation time, Tony had little or no contact with his director before shooting began.

'Tony was surprised to learn that Hitch and I had meetings prior to filming,' Janet Leigh observed. 'But I wonder if it wasn't because he wanted a kind of distance, a not-quite-worldly quality on how Tony played Norman.'

Yet Hitchcock wanted as much sympathy to go to Tony's character as possible. First, he hoped audiences would want Janet Leigh to get away with the robbery, and then, by the time the car sinks into the swamp with her body in it, they should be rooting for Norman. This could only have been achieved because Tony does not convey the characteristics of a conventional movie monster, but those of a likable boy next door.

'He let me make several changes and suggestions,' Tony enthused. 'I haven't been treated like that before or since. Hitch thought it was time he worked with an actor rather than get the actor to work with him . . . Even as the first day proceeded I could see he wanted to know what I thought and what I wanted to do and I was really very surprised by this. I tentatively made some small suggestion about something I might do. He said, "Do it." I was confused at first. When we started the picture I had met Hitchcock but once and I was very apprehensive about making any statements about what I thought, what I felt about the character and about the different scenes. I got to relaxing more with him and making more and more suggestions.'

From Tony's remarks, and because his two best performances were given for the two best directors he worked with – Hitchcock and Orson Welles – it is apparent that he, more than most stars, needed to be accorded a sense of his personal worth, not only as an actor, but as an intelligent man with opinions of his own.

'It was clear right from the start that Hitchcock wasn't turning his back and that we were all in this together,' observed Tony. 'He was so painstakingly interested in what I had to say and was so eager to accept ideas of all kinds to the point when I would sometimes come into his dressing room in the morning with the rewritten pages and I would offer these to him, and he would turn away from the London *Times* and say, "Are they any good?" I'd say, "I don't know, shouldn't we be saving time if you would go over them now." He'd say, "I'm sure they will be very good." I said, "Don't you want to see them now?" He replied, "Enchant me later!" '

One of Tony's suggestions was that Norman should be a compulsive candy-eater, which also indicates the killer's infantile nature. The sound crew had to mask the constant chewing noises, but Hitchcock emphasized this bit of business with a large close-up of Tony's gulping gullet, shot from below at a tense moment.

For the confrontation between Martin Balsam as Milton Arbogast, the private detective, and Norman Bates, Hitchcock encouraged the two actors to find their own rhythms and overlap each other's dialogue. The first time they did it in one take, the crew applauded spontaneously. This is another instance that lays the ghost of Hitchcock's notorious and ill-judged 'actors are cattle,' remark.

'Tony was and is a very private person,' observed a Hitchcock associate. 'but he was very taken with the whole movie, wanted to be part of everything. Hitchcock liked that and helped him a lot. Tony was very serious about the whole thing.'

Wardrobe expert Rita Riggs observed: 'I think Mr Hitchcock liked Tony a lot, but he was a very shy, quiet young man. And many of us only got to know him because we could see how his mind worked through that wonderful game.'

'That wonderful game' was one that Tony was said to have invented called Essences, which was a little like Twenty Questions. The person who was 'it' chose a literary or historical character while the others had to guess the identity by asking questions like, 'If you were a car, would you be a beat-up Pontiac or a Ferrari?' The guessing sometimes went on for days and got so heated that the crew could hardly wait to finish work and get back to the game.

Since the shower sequence did not require the services of Tony, he was released to fly to New York for rehearsals for the Frank Loesser Broadway musical *Greenwillow.* Hitchcock confided to Stefano that Tony, whom he thought 'excessively shy around women,' should be spared any unnecessary embarrassment. 'It just wouldn't be very nice,' he commented.

Thirty years later, Tony, on learning of the qualms of the director, observed: 'That was sweet of him. Typical of his generosity.

Whether imaginary or based on fantasy, still it was awful nice of him to have the idea. I said, "Look, I've got to take some of these rehearsals," and, through special graciousness on Hitchcock's part, he said, "Go ahead, we don't need you for this." You have only to see the film to see the silhouette coming in that door has as little resemblance to me as any silhouette could . . . I'm left-handed and the stabbing is made by the right hand. No-one took into account that I was not there for that sequence. Hitchcock was absolutely determined to play fair with the audience and all the entrances and exits made by the dual personality of Norman were timed with a stopwatch, to make sure there was plenty of time to get in and out of clothes. He did not want to cheat the audience in his mis-en-scéne. But I'm not positive that the right-hand issue was ever raised.'

Stopwatch or not, real time (as distinct from the illusory screen time) denotes that Norman was a skilful quick-change artist, in that he would have had to go all the way up to the house, put on his mother's clothes, grab a knife, get down to Cabin One, and enter the shower room in just two minutes and twenty seconds flat. After he has stabbed Marion, he has only one minute and ninety-five seconds to return to the house, argue with his 'mother' upstairs, take off the dress and return to find the body.

Another deception, acceptable within a plot that relies on surprise and keeping audiences in the dark (an appropriate idiom for Hitchcock cinemagoers), is that Mother's voice was plainly not Tony's. One of her voices was that of twenty-three-year-old Paul Jasmin, a budding actor and friend of Tony's.

'Hitchcock had decided that if Tony did the voice right from the beginning, it might give away the whole thing,' Jasmin explained.

In addition, the voices of two actresses, Jeanette Nolan (Orson Welles's Lady Macbeth in his 1948 film) and Virginia Gregg, sounding more grandmotherly than motherly, were spliced in at different moments. It was twenty-four-year-old stuntwoman Margo Epper who portrayed Mother in the shower sequence, although various other doubles were used to represent her in other parts of the film. Rita Riggs who dressed Epper, commented, 'Margo, because of her horsemanship, is long and lean and had almost a male set of hips. Of all the people possible, she came closest to having Tony's square shoulders and thin hips.'

For the second murder, Hitchcock used Mitzi, a Lilliputian, to double for Mother.

'The reason she was hired was that Hitch was particularly worried that the audience was going to see through the whole thing,' observed Tony. 'Remember, this scene comes a little more than halfway through the picture. In order to strengthen the illusion, he engaged a woman who was very small and, physically, totally unlike anyone else [who appeared as Mother] in the picture.'

'I'm sorry, I didn't hear you in all this rain,' are the first words Norman Bates says, after running down the stairs from the house to the motel to greet Marion Crane. He is a good-looking, clean-cut young man, who soon reveals himself to be charming, confident and witty. There is nothing about him to suggest a homicidal psychopath. He hesitates slightly on deciding which room to give his guest, but settles on Cabin One, conveniently next to the office and the peephole.

By initially presenting the audience with such a 'normal' Norman, who even makes ironic remarks like, 'There's hangers in the closet and stationery with Bates Motel printed on it, in case you want to make your friends back home feel envious,' Hitchcock loads the dice. Where does such an isolated momma's boy get that sophisticated patter? We only get an inkling of his puritanism, when Norman gulps with embarrassment when indicating the bathroom.

> Norman: – and the uh –
> Marion (rather amused at his discomfiture): The bathroom.
> Norman: Yes. Well, uh – i – i – if you want anything just – just tap on the wall.

A further clue to his inhibitions comes when he stumbles over the word 'mother', and when Marion asks if he goes out with friends, he replies, 'Well, uh – a boy's best friend is his mother', without irony, as if it were an axiom, unlike his other jokey remarks.

Birds hover everywhere, stuffed ones and in pictures, as Norman grins and cranes his neck while watching Marion Crane from Phoenix eat 'like a bird'. (It was a natural progression from *Psycho* to *The Birds* for Hitchcock.) The ornithological theme is accentuated by Norman's resemblance to a bird – the shrugging shoulders, the fanning hands, the falcon's neck, and the rapid chomping on his Kandi Korn.

He remains unblinking as Marion suggests putting his mother away 'some place', while his adam's apple performs, before reacting with repressed anger. A short while later, Norman goes to his peephole behind the painting (Rembrandt's *Susanna and the Elders*, which portrays the story from the *Apocrypha* of a girl brought to grief by being spied on) to watch Marion undress, his eye in large close-up (echoed by Marion's after the murder). Now, for the first time, he reveals himself to be slightly touched. Marion enters the shower and, with Tony safely away in New York, Norman Bates, taking on his dead mother's identity in grey wig and frock, stabs her a number of times, in one of the most celebrated passages on film.

After the murder, Norman, clenching his teeth and setting his jaw, undertakes the task of meticulously cleaning up the bathroom, getting rid of all the blood and the body. During the nine-minutes-forty-second wordless sequence, Tony indicates that Norman, for the moment, is no longer a boy but a determined man with serious business on hand. Biting his lower lip, munching candy, and looking around warily like a bird of prey, he watches as the car sinks into the swamp. A flicker of a smile plays upon his lips, and he gives a look of satisfaction.

When the detective (Martin Balsam) starts asking questions, Norman, holding sheets and chomping nervously on his candy, suggests a little boy caught cheating in school.

When Arbogast implies that Norman had been used by Marion, he retorts, 'I'm not capable of being fooled! N-not even by a woman!'

'Well, it's not a slur on your manhood,' says Arbogast.

When the detective leaves, Norman smirks mischievously. He again flashes his devastating smile,when Marion's fiance (John Gavin) and sister (Vera Miles) arrive to investigate, pretending to be clients wanting to stay. But he gradually gets more flustered and strained with the large, masculine presence of Gavin looming over him, making Tony look almost short. He taps his fingers on the desk as he chews rapidly, then noticing Vera Miles' absence, his voice rises to the height of Osgood's in *Scarface*.

'Where's that girl you came here with? Where's that girl?' he wails.

After Norman Bates is exposed, his mouth twisted as his wig falls off when Gavin wrenches the knife away in the nick of time to save Miles, he sits like Whistler's *Mother*, dark lines under his eyes, against a blank wall at the court house. His mother's voice is heard in his head. A fly rests on his thumb.

'Let them see what kind of a person I am – not even going to swat that fly. I hope they are watching, they will see, they will see and they will say, "Why, she wouldn't even harm a fly.'

Anthony Perkins in the final shot of *Psycho* (The Ronald Grant Archive).

The split-second dissolve superimposes the mother's skull upon Tony's head, and the film ends.

The films of Alfred Hitchcock do contain streams of superb performances – though most of them are given by established actors playing polished heroes – Robert Donat, Michael Redgrave, Cary Grant, James Stewart, and cool blonde heroines like Madeleine Carroll, Joan Fontaine, Ingrid Bergman, Grace Kelly and Tippi Hedren, but even these had shadows of doubt lingering over them. Norman Bates is the most disturbed of all Hitchcock's protagonists, but he is only the culmination of such characters as Joseph Cotten's merry widow assassin in *Shadow of a Doubt*; Gregory Peck's mental patient in *Spellbound*; the two homosexual young men who commit a gratuitous murder in *Rope*; and the shrewd psychopathic Robert Walker in *Strangers on a Train*, who wants his father dead so that he can have his mother to himself. The latter comes closest to Tony's portrayal in insinuating, charming menace, demonstrating 'that one may smile, and smile, and be a villain.'

Robert Walker was a handsome open-faced young actor (he was thirty-three with only months to live) whose roles up to then had been free from complexity or trauma. Although Hitchcock perversely claimed it was typecasting, because he found Walker as strange in real life (something he only realized after shooting the film), it was as uncharacteristic a role as Tony's Norman. What the director was actually reacting against was the conventional idea of evil cloaked in evil-looking clothes.

Norman Bates is an extraordinary creation, because this serial killer, this dysfunctional murderous youth, is sensitive and distressed. Charm is an overworked word, especially when attached to Tony's personality, but it has the devastating effect Hitchcock intended when used to describe a killer such as Norman Bates. Audiences were attracted by his little-boy-lost looks and behaviour, while recognizing that 'matricide is probably the most unbearable crime of all – most unbearable to the son who commits it.' But Orestes, one of the heroes of Greek literature, murdered his mother and her lover, and although pursued by the Furies, was later acquitted by the Areopagus, the highest council of the Athenian state, famous for its wisdom and impartiality. Tony's performance and Hitchcock's mise-en-scène go far deeper than the half-baked surface psychological explanation offered by Dr Richman at the end.

'You can feel your loneliness through Norman, your ostracism through him. The next thing you know, you've got the knife in your hand', remarked Dennis Christopher, Tony's actor friend, revealing, to a potentially dangerous degree, how much empathy Tony/Norman engendered.

Over two decades later, Jeffrey Dahmer, one of the United States' grisliest serial killers, was being sent donations and letters from well-wishers. Most of the benefactors were women. A seventy-four-year-old nun in correspondence with Dahmer explained, 'He did awful things but way deep down he isn't a mean kid.'

This describes the general reaction to the character of Norman Bates, as impersonated by Tony. Consequently, Tony and Norman would be forever linked, as much as the two interconnected young men in *Strangers on a Train*, originally a novel by Patricia Highsmith. In the novel, she writes: 'Nothing could be without its opposite that was not bound up with it. Each was what the other had not chosen to be, the cast-off self, what he thought he hated but, perhaps, in reality, loved . . . Two people in each person. There's also a person exactly the opposite of you, like the unseen part of you, somewhere in the world and he waits in ambush.'

'My screen persona changed in 1960 with *Psycho.* I suddenly abandoned being the young leading man but became this quirky, nervous tic-ridden juvenile. The film was too good, the part was too well-written, the performance was too well-directed by Hitchcock, that it left a lasting impression on moviegoers who were more interested in seeing me in roles like that than in anything else.'

For years after *Psycho*, whatever Tony did, he would still be associated with Norman Bates. Everywhere he went, people kept telling him that their wives or girlfriends were afraid to take a shower because of him. He had a stock reply.

'Tell them to get dry-cleaned.'

During a visit to Rome to publicize *Psycho III*, he decided to take a shower in his hotel room before going out to give interviews.

'It was a stormy afternoon. There was something particularly eerie about the weather that day. It hadn't quite rained yet. I stepped out of the shower before turning on the water and I locked the bathroom door because it occurred to me that if some freak who knows I'm here decides to put me to the ultimate test, would my heart stand it. I know what it feels like to be scared of Norman Bates.'

Tony's son Osgood commented, 'I remember my surprise one day in school when a friend asked me if I wasn't afraid to take a shower at home when my father was in the house . . . I had to see the movie *Psycho* in order to understand the allusion to the murder in the shower. That sort of reaction made us laugh a lot, but we didn't attach too much importance to it.'

When Tony was shooting *Psycho III* in September 1983, he explained how he would reassure his sons about his alter-ego.

'Look, you're living in the same house as Norman Bates, you're under the protection of the owner of the house and the motel. What the heck can happen to you? They nod right off.'

But there was no way he could ever escape that man, whose

features were superimposed upon his, like the mother's skull at the end of *Psycho*.

At the 1992 awards lunch of the Publicists Guild of America, traditionally held three days before the Oscar ceremony, Guild president Henri Bollinger committed a Hollywood-style Freudian slip when introducing his star guest.

'Here to present our Showmanship award, the Guild's highest honour, is one of this year's Academy Award nominees for Best Actor – Anthony Perkins.'

Anthony Hopkins stepped up to the microphone and said menacingly to Bollinger in his Hannibal Lecter voice, 'Where are you having dinner tonight, Henri? I'll be right round . . . wrapped in a shower curtain.'

Six months later, Tony died, but Norman Bates lives on, and will continue to do so. Even now tourists are gaping at the Bates house on their tour of Universal Studios, and the killer himself looms out at people every day from a giant screen at Epcot in Orlando, Florida.

'Norman appears on request,' Tony used to say. 'I would even say on demand. I can dial my own personal 800 number and Norman will reply.'

In fact, those who wish to contact Norman Bates, can write to him c/o Bates Motel, 4019 Highway 113, Fairvale, California. Tel: (805) 555–9130.

13

'NEVER WILL I MARRY'

'Born to wander solitary, wide my world, narrow my bed' – Gideon Briggs in *Greenwillow* (1960)

While his female doubles were busy slashing up Janet Leigh in the shower back in Hollywood, Tony returned to his two differently utilized apartments in New York, and prepared to star in his first Broadway musical.

'In one way, it was a sense of failure that made me want to sing on Broadway . . . I made some records a few years ago of a very low soft singing that I was ultimately, if not immediately, dissatisfied with. I wanted to prove – to myself at any rate – that I could sing better than I sounded on those things you can pick up for $3.49 at the corner store. I knew I could. I knew my voice was better than it sounded on those records.'

Frank Loesser's *Greenwillow* gave Tony the chance to do just that.

'Frank brought the book around to my apartment himself, since the apartment practically adjoins his office and there he was,

Anthony Perkins browsing at a Fourth Avenue bookstall (Photofest).

standing at the door in his blue overcoat, and I didn't know it was he and he didn't know it was I. I read the book and then we talked about directors. He wanted someone like Moss Hart. I countered with George Roy Hill, who directed me in *Look Homeward, Angel.* I knew this was going to be a brand new thing for me and that I'd be happiest if I could be directed by someone I'd worked with, someone I was sensitive to and who was sensitive to me.'

'Tony wanted me to direct, but I wasn't sure I wanted to' said George Roy Hill. 'I think Tony was afraid to tackle a big singing role, and he wanted me there very much, so I went against my better judgement.'

'They had Anthony Perkins in mind for Gideon from the beginning,' wrote Susan Loesser, the composer's daughter. 'He projected an innocent rather fey quality, this tall, gangly male ingenu, and also a sense of moral integrity, all of which strongly suggested Gideon to the authors. But could he sing well enough to carry the role? They decided to take a chance on him, and my father spent many hours coaching Perkins through his songs, telling him when and how much to tilt his head, move his hands, take a breath. He introduced him to the Loud is Good school of musical theatre and made sure he pronounced every Loesser lyric so that it was clear to the back of the house. This did not endear him to the actor.'

Susan Loesser thought that the reason Tony became demanding and critical of his material, as well as objecting to Frank Loesser's constant coaching, was because he was insecure about his singing. Tony, Loesser and George Roy Hill, the director, argued over their respective concepts, almost coming to blows at times.

Ten years later, Tony told Rex Reed, 'I thought the book was very naive and I'd say, "These lines are terrible!" and they'd yell, "Say 'em!" and I said 'em, and I was the star!'

Despite some of the difficulties in the songs, Tony refused to have a voice coach.

'People ask me now, "Who are you studying voice with?" Well, I'm not,' Tony explained to the *New York Times* during the tryout road tour in February 1960. 'I felt that if I did, it couldn't but force me into a specific style, so that when I was singing I'd really be thinking about some half-realized technicalities instead of about the song. Also, it probably wouldn't have done much good. I know that so far I'm getting across. I always ask the girls who come back after the show where they were sitting, and to date they've said they've heard me, no matter where they were.'

Although on his records his voice tends towards a baritone, here with a higher *tessitura*, he has a pleasant tenor which gets the high notes with not much strain.

'As for the songs, Loesser told me that the only time a song should occur is when emotion has become so intense that it's no longer sufficient to explain it in speech. I try to bear that in mind when I'm doing a number, I try to remember that it's a moment so intense I can't speak it.'

Tony's role was Gideon Briggs, a young man from the sleepy town of Greenwillow, cursed with the 'call to wander'. He fears that falling in love will prevent him from realizing his ambition. But he is finally persuaded not to roam by 'The Music of Home', accompanied by rather corny lyrics.

Much better were the two stirring solos Tony was given to sing – the lyrical 'Summertime Love' and the anti-romantic 'Never will I Marry'. The latter, in which he warns women not to waste their time on him, with its hauntingly syncopated melody ending with the word 'marry' on a high note, was sung with real gusto.

One night, Cecil Kellaway, who was Reverend Birdsong, said, 'That's your cue, Hideous,' instead of 'That's your call, Gideon.'

Commented Tony, 'Shows what he thought of me.'

In fact, Tony was perfectly cast in the atmospheric but rather whimsical tale, which was too slight for most tastes. Although *Greenwillow* captured the spirit of rural America by celebrating its small-town customs in an unpretentious and endearing manner, there was something contrived about the simple, lyrical songs, à la Rodgers and Hammerstein, coming from a sophisticate like Loesser, whose best work was the brash metropolitanism of *Guys and Dolls* and *How to Succeed in Business Without Really Trying*. Critics thought the musical the major disappointment of the season, generally considering it too untheatrical and thin. Kenneth Tynan in the *New Yorker* was the cruellest, calling it 'a simple-minded extravaganza'. However, Brooks Atkinson in the *New York Times*, praised both the show and its star.

'Until Anthony Perkins started to sing the pensive "A Day Borrowed From Heaven" and the moody "Summertime Love", none of us would have imagined him as the chief performer in a major musical show. But Mr Perkins turns out to have a sufficiently flexible voice to make songs sound like music . . .'

Greenwillow, which opened at the Alvin Theatre on 8 March 1960, struggled on for ninety-five performances, closing on 28 May. On closing night, the company received a cable from Loesser, which read, 'Oops, sorry.' Thankfully, during the first week of the run, the cast recorded an album, which was issued with the striking all-green willow cover of the posters, and a photo of Tony in a green jerkin.

While Tony was rehearsing *Greenwillow*, he met Alan Helms, a good-looking young man who was starting his career as an actor and model. They were introduced at a party given by Michael Kahn, then at Columbia University, and much later Artistic Director of the Shakespeare Festival at Stratford, Connecticut.

Tony and Alan took to each other right away. They both

ALAN HELMS

(PHOTO PROVIDED BY ALAN HELMS).

happened to be reading Lawrence Durrell's *Alexandria Quartet* at the time. As it was yet to be completed, Alan guessed, quite correctly, that the fourth novel would be titled *Cléo*. This impressed Tony no end, and he gave Alan his phone number and asked him to call him the next evening at seven o'clock.

'I waited for seven minutes, because I was very nervous about appearing overly eager to talk to a famous movie star Anthony Perkins,' Helms recalled. 'He answered not by saying hello, but by saying, "Seven minutes, hey? Very good. Very good." '

They met for a drink, and Tony invited Alan to what the latter calls, 'his shack-up pad' on 55th Street, a block away from the apartment he shared with Helen Merrill.

'He would have been uncomfortable taking men back to the apartment where he lived with Helen,' commented Helms. 'It was impossible to take anyone to Helen's, because his bedroom was in the very back of the apartment and the only way you could get to it was through hers. Whenever we met for sex, it was in the 55th Street place. We spent one night at the 56th Street apartment when Helen was out of town. Tony took me to meet her once and I had the feeling that it was very important that I meet with Helen's approval, and if there was any reason I didn't that would affect our relationship.'

Owing to his reticent nature, Tony never mentioned his mother to Helms, nor did he mention his relationship with Grover Dale.

'I didn't realize I had intruded on his relationship with Grover. It was only later that I discovered that they were lovers. He never told me. Once when we had a date for lunch, I went to fetch him at the theatre. We met backstage. While he was showing me the sets we turned a corner and there was Grover who was clearly uncomfortable. I didn't know why.'

Tony and Alan spoke at least daily and saw each other every second night, although they were rarely seen in public together.

Once, when Tony had to postpone a date because he had been called to a *Greenwillow* meeting, he asked Alan what he was going to do. Alan replied that as he was unable to see Tony in the flesh, he would go and see him in *On The Beach*, which had just opened at the Astor Theatre, on Broadway and 45th.

'When the lights came up there was a huge commotion in the balcony,' Helms remembered. 'I thought nothing of it, and went home. Tony called later to say that the meeting ended sooner than he had expected and he had gone to the theatre to fetch me, and found himself in the balcony. When the film ended, people turned round and saw the man they had just seen on the screen. I was struck by that, because Tony hated to be recognized.'

The brief love affair ended before *Greenwillow* opened on Broadway.

'I visited Tony out of town when *Greenwillow* was on the road. I spent a weekend with him in Philadelphia. And I ran into Grover again under the marquee of the theatre. There was something very strained about Tony that weekend. There even seemed some effort involved in the sexual part. I think the sexual part was most of the glue of our brief relationship and I had the sense when I left the next day that our affair was over. Yet, the great pleasure of the relationship for me, after the cheap thrill of having an affair with a movie star, was that Tony was so bright and was such a good conversationalist.'

There was enough of a remaining connection that when *Greenwillow* opened, Alan went backstage to see his ex-lover. He knew that Tony got a thrill from having his name up in lights outside a Broadway theatre, mainly because of his father, and also because he always remembered that Osgood had marked him out for stardom at his birth by deliberately giving him a seven-letter first name so that it would balance his last name on a theatre marquee.

'I went down on opening night and counted the number of light bulbs that made up his name and sent a telegram to tell him the result. We never saw each other again by design after that.'

A couple of weeks after they broke up, Alan and Tony ran into each other near Helen's apartment on 7th Avenue, and they were both carrying copies of *Cléo*, the last volume of the Durrell work that had sparked off their friendship.

'The last time I saw Tony was one night in Boston about twenty years later,' Alan remembered. 'We passed each other on a deserted street, and I turned around and called "Tony!" He kept on walking. I yelled "Tony!" He kept on walking. I yelled again. "Tony! It's Alan Helms." He kept on walking.'

14

AIMEZ-VOUS TONY?

'I've just realized I've never been in love' – Philip Van der Besh in *Goodbye Again* (1961)

Only a month after *Greenwillow* closed on 28 May 1960, Tony went into rehearsal for another musical, *Damn Yankees*, for a two-week summer stock run at the Carousel Theatre, Framingham, Massachusetts. This 1955 Richard Adler-Jerry Ross Faustian musical had been filmed two years earlier with Tab Hunter, Tony's former lover, in the role of baseball ace Joe Hardy.

Cathryn Damond played the part of Lola, the Devil's handmaiden given the job of vamping Joe (Tony), a rookie on the Washington Senators, while the Devil (Murray Matheson) tries to fix it so that the Senators can beat the Yankees for the AL pennant and so causing millions of people to go mad. Harry Stanton played middle-aged Joe Boyd, who sells his soul to turn into the youthful Tony Perkins.

Here was Tony, the epitome of all-American clean-cut cuteness as a sporting hero, having just appeared green and willowy in a folksy bit of Americana on Broadway, his image as yet unbesmirched by Norman Bates. The portrayal of a maniacal murderer was only beginning to hit the public just as *Damn Yankees* ended. Tony decided it was a perfect time to leave the country and Norman Bates behind him. Like Gideon Briggs he would satisfy his 'call to wander'. Fortunately, he had been offered work in Europe which he accepted with enthusiasm.

Tony arrived in France in September 1960, having signed to play in a film version of Françoise Sagan's *Aimez-Vous Brahms?*, the third of the French author's slim, romantic novels to be filmed after *Bonjour Tristesse* and *That Certain Smile.* It would be the first of nine films Tony was to make in France, where he would live intermittently in the 1960s.

There he met Anatole Litvak, the Russian emigré director, who had just settled permanently in Paris after a long sojourn in Hollywood. When Litvak told Tony that they were looking for an English title that American audiences could understand – presuming they would find all three words of the French title incomprehensible – the actor came up with *Goodbye Again*, one of his father's Broadway successes. Because there were very few people around in 1961 who would remember the 1932 play or the 1933 film version, there would be no confusion between Sagan's chic romance set in Paris and the farcical comedy in which Osgood (Warren William in the film) had performed with such dexterity (alone) in bed.

Tony's co-stars were to be Yves Montand and Ingrid Bergman. Montand had just returned from making two films in America, and was now known over there. Bergman had not made a film since her marriage to Swedish stage producer Lars Schmidt two years previously. According to Tony, at his first meeting with the Swedish star she had said, ' "So, you're Tony Perkins. I hear you're pretty good. I guess maybe I better watch out for you". . . Ingrid started talking about how as an actor she always kept her ego out of it. She said how she'd done a play and she went up to someone and said, "I understand you can be very hard to work with and are very competitive and I don't work that way." I was grateful to her for her frankness and having the first salvo – how wonderfully air-clearing.'

Nevertheless, competitive or not, Ingrid was an astute judge of actors and she knew that Tony was so strong that 'he could steal it'. As for Tony, although he called Ingrid his 'idol', he went into the picture like a boxer going into the ring with a champion.

'I wanted to remain on my feet,' he said.

Shooting on *Goodbye Again* started on 19 September and was completed on 13 December. Most of it was filmed at the Studio de Boulogne in Paris with sets by Alexander Trauner. There was a single sequence in London, one in Deauville, and another at the Salle Pleyel, where Tony and Ingrid go to hear the First and Third Symphonies by Brahms.

Soon after the cameras started rolling, just before their first kissing scene in the film, Ingrid called Tony into her dressing room.

'It'll take time, the kissing,' she said in her most profound voice. 'We'll get it wrong. Let's practise kissing.'

Years after, in a lengthy interview with a reporter from *People*, Tony remembered how Ingrid had attempted to seduce him, an occupational hazard that Tony seems to have often encountered. ('She finds all accused men attractive . . . accused men are attractive' – *The Trial*.)

'She would have welcomed an affair. Every day she invited me to her dressing room to practise a love scene. I insisted on standing near the door, which I kept open.'

However, Tony later asserted that the quotation was 'a presumably undeliberate distortion of me'.

Ingrid Bergman's side of the story was told in her autobiography.

'I took Anthony Perkins into my dressing room – he was supposed to be my young lover – and I said, "Because we've got to do it later in the film, and I don't know you, I'm hardly acquainted with you, and I'm shy and I blush. Much better we do our rehearsal in my dressing room, so that I shan't start dreading the moment when we have to do it in front of a hundred technicians." He grinned, and understood, and said, "Okay," then kissed me, and said, "That hurt? No? Good." He was very sweet, and it was easier for me after that. I knew him. We were friends. You see, although the camera has no terrors at all for me, I'm very bad at this sort of intimacy on the screen, especially when the men are practically strangers.'

In the film, they do sleep together, but this is only indicated the morning after. From a letter quoted in the same book, Bergman writes:

'These two actors [Montand and Perkins] are wonderful for their parts. It's a long time since I worked with *two* actors I enjoyed so much. They are both charming, both great personalities and very different, and you understand why I – in my part as Paula – love them both . . .'

Variety described *Goodbye Again* as having 'strong appeal for a middle-aged distaff audience.' In other words 'a woman's picture', a discredited genre (sometimes unfairly so) that can offer better examples than this superficially sophisticated soap opera. 'The middle-aged distaff' audience might have enjoyed seeing Ingrid Bergman as a wealthy forty-year-old interior decorator (the actress was actually forty-five), dressed by Dior, falling for a wealthy younger man, twenty-five-old law student Perkins (he was twenty-eight), while her lover of five years, wealthy womanizing businessman Yves Montand (wooden) is abroad and with a broad. When Montand returns he promises to sacrifice his cherished freedom and make an honest woman of her, so she tearfully gives up Perkins, though Montand continues to philander.

All this was enacted in an elegantly photographed Paris of dinners at Maxim's, smart hotels, chic apartments and fast sports cars. The original title came from the question Tony asks Bergman.

'Do you like Brahms?'

'I don't know, it was so long ago,' she replies crassly.

Yet, in her apartment, she has a record of the Brahms Third symphony, the *andante* of which provides the film's theme tune. When they do go to a concert at the Salle Pleyel, her mind wanders during the Brahms First symphony, remembering how Montand first picked her up in a café. They are then so caught up with each other during the interval, that they have to hurry back just in time to catch that *andante.* It turns up again in various forms throughout the film – played by a jazz combo and sung by Diahann Carroll at a nightclub as 'Love Is Just A Word'.

The word 'love' is much used in this trite triangle. 'Love is no more than the touching of two skins,' and 'I've just realized I've never been in love,' Tony tells Bergman, before he is completely smitten. Later, he agonizes, 'The worst sentence is to be alone and without love.'

However, Tony's youth is once again an impediment. 'There's a man. A real man,' he says, referring to his rival.

'He's just a boy, and terribly unsure,' she tells Montand.

A toy boy, in more recent parlance, who hears someone whisper, 'How old is she?' when he and Bergman are out at a restaurant together.

As a pampered puppyish boy called Philip Van der Besh (rich people in Hollywood films are frequently called Van something), of whom his mother (Jessie Royce Landis) says, 'He's quite bright but I haven't the faintest idea what goes on in his head,' Tony displays his skill in off-beat humour. He is at ease in the lighter aspects of the role, when drunk, or doing a burlesque of a D.A.'s courtroom technique, or revealing a self-mocking Oedipus complex, though he is sometimes ingratiatingly irritating. He is at his weakest in the romantic and weepy melodramatic moments. They do not come naturally to him, and without a strong director's hand, they seem forced.

'I was sort of an interlude. Dammit. Damn him. Damn everything,' he cries, walking tearfully through the streets, after Bergman has thrown him over for the more mature Montand.

Tony was disappointed when he saw the rushes of one of his best scenes, a monologue in which he analyzes his actions.

'I felt somewhat betrayed by the camera operator. I had wanted my gestures in that scene to reach the limits of the screen and in rehearsals, on discussing this particular point with him, he cautioned me to stay within such and such limits. Well, his limits were conservative to the extreme, and I have always felt that that would have been more effective if my gestures had been more pronounced.'

Bosley Crowther in the *New York Times* wrote: 'Of the actors, Anthony Perkins not only has the most engaging role but he also plays it in the most engaging fashion and almost carries the picture by himself. As the nervous-eyed whimsical young fellow . . . he ranges from boyish excitement to deep and tear-popping grief and makes it believable and cogent. It is too bad they throw the play to the woman at the end.'

'Oui, Brahms', was one critic's response to the film's French title, and many others followed the same line, though *Goodbye Again* was a big box-office success, one of Tony's last. And this is 1961, twenty years away from his final film!

'When they started making it they had a problem of whether to try to appeal to American or European audiences,' Tony remarked. 'Because customarily love stories have to be keyed to fit either the realistic side of life and love, or the slightly more palatable and Americanized version. Well, they decided to make it the American way, slicker, slightly less down-to-earth, glossied, a more movieish way . . . in the writing, sets, costumes, photography, in the entire image of the picture. What is so strange is that it ended up appealing more to Europeans than to Americans. So perhaps if they had made it in the so-called European manner it would have appealed more to the Americans! No one could have been more surprised than United Artists when this picture turned out such a success.'

Tony's performance won him the Best Actor award at the Cannes Film Festival, as well as the Victoire de Cinéma, Germany's Grosse Otto and Italy's David di Donatello (shared with Spencer Tracy in *Judgement At Nuremberg*).

All the way to the Theatre de Champs-Élysées to receive his Victoire de Cinéma award, according to a reporter in *Cinémonde*,

'Tony kept repeating non-stop the little speech he had written himself with the help of a French dictionary. All afternoon he had worked on the speech like a good student in order to thank those who had elected him Best Actor two years in a row. [He had received one for *Psycho* the year before]. Unfortunately, the programme was so long and Tony so nervous that all he could get out was "Merci . . . Merci beaucoup . . . Je suis si content . . ." That was not up to snuff for him, but he nevertheless has a happy memory of that evening and talks about it often, because "you see, in a single evening, I met all the artists of Paris!" He wrote down his impressions in his black-bound journal.'

Despite Norman Bates, *Goodbye Again* pushed Tony into the position of a romantic leading man of the 1960s, someone who definitely appealed to the younger generation, especially in France. Yet he continued to be self-derogatory.

'I'm not really suited to be a movie star. I have no confidence in myself. I'm not interested in money. I'm not good looking. I have a hunch in my spine. I can't see worth a damn. I have a very small head. I haven't many opinions. I have no string of French girls. I'm not tough. I haven't a single quality a movie star should have. Not a single one.'

This was a mixture of pose and sincerity, but there was a deeper sense of being an imposter, an uneasy feeling that he would be found out.

15

OEDIPUS AT HOME

'Mother! Oh God! Mother, mother! Blood, blood!' – Norman Bates in *Psycho* (1960)

Tony had returned to the USA from his stay in Paris after hearing that he was on David Lean's shortlist for the title role in *Lawrence of Arabia*, due to start shooting in March 1961. ('My mouth is so dry, they could shoot *Lawrence of Arabia* in it' – *The Last of Sheila*.) Tony, who had read *The Seven Pillars of Wisdom*, thought that he might be able to approach the complexities of the sexually ambiguous hero. Albert Finney had quit after four days, and, after serious consideration, Marlon Brando was deemed unsuitable. Meanwhile, Tony's friend Monty Clift was busy phoning Lean in Madrid almost every day, begging to be allowed to play Lawrence. Although it now seems inconceivable that an American, or anyone other than Peter O'Toole, could have taken the role, it is not difficult to see why Tony might have been deemed a likely candidate, nor why Clift could not have been a possibility, despite his being on the edge of a crack-up.

However, instead of Arabia, Tony was offered a chance to go to Greece to make *Phaedra*. Jules Dassin, the American emigré director, living in Greece with Melina Mercouri, was looking for a young lead for his updated version (from 428 BC to AD 1961) of *Hippolytus* by Euripides (the same source material as *Desire Under the Elms*).

Set among the upper crust in modern-day Greece, it was about Phaedra Kyrilis, the second wife of a shipping magnate (modelled on Onassis), who falls passionately in love with her stepson, Alexis. After Dassin had seen Tony in *Goodbye Again* he thought he would be ideal as Alexis. Even though he was not Greek, his accent could be explained away by giving him an English mother. Anyway, Dassin had already signed up the Italian actor Raf Vallone for the father.

Dassin rang Tony at his New York apartment.

'A friend answered the phone, and told me that Tony was in the country,' recalled Dassin. 'I said, "I'm sending him a script and I command him to like it." I then posted off the screenplay of *Phaedra*, written by myself and Margarita Liberaki. It was not long before Tony replied that he would do it.'

Never having been to Greece, Tony was not concerned that he was following directly on a similar role where he is the object of the desire of an older woman. When he accepted, he was ignorant of the fact that the producers, United Artists, were not keen to have him at first, thinking him not 'masculine enough.' But Dassin had insisted and won. Yet some critics later bore out UA's fears.

One reviewer, who considered himself an expert on women's sexual tastes, thought Tony 'too willowy to excite a woman like Mercouri.' Pauline Kael, also taking the conventional gender line, commented that Tony's career 'was undermined by a lunatic piece of miscasting . . . when Melina Mercouri swept him up in her arms, he was made to seem ludicrous. People left theatres giggling at the idea that a woman might prefer this skinny boy to her husband, when the husband was played by Raf Vallone. Perkins hasn't been a star since.'

Dwight McDonald wrote: 'The wispy Perkins . . . becomes more fragile and epicenely contorted with each new film. He is so outmatched in every way, from breadth of shoulders to manliness of voice, that during the love scenes I had the unsettling feeling they were both in drag.'

Phaedra, called on the posters 'a violent drama of profane love,' reveals Tony in England, where he should be studying at the London School of Economics. Instead, he spends his time sketching Greek statues at the British Museum. Vallone has sent his attractive wife to London to fetch him back to Greece, in order to take his place in the family shipping business.

Stepson and stepmother meet while he is casually drawing Aphrodite. He turns on his charm, and the two of them are soon dancing at a nightclub.

'Don't call me mother,' she says to him as they whirl round the dance floor.

She persuades him to give up painting in London and return to Greece. Meanwhile, they start an affair in Paris, where they naturally visit Dior.

Back in Greece, Melina's (lesbian?) maid warns her, 'Put that boy out of your heart or everything will fall.'

Being a tragedy, of course, everything does end badly, with Tony's death, her suicide, and the sinking of the S. S. *Phaedra*, perhaps symbolic of the whole enterprise. The overwrought performances were observed by a chorus of bemused, black-shrouded wailing women. Dassin himself (uncredited) played an Old Greek.

Much of the powerful plot was undermined by some of the lines uttered, an example of which was: 'I love you, and when I say I love you I mean I'm in love with you.'

nxiety in close-up, while Tony gave another yal of arrested development, smiling with venself around pillars, kicking his heels on the the floor like a cat.

Iidnight (whatever that meant) did very little for on, and was a worm that was beginning to bite Nevertheless, he was happy to be living in Paris, to visit a number of clubs. It also led to his work-Welles.

When Vallone discovers the situation between his wife and son, he cries, 'Get out of Greece! Carry my curse wherever you go.'

Tony replies, 'I love you.'

As he drives to his death, Tony shouts, 'She loved me like they did in the old days. Goodbye Greek light, Goodbye old sea!' in a manner, according to one critic of 'a boozed American tourist'.

Tony remembered it as 'an awkward and difficult' role, because Dassin was particularly anxious that he did not repeat what he had done in *Goodbye Again.* The director, therefore, explained to Tony that he would like Alexis to be made less attractive and, though not villainous, to have his unappealing characteristics identified.

'I think the picture had great originality,' Tony recalled. 'We shot it under the adverse conditions that Dassin particularly seems to enjoy. He is a singular director in that the thing that makes him work most heatedly . . . is to have technical and, well, any kind of problems that can seem insurmountable, and in the conquering of these problems he finds his inspiration to film . . . The most difficult [part was] literally lugging equipment ourselves up the rocks and over the mountains, that's the kind of thing he likes.'

The steamy love scene between Tony and Mercouri was shot in a half abstract half realistic manner, in which the bodies, seen as Greek statues, seem to melt. Although Mercouri was over ten years Tony's senior, it was he who, according to Dassin, 'protected her'.

'He was cleverer than Melina as to film technique. He would nudge her into a better light so she would look better.'

In the ancient tragedy, Hippolytus is killed when racing his chariot along the beach and attacked by a sea monster. In Dassin's version, the young man drives his sports car over a cliff. He seems to love the car, which he kisses and calls 'my girl', as much as any woman.

'The car scene . . . was filmed in the most dangerous, foolhardy way,' Tony commented. 'We were in a car with the camera mounted on the hood which made it absolutely impossible to see. I was driving at breakneck speed around the mountain turns, yelling and crying the dialogue. It could have been done in any number of a hundred different ways just as well, but this was the hardest way and this was damn well the way he wanted to make it, and I think it was good for the picture.'

'Tony was the worst driver ever,' according to Dassin. 'An Aston Martin can run away with one. I sat beside him with the mike. The emotion of the scene made him close his eyes, and I'd have to kick him to watch the road.'

There must have been something in the Greek air, and in the warm and open nature of Jules Dassin and Melina Mercouri, who were to marry five years later, that drew the normally shy and solitary Tony out of himself.

'Making *Phaedra* with Melina Mercouri and Jules Dassin was an emotional circus – to cohabit with their vitality is unforgettable. They were at that pinpoint in time when they were riding high after their success in *Never On Sunday*, and during our last day of shooting the three of us cried so much that we had to reshoot the next day – our eyes were so puffy.'

But Dassin has second thoughts about the film.

'I would have liked to have made it in Greek and closer to the Euripides tragedy, but as it was it became merely a melodrama. My idea was to replace the kings with the shipping magnates. Onassis liked it, but thought he was better looking than Raf Vallone.'

Dassin said he found Tony an excellent working partner. 'At the risk of speaking in clichés, I would say that there was not a single moment that wasn't enjoyable. Everybody liked him. On Hydra, where we filmed, the islanders would bring him nuts and honey.'

Still enjoying th
returned from G
vak once more af
years and eight film
on screen with Soph
was to play her husba
French title being *Un*
Wound).

Although his role see
young men he had been p
regressive portrayal of a spo
lousy. As for Tony's looks, he
Desire Under the Elms, in whic
of a five o'clock shadow.

As Loren said, 'When I play op
his mother, even though I'm youn

Melodramas do not come much
night. The plot so far . . . Tony Per
ren, is the only survivor of a plan
Casablanca. He returns to his wife's a
shevelled but still alive and smiling wi

'Airplanes,' he reflects, 'do funny thing

'You're hurt!' she exclaims.

'Oh, it's nothing. Just a bit of gangrene.'

'Would you like me to warm up somethin

He tells her to hide him while she collects th
gets the money and drives him to the Belgian
runs him over with her car, and dumps the body
telling her tale to lover Gig Young, she gradually

Producer-director Litvak merely added to the
chanics of the movie by approaching it in an hyste

16

ANTHONY P. AND JOSEPH K.

'Why am I always in the wrong, without knowing what's wrong or what it's all about?' – Joseph K. in *The Trial* (1962)

'Someone must have been telling lies about Joseph K., for without having done anything wrong he was arrested one fine morning,' is the arresting opening sentence of Franz Kafka's *The Trial.* By a strange coincidence, the bank clerk Joseph K. is arrested on the morning of his thirtieth birthday, the exact same age as Tony was when he took the role in Orson Welles's version of the unfinished 1925 novel.

Tony must have been conscious of the close connection between Kafka's paranoid hero and himself, almost as much as he was aware of some of the parallels between the inner life of Norman Bates and his own. Whether Orson Welles was aware of this analogy when he chose Tony for the role is not clear, but Welles had seen *Psycho* and admitted to recognizing something of Bates in Joseph K.

Kafka indicates that Joseph K.'s sexual development has also been arrested, and at the age of thirty he has not grown up sexually. There are moments when one wonders if the trial he is about to undergo, which unfolds like a nightmare, is connected with this. K.'s own introspection has begun a process of self-appraisal and self-condemnation, and he is powerless to stop it.

There cannot be a person in the Judeo–Christian world who has not at some time or another felt they have been unjustly accused of something they did not do, or harboured a guilty secret they would be terrified of having exposed. More specifically, keeping one's homosexuality hidden from the world at large, and afraid of the consequences if it were revealed, would have been sufficient for Tony to understand Joseph K.'s fears. Though both could be accused of 'having delusions of persecution'.

For obscure business reasons of their own, Alexander and Michel Salkind, Paris-based Russian independent producers, wanted Welles to make a film of any out-of-copyright classic he cared to pick, to be shot quickly in Yugoslavia. Welles perused the list of non-copyright possibilities they sent him, and decided that the only one that remotely interested him was the Kafka novel. However, Welles would have been more in tune with *The Castle*, because its hero, K. is an aggressive protagonist unlike Joseph K., the passive victim in *The Trial*, and because it is more an allegory of Power, the sustaining motif of the director's *oeuvre*.

Welles made an updated adaptation, and rounded up a group of his friends, including Akim Tamiroff, Jeanne Moreau, Romy Schneider, Suzanne Flon and Katina Paxinou (vanished from the final cut) to appear in it. Happily, Tony was in Europe when Welles approached him to play Joseph K.

'I did *The Trial* because I wanted to work with Orson Welles. It was one of those crazy unplanned things . . . I got a call from [Anatole] Litvak saying, "Orson Welles wants to get in touch with you." He acted as a kind of go-between between Welles and myself. I never thought that I would work with Welles, it has always been one of the dreams of my career since I was fourteen years old.'

In retrospect, this seems a rather precocious ambition, as Welles, who had only directed two films a few years earlier, had little reputation in 1946. It is doubtful whether Tony would have seen *Citizen Kane* or *The Magnificent Ambersons*, and even if he had, it seems unlikely that at fourteen he would have responded to them. But in 1962, despite the slings and arrows of outrageous fortune, Welles loomed large for most film-lovers.

'We discussed the picture at length, and he paid me the great compliment of saying he would like to know whether I would make the picture because if I wasn't going to make it, he wasn't going to make it either,' Tony remarked. 'I'll never know if that's the way it really would've been or not, but I prefer to take it as the truth and I will always want to believe that.'

Shooting of the exteriors began towards the end of March 1962 in Zagreb, whose run-down, East European look seemed ideal for Kafka's grim world.

'When we worked on *The Trial* we basically lived, breathed and ate and slept together for three months,' recalled Tony with exaggeration. 'I was fastened to him. We were all alone. We were the only English-speaking people in Zagreb. You have to be tight with somebody when you're in a place like that. Most of the crew members were Yugoslavian, and they were an affable bunch but we just didn't know how to talk with them.'

There is no doubt that the large, ursine, extrovert Welles and the slender, sheepish, introverted Tony were thrown together a great deal of the time and worked closely, but during Welles's brief stay in Zagreb, he found time to meet Oja Kodar, a Yugoslavian sculptress and writer, who was to be his constant companion and assistant for the rest of his life.

ANTHONY PERKINS IN *THE TRIAL*, 1962 (PHOTOFEST).

William Chappell, the American actor who played the painter Titorelli, gave a vivid description of Orson Welles directing Tony in Zagreb.

'"You are pinned to the wall like a thumbtack. You are like a sick moth," and the lines of Tony's back obediently shrink into a thin dusty shape. He roars approbation at the speed with which Perkins responds to direction. Perkins is 150 per cent an actor, and he is also consumed with being an actor. Is he not too rare for Joseph K.? small intensely mobile face, his urchin thatch of dense black hair, his high-pitched voice, his gangly elegance with long, long legs and an Egyptian torso unnaturally broad in the shoulder and small in the waist and so flat it is almost one dimensional. He never seems to tire.'

After a few weeks in Zagreb, word came suddenly from Paris that the Salkinds had run out of money and were unable to provide the part of the budget the Yugoslavians had agreed to match. So no sets could be constructed in the Zagreb studios, no pay was forthcoming for the cast and crew, and the only thing to do, according to the Salkinds, was to abandon production.

They had, of course, underestimated Welles, who was all too used to shooting with no money at all, wherever and whenever he could. The answer to their dilemma, he at once recognized, was a moonlight flit to Paris. Once there, it should not be too impossible to improvise. And improvise he did!

'The only thing we didn't have was studio space, hence the oft told, but true story of Welles finding the Gare d'Orsay,' Tony recounted. 'I had it from Welles the following day so if it is apocryphal it is a story he thinks enough of to have thought out twenty-four hours in advance! Welles has always been very much attracted by the moon, he gets his inspiration from the moon. When the moon comes up and goes down – this is important to him. In this case, he was standing on his balcony at the Hotel Meurice [in the rue de Rivoli] . . . we had been thrown out of the studios at Boulogne because we didn't have enough money. He's standing there on the balcony looking at the full moon. But the moon isn't moving, it's neither rising nor falling. The trees in the Tuileries Gardens obstruct his view. Finally he goes up onto the roof of the hotel and sees it isn't the moon at all, it is the face of the clock at the Gare d'Orsay. Well, there's nothing for it but to go right over there at four o'clock in the morning, talk to the caretaker, who says, "we don't use 90 per cent of this rambling structure anymore". . . Well, that was it. He gave the man, I think, a couple of thousand francs to go in and take a look at it, and saw this rotting superstructure, this Victorian nightmare of passageways and grillwork, dust, dirt and decay. And he said, "That's it." '

Thus, not being able to afford studio space, let alone the sets he had designed, Welles had the inspiration to move into the grand, abandoned art nouveau-style Gare d'Orsay (built in 1900 and now the Musée d'Orsay) on the Left Bank.

Aside from the scenes already shot in Yugoslavia, there were others filmed in Italy, so that when Tony walks out of the Gare d'Orsay in Paris, he is in Zagreb and walks across the street into Milan. Working at fever pitch, Welles finished the shooting by 2 June, in under nine weeks. He was then able to edit the film just as he wanted, and had it ready for its Paris première by 21 December 1962. On the final day of shooting, Welles was in a wonderfully exuberant mood, realizing he had finished another film against all the odds.

'We used to call each other the Ever Ready Players because we never really knew what scenes we were going to be shooting due to financial difficulties, difficulties with sets, or with actors stuck in Zurich overnight,' said Tony. 'So I memorized the entire script which was so thick it was written in two volumes – it is the only script I've ever known that was in two separate books. We cut a lot.'

One of the scenes excised was one in which Tony, who is almost never off the screen, has his fortune told by a computer.

'I suppose a computer is rather like a judge . . . Yes, why not? Why shouldn't an electronic brain replace a judge? That would be a great step nearer to perfection. Errors would no longer be possible and everything would become neat, clean and precise. Instead of trying to take advantage of us behind our backs, lawyers would be forced to be as exact as accountants or scientists. Imagine a tribunal working like a laboratory. . .'

The director and leading actor continued to spend around sixteen hours together every day.

'We got up in our respective hotel suites and met for breakfast and drove together to the set with my car following empty just behind. We had lunch together and dinner and then went out nightclubbing, until the wee hours. He drank, I didn't.'

But when time became shorter, the hours of shooting became longer. The biggest problem for Tony was his dislike of working at night. He always claimed to do his best work before noon, the earlier the better, but *The Trial* was frequently shot all night long. Yet Tony was taken with the way Welles listened to any suggestion he made, just as Hitchcock had.

As Tony observed, 'He's extremely good with actors, he never loses his temper . . . he had a field-marshal's affection for the troops – the crew, the actors, the extras. He's a wonderful manipulator – and I mean that in the best sense – of people and their soft spots and the ways to get them behind his vision of things.'

Nevertheless Tony, who always claimed to believe 'in the firm hand of the director', was in conflict with Welles's conception of Joseph K. He believed K. to be guilty and Tony did not. When Tony voiced his misgivings, Welles replied, 'He's guilty. Guilty as hell.'

'I don't think it's a successful film as a whole, primarily because Welles and I disagreed about the delineation of the character,'

Tony commented in retrospect. 'Early on I understood that he wanted to have a guilty, cringing, obsequious, nervous, anxiety-ridden and completely burnt out Joseph K., who was in fact guilty of everything that was accused of him, although this is a radical departure from what I believe are the absolutely clearly observed wishes and motivations behind Kafka's work. I had to go along with it, because he was the director. Not only was he the director but he was Orson Welles and you just don't fly in the face of that. So I played it that way. I played it with a sort of suspicious undertow. He wanted, not a Norman exactly, but he wanted a guilty guy. And I thought that was really antithetical to the piece. I was surprised that he wanted it but naturally I supplied him with it. That's the way I would work with any director that I had admired.'

Like the novel, the film is open to more than one interpretation, and if Welles had wanted Tony to play guilty, the portrayal does not necessarily discount Joseph K.'s innocence.

'I'd still feel guilty, even if I haven't done anything at all,' says K.

He is guilty of not asserting his innocence, or, as Kafka suggests, no man is completely innocent.

'Unless your thoughts are 100 per cent innocent, how can anyone avoid feeling guilty.'

Tony does not play Joseph K. guiltily but defiantly. Looking like an animated stick man or as if a spring is coiled inside him, he gives a kinetic performance. Though his American accent makes him seem more middle-American than mittel-European, he delivers his lines with wonderfully variable intonations and rhythms, most of which come out of the side of his mouth. When wound up with emotion, the voice takes on a rasping tone, he gnashes his teeth (as Norman Bates was wont to do) and clenches his fists. A tall man under low ceilings, dressed in a smart three-piece suit, tie and pocket handkerchief, he walks as though on a rolling ship as he moves around the labyrinthine rooms, magnetically drawn to the walls. But his gait is mostly as graceful as a deer, whether serene or startled. (Tony once explained that when he walked in films, he often imagined that the air was as thick as water, so a certain effort had to be expended when making his way through the atmosphere.) Tony's consummate comic timing is also given full rein. Welles was disappointed that people failed to see how funny *The Trial* was.

'Tony Perkins and I were laughing all the way through the shooting,' he stated, though, alas, not all the way to the bank.

Tony's Joseph K. is never gloomy, nor is he pathetic, and at the climax he becomes a tragic figure, more Welles's K. than Kafka's.

'I have changed the end,' Welles stated. 'In Kafka, K. dies a beaten man. In my version he protests to the very end.'

Unlike Kafka's K., he refuses to take his own life with the knife provided by the two hired assassins on the waste land, not because they 'had not left him the remnant of strength necessary for the deed', but because he will not do the work for them.

'You . . . you . . . you . . . you dummies,' he protests. 'You'll have to kill me.'

They throw dynamite in the pit as he laughs hysterically and the mushroom cloud is seen. By strengthening K.'s contumacy, Welles has made him, through Tony's tour-de-force portrayal, a more sympathetic character and one that makes his appeal to women more plausible than the greyer K. of the novel. As the Advocate (played by Welles) says about his mistress/assistant Leni (Romy Schneider), 'She finds all accused men attractive . . . accused men are attractive, not that being accused makes any immediate change in a man's personal appearance, but if you have the right eye for these things you can pick out an accused man in the largest crowd. There's just something about them . . . something attractive . . . it can't be a sense of guilt . . . we can't all be guilty. Some are more attractive than others.'

But this bemused critic Penelope Gilliat. 'It is peculiar that women should throw themselves at Perkins, who belies all [that is said] about the attractiveness of accused men. Does he have some quality of which I'm not aware, so that he keeps getting cast opposite tiger-women like Sophia Loren and Melina Mercouri? Or is it just that he is tall enough?'

Unfortunately the casting of Tony was the target of much critical flak. Dwight McDonald in *Esquire* thought, 'Anthony Perkins is a calamity, and an unavoidable one, since as Joseph K. he appears in every scene.' McDonald took up the refrain elsewhere: 'Finally Welles has made his greatest casting mistake to date . . . Anthony Perkins. Kafka made Joseph K. a sober solid citizen, a valued employee, since this makes his arrest and trial all the more absurd, in the existential sense. But Mr Perkins is more like a sensitive adolescent in an Inge play than a stable young career man and he expresses guilt the instant the detectives invade his bedroom; he flutters, he writhes, he teeters on the verge of hysteria. But if Joseph K. feels and acts guilty from the beginning, then the major dramatic point of the story is lost; there is no problem, no mystery, no tension, no movie. And in fact there isn't.'

Welles answered the criticism of the so-called miscasting.

'I think everybody has an idea of K. as some kind of Woody Allen. That's who they think K. is. But it's very clearly stated in the book that he is a young executive on his way up – "a bright young man, one of the brightest."' It was K.'s 'aggressiveness' that Welles said he specifically had in mind in casting Tony, and against which he is convinced people reacted.

Far more contentious was Welles's approach to the subject, which might have benefited from a cooler technique. Impressive as it is, the film is too sumptuous and baroque. The vast setting of the Gare d'Orsay, the music (the overridden war horse – Albinoni's

Adagio), the expressionistic camera angles, overheat the picture. Whereas Kafka adroitly describes a drab and realistic world inhabited by strange people, in the film, real people inhabit a nightmare world. There was a further miscalculation in the attempt to place it in a post-war setting, with its allusions to concentration camp victims (Welles said he conceived K. as a Jew, representing an outsider in society, though this is not discernible in Tony's performance), and the Atomic bomb.

'I suppose the film's greatest weakness is its attempt at universality,' Welles later admitted. 'Perhaps on one level a picture always loses by being deliberately universal.'

It is a sad fact that *The Trial*, whatever its flaws, was perhaps the last film of any significance that Tony made in a career that continued unabated for almost another two decades and another thirty films. Nevertheless, after an end came a new beginning.

17

THE TWO MASKS

'Look, if you don't work, you don't eat. If you don't eat, you get very skinny, you fall down and then you're dead' – Andy Hobart in *The Star-Spangled Girl* (1966–1967)

In the late summer of 1962, Tony returned from Paris to New York, where he had bought a carriage house on West 55th Street. He and Helen Merrill had decided that her apartment on West 56th Street was rather too small for both of them, and that they both needed more space. Leading a double but not duplicitous life – most of his friends knew of his liaison with Grover Dale – Tony and Helen continued to live together platonically.

Although his mother was still very much an influence, Helen, who was not much older than Tony, fulfilled the function of a mother figure as well as surrogate wife, providing him with a certain social acceptability even among the bohemian crowd in which they moved. What is more, Helen was aware and tolerant of his sexual leanings, whereas it was inconceivable that his prim and proper mother had any intimation of them. Tony was more

Anthony Perkins (left) and Sidney Armus in *Harold* on Broadway in 1962. (New York Public Library at Lincoln Center).

often seen out at restaurants, theatres and movie theatres with Helen rather than alone with Grover, with whom he was having an 'affair', the word to describe their relationship by those who knew them at that period.

He did have other sexual partners, but, in Alan Helms's words, 'Tony cared too much about his profession to ever put it into jeopardy by being promiscuous. He was also too fond of his privacy to risk letting it be known that he was gay. That he could never have borne.'

Yet he did not seem to suffer the same constraints abroad. Of the time when Tony was making *Phaedra* in Greece, Jules Dassin said, 'It was never much of an issue with Tony, and was only touched upon. They are slightly more tolerant of homosexuality here.'

In Paris he was quite relaxed about appearing at the Café Flore with beautiful young men, and he also frequented smart gay bars such as Le Fiacre and La Reine Blanche in St Germain dés Prés. One of his brief sexual encounters was with the recently defected Russian ballet dancer Rudolph Nureyev, then making full use of his new-found freedom in Paris in the days when few sexual practices were considered unsafe. (Nureyev died of AIDS in 1993.) Claude Chabrol, who later directed Tony in two films, remarked: 'He told me he had to hide his sexuality less in France. We all knew about it, but we didn't give a fuck. He even brought a young American friend onto the set with him sometimes.'

In October 1962, Tony opened the Osgood Perkins Art Gallery at 137 West 55th Street, built in homage to his father. Osgood was a talented water-colourist who handpainted his Christmas cards, and whose favourite subjects were landscapes of the French countryside where he and his wife spent a few holidays before Tony was born. The gallery, which showed the work of contemporary American artists, lasted but a few years.

At Helen Merrill's instigation, Tony then decided to try his luck on Broadway again in *Harold*, a comedy in two acts by Herman Raucher. It was directed by Larry Blyden, and the cast, apart from Tony in the title role, consisted of Nathaniel Frey, John Fiedler, Don Adams and Sudie Bond. It ran for a mere twenty performances, from 29 November to 15 December, at the Cort Theatre.

'I think and still think that it was a very amusing comedy, all about a gawky young man whose friends get together and try to improve him so that he can get what he wants out of life,' Tony reflected. 'Think of Eliza Doolittle as a man and not a girl, with several Henry Higginses remodeling his character. That was the idea, but somehow it didn't come across and we had a very short run.'

The play was, according to one critic, 'a tepid variation on the Pygmalion theme,' in which three Bronx buddies form a syndicate to launch an unsophisticated neighbourhood kid into high society. Harold finally asserts himself when he falls in love with Iris, a girl his mentors had intended as no more that a practice date. Still, he buckles under to pressure and pretends to go to the society ball for which he was groomed. Only after roaming the streets of New York for two hours in a Prince Charming costume does he return to face them down.

It would seem that Tony, at thirty-one, was now a bit old to play a nineteen-year-old, and there were those who said so. Walter Kerr wrote: 'Nothing against Mr Perkins himself, of course. He is a fine actor, with shoulders which hike nervously as though they were suspended on puppet strings, and he can let his shirt buckle out at the belt or shift his furtive eyes in an entirely convincing evocation of high adolescence. I think he should stop doing it though, at least in plays like this one. To put so much skill into what he could have played equally well, and then left behind him, at summer camp twelve years ago reduces honest performing to not much more than a stunt. Mr Perkins is using genuine adroitness to prove he can ride a scooter-bike.'

While *Harold* was limping towards the end of its two-week run, executive producer Ely Landau sent Tony a novel by Helen Eustis called *The Fool Killer.* The film adaptation was to be directed by the little-known Servando Gonzales, born in Mexico City in 1925, whose first feature, *Yanco,* had been given a limited release in 1961, a couple of years previously.

'Although I read it [the novel] and was impressed, I didn't see it as a part for me,' Tony recalled. 'Then I was sent the script on the assumption that I'd like it better. It was quite right for the picture yet I didn't feel I could do it properly. So I considered it a dead issue until Landau told me that he was screening *Yanco* . . . I clearly remember leaving this screening, going straight to the nearest phone booth, calling Landau and saying, "I'll do the picture." I felt that with this director who is so particularly and strongly visual that he could make this picture as unusual as my casting in the part would require it to be. I think he's an extremely gifted man.'

In Tony's estimation, *Yanco,* directed by the 'extremely gifted' Gonzales, was 'one of the most beautiful movies I've ever seen, presented with the simplicity of the artist. I could never forget it.'

There are very few people who could contradict him, because not many have managed to see the film. *Yanco* (produced, directed and written by Gonzales) is a rather self-consciously poetic and slightly mawkish tale of a young Mexican peasant boy who is taught the violin by an old man. Gonzales followed it with a film called *Los Mediocres,* an epithet many critics applied to *The Fool Killer.*

Working with Gonzales, Tony found, 'He doesn't speak English and I don't speak Spanish . . . actor and director were in complete harmony.'

Actually, when there were problems of communication, Tony

was assisted by his eleven-year-old co-star, Eddie Albert Jr, the bilingual son of Mexican actress Margo, and Eddie Albert.

Young Eddie, making his screen debut, was sent along for the part when the producers contacted his parents.

'I read for it, along with many others and got it. My mom helped me work on the character . . . After spending twenty-eight weeks making that ill-fated romantic fable and living in a Holiday Inn room in Knoxville, Tennessee – I realized that I could not yet handle the business of being an actor.' (He later came back at twenty-one as the lead in *Butterflies Are Free*, on Broadway and in the film.)

The Fool Killer, set in post-Civil War America, tells the tale of a twelve-year-old orphan who leaves his foster home to set out on a journey. He meets a crotchety old farmer (Henry Hull) who tells him the legend of the 'fool killer', a tall axe-murderer, who wishes to rid the world of fools. The boy later befriends an odd, introverted veteran called Milo Bogardus (Perkins). Together they attend a revival meeting, but the disturbed, anti-religious Milo leaves. Afterwards the preacher is found hacked to death. Naturally the boy suspects Milo, who begins to fit the 'fool killer' description. After the boy is taken in by a kindly couple, their lives are threatened by the enraged Milo. The boy pleads for their safety, and the finale comes when the killer takes a fatal fall from their roof.

Although the film was made in 1963, it was only released two years later. In 1969, Jack Dreyfus Jr bought the rights, re-edited and released it, though it was badly cut. *The Fool Killer* was, in fact, only Tony's first post-*Psycho* psycho role, yet he was the victim of critics reviewing it retroactively. Thus Tony was 'typecast as a controlled psychotic', and he 'excels again as the cinema's most exciting psycho.' The *New York Times* which got round to reviewing it in June 1969, six years after it was made, thought the film 'describably bad . . . [in which] Gonzales has anthologized almost five decades of cinematic cliches – obtrusive wipes, wobbly dissolves, bizarre camera angles . . .'

This off-beat portrait of Americana has splendid, though rather self-consciously aesthetic black-and-white photography, while much of the dialogue strives for poetry. Tony, lying face down on the ground, announces he can feel the grass grow, and the boy says of a beating by his stepfather. 'It ain't the pain of it, or the hurt. It's the shame.'

'*Fool Killer* is rather folk-lorish and folk-legendish. I think very much to its credit,' Tony claimed. 'Somebody said it was a cross between *Friendly Persuasion* and *Psycho.* That's a little glib, but it certainly sounds good.'

If a comparison were to be made – much to its disadvantage – it would be to Charles Laughton's masterpiece, *The Night of the Hunter.* What *The Fool Killer* revealed was the dark side of Tony's talent that would later obscure the sunnier side. It was Norman Bates, above all, that producers saw when casting Tony.

Of Norman Bates, Tony commented years later: 'It was such an original role and its impact was so enormous that people inevitably started to think, "Oh well, we've seen him in other roles but this is the one that's really him. Look he just seems to be doing it, he's not even acting." My performance as Norman Bates passed for naturalistic acting in those days, but it seems very mannered to me. It made people feel that this was the thing for me and that this was what I could do best. It was a struggle to avoid those roles.'

Tony would eventually give up the struggle, but he still had a range of characters within him, comic and tragic, that he was determined to embody.

18

AN AMERICAN IN PARIS

'It's exactly how I thought Paris would be. Checked table cloths, red wine . . .' – Warren in *Is Paris Burning?* (1966)

After *Harold* flopped on Broadway, and *The Fool Killer* had been shelved, it seemed a good time to take up a couple of offers from France and return to Paris in the autumn of 1963. Both the French-language films were very different in tone, but neither was of much consequence.

The first was a police investigation drama called *Le Glaive et la Balance*, given the title *Two Are Guilty* for distribution in the USA. It was directed by fifty-four-year-old André Cayatte, who had been a journalist and lawyer before becoming a director of rather flat, didactic films, most of which criticized the French legal system. This was his first picture since *The Crossing of the Rhine*, which had unaccountably won the Best Film award at Venice three years earlier. Cayatte, therefore, thought he might profit from his wider recognition in the English-speaking countries, and also from Tony's reputation in France.

The title, *Two Are Guilty*, refers to the fact that three young men (Tony Perkins, Jean-Claude Brialy, Renato Salvatori), of similar looks and all similarly dressed, are arrested for murder. It is established that two men carried out the crime. The problem for the investigators and the jury is to determine which of the three is innocent.

Both Brialy and Salvatori, like Tony, already had their best days in the cinema behind them, and this pedestrian whodunnit, which rambled on tediously for a hundred and thirty-one minutes, did nothing for any of them. However, it was lightened up slightly by Tony as Johnny, a transplanted American song-writing cad. At one point, he sings a seductive song to his girlfriend, explaining that she is the first person to hear it, though a little later, she catches a black chanteuse humming it. Tony explains, with artless charm, that he meant he had intended her to be the first.

Une Ravissante Idiote (*A Ravishing Idiot* aka *Adorable Fool* aka *Bewitching Scatterbrain*) was a change of pace, but the film was not much better. Yet the piquant combination of Brigitte Bardot, the French 'sex-kitten' and Anthony Perkins, the American 'sex-puppy', aroused a certain amount of interest, despite the slow decline of both stars' film careers.

Of his thirty-year-old leading lady, with over thirty films behind her, Tony, the supreme professional, remarked: 'You have to make movies a game for her because she just can't take them seriously. She doesn't like to rehearse; she doesn't like to do more than one take, maybe two. So everybody is on their toes all the time and you get a real feeling of spontaneity which shows up on the screen.'

There is a certain amount of spontaneity in the performances, though Bardot, in the title role, plays a dumb blonde with an irksome hyena's laugh for most of the way. She is Penelope Lightfeather who cutely meets Tony in a restaurant when he chases a dog under a table to retrieve her shoe. The confusing plot concerned spies attempting to obtain a secret document from a safe in the house of a minister at the war office, the combination of which is B. A. B. E. Everybody turns out to be a spy or counterspy, with Tony pretending to be Harry Compton, a British secret service agent, revealed as really an incompetent Russian agent called Nicholas Mukouline, and Bardot a lieutenant in the secret service.

At the height of the James Bond craze everybody started making Bond spinoffs, and the director, thirty-five-year-old Edouard Molinaro cashed in (figuratively) on the fad. Despite being a contemporary of many of the New Wave directors, he had chosen to go in for commercial, mainstream French cinema, although here he uses the fashionable free-wheeling style.

It is all singularly 60s, and is set in London (though only a few exteriors were shot there) at the time when the English capital was still swinging. Everybody, however, speaks in French, including the omnipresent British bobbies. The only words in English are 'Son of a bitch!' spoken by Grégoire Aslan as an agitated double agent. One could presume it to be France's revenge for all those English and American films supposedly set in France.

In a Beatle cut and with a slightly American-tinged French accent, Tony is obviously enjoying playing comedy on screen again. He double-takes (as a double agent), falls over, bumps into things, and quickly puts on his spectacles for a moment when Bardot's skirt accidentally slips down. As he is supposed to be an 'English gentleman', he is terribly shocked when B. B. asks him to kiss her in the park. At one stage, exclamation marks and dots come from his eyes to her chest, an indication of the film's jocular tone. Tony provided expert farcical playing in a film as light as a feather and as broad as the Champs-Elysées.

Une Ravissante Idiote managed respectable box-office receipts in France and Italy, mainly because of the names of the two stars – though some of the fan magazines in Hollywood had found new teenage idols to pursue, Tony still had a large female following in France – but it would be fourteen years before *La Cage aux Folles* provided director Molinaro with an international hit.

Tony had always felt more carefree in Paris, but as a career move it was in a downward direction. Thus, after the two French films of little merit, he returned to New York and the home he was sharing with Helen Merrill. He was content to help decorate the house, go to dinner parties, and see his small circle of friends. While he had been in France, Grover Dale had kept occupied in Hollywood by appearing as one of the principal dancers in *The Unsinkable Molly Brown*, starring Debbie Reynolds.

Because he had not been seen on American cinema screens since the disastrous *Five Miles To Midnight* in 1963, two years previously, he was all but forgotten. His last success had been *Goodbye Again* in 1961, and the phone failed to ring with either film or stage offers.

However, while Tony was in Paris, British director Tony Richardson was keen to stage a Broadway revival of Tennessee Williams's *The Milk Train Doesn't Stop Here Anymore* with Katharine Hepburn as Mrs Goforth, an aging millionairess who takes a young poet as her last lover. In the role of the poet, who turns out to be the Angel of Death, Richardson thought Tony would be ideal. When Hepburn refused because Spencer Tracy was ill, and Tallulah Bankhead took over, Tony turned down the role on the grounds that it would be another older woman-younger man plot. Perhaps he was intimidated by the prospect of working with the formidable Tallulah, with whom Osgood had appeared in George Cukor's *Tarnished Lady* in 1931. He did, nevertheless, suggest his friend Tab Hunter for the part of the 'beautiful young man', and put Richardson in touch with him. But the camp combination of Tallulah Bankhead and Tab Hunter in Tennessee Williams was not enough to carry the play over more than a few nights.

Meanwhile, Tony got a call from record producer Ben Bagley. At the time, Bagley was living with Montgomery Clift in a house on 62nd Street. Clift's career was virtually over, and he had not made a film since *Freud* three years previously. Bagley, who liked to mix actors who could sing with singers who could act on his albums of evergreens, wanted Clift to croon a Jerome Kern song, 'I Have The Room Above', for one of his compilation discs. Unfortunately, Bagley had a problem getting Clift out of bed before noon. It was the period when the actor had lost most of his confidence, and was also terrified of making a fool of himself, although he had a pleasant singing voice. So Monty invited Tony, who was a friend, and whom he knew to have recorded a few numbers himself, to come over to his house to give his advice.

After Clift had delivered the number, Tony told him that he should have no qualms about recording it. But when Bagley proposed his friend to the record company, they rejected the idea. They reckoned that the once shining star was well and truly washed up. So Bagley suggested Tony, who delivered a couple of numbers for the 'Jerome Kern Revisited' album, the first of half a dozen recordings Tony would do for Bagley over the years.

In fact, he followed it almost immediately with a George Gershwin album, in which he breezily sang 'Under A One-Man Top' and 'Changing My Tune' (both with Barbara Cook).

A short while later, Tony's brief dry spell was broken when he got a call from Paramount to join an all-star cast for *Is Paris Burning?/ Paris brûle-t-il?*, to be shot in the city of the title in the spring of

1966. It was to be made by one of the few directors Tony was to work with more than once – René Clément of *This Angry Age.*

Since that Indo-Chinese epic, Clément had had a great success with *Plein Soleil* (*Purple Noon*), starring France's glamour boy, Alain Delon. Delon with Jean-Paul Belmondo, Charles Boyer, Leslie Caron, Jean-Pierre Cassel, Yves Montand and Simone Signoret were among the French stars recruited for the new film; Kirk Douglas (General Patton), Glenn Ford (General Bradley), Robert Stack, Orson Welles and Tony were the principal Americans. The sprawling episodic screenplay was by Gore Vidal and Francis Ford Coppola, and despite all the star faces cropping up every few minutes, Clément took a realistic approach to the subject, shooting it in black and white and often using actual documentary material.

Those keen to see Tony had to wait almost the film's full one-hundred-and-sixty-five minutes before he appears near the end as an American sergeant, part of the force liberating Paris. This is the sum total of his role:

'I never thought in a thousand years I'd get to see Paris,' he says excitedly as they are ready to move in.

'See Paris and die,' his fellow GI (Skip Ward) remarks jokingly,

'No, that's Naples,' Tony replies, giving a nervous smile. 'What do you think happens when you die?'

'You go to Naples.'

'Funny.'

When they finally enter the city, a French girl climbs onto Tony's lap in the jeep.

'We waited for four years for you to come,' she says.

'But America has only been in the war three years.'

'It doesn't matter.'

Then the naive GI catches sight of the Eiffel Tower and is thrilled. But before he can do any further sightseeing, he is helping a French resistance fighter, who wants him to use his bazooka on the Germans, though he continues to ask questions about Paris.

'Yeh, the Latin Quarter. That's not a nightclub. That's where the students live, right?'

After knocking out a German tank, he and the Frenchman go into a bar to celebrate.

'I never tasted wine till we got to Normandy. It's exactly how I thought Paris would be. Checkered table cloths, red wine . . .'

But his joy, and his life, are terminated by a shot from a German sniper. Exit Tony Perkins.

It was certainly prestigious for Tony to have been included in this starry jamboree, despite having such a small, but touching, role.

After doing his bit in *Is Paris Burning?*, Tony was approached by Claude Chabrol to appear in *Le Scandale (The Champagne Murders)*. Chabrol, one of the instigators of the French New Wave and the co-author (with Eric Rohmer) of a book on Hitchcock, had met Tony some years before at a dinner given in Paris for Hitchcock, when the British-born director came to receive the Legion of Honour in 1959 just before shooting on *Psycho* began.

'We talked a little, and he told me how much he would enjoy working in France,' recalled Chabrol.

Knowing that Tony spoke French well, though 'with an American accent you could cut with a knife', and was in Paris, Chabrol sent him the script of *Le Scandale*, which the actor readily accepted, saying he took the part mainly to find out whodunnit. (Obviously, he had neglected to read the full script.)

Initially, Chabrol was going to make a film in English for Universal in London. The producer wanted a scene of a murder which takes place in a nudist camp.

'I thought we'd have some fun in finding a place to hide the murder weapon,' Chabrol joked.

But the script was radically changed, the locale switched to France (it was filmed at Rheims in the Champagne country), and shot in two languages, with Tony dubbing his own voice in French.

The director found Tony very agreeable, though a little tense to work with, and they became good friends mainly because they had in common a fanatical enthusiasm for the mystery novels of John Dickson Carr (alias Carr Dickson and Carter Dickson) – thrillers with titles such as *Poison in Jest*, *Cut-Throat* and *The Dead Man's Knock* – and they would send each other his books across the Atlantic over the years.

'It was something that bound us,' Chabrol remarked.

Le Scandale told of the wealthy owner of a champagne company (Yvonne Furneaux), her husband, a former gigolo (Tony Perkins) and her secretary (Stéphane Audran, Chabrol's wife), plotting to make an eccentric playboy (Maurice Ronet), who holds the key to a profitable takeover bid, believe himself to be a murderer.

Tony again played an immature American in Paris (as in the two Anatole Litvak films, *Goodbye Again* and *Five Miles to Midnight*), an unpredictable, temperamental pouting toy boy, seemingly more attached to his male friend than to his wife.

'When I worked at the Carlton Hotel, I fulfilled a function, huh? Anybody could rent me, and do what they liked with me. Now I'm the champagne king. Who is he? Where's the – thing – that justifies my life?'

At bedtime, as she kisses and massages his bare back, his elbows jutting into her face, he rebuffs his wife's advances, preferring to do the *Herald Tribune* crossword.

'I'm sorry, dear, I really don't feel too well. I'm tired. It's always like this when I don't get enough television,' he says drily.

The erratic Chabrol flounders around in this grotesque and unpleasant thriller, using some clever contrivances and achieving a showy, extremely high overhead final shot, as Tony, Ronet and Audran scramble for a revolver. Happily, with *Les Biches* (1968), the director would return from the wilderness in which films like this had placed him. Tony's film career, however, would remain in the doldrums for some time.

At least he had been relatively happy working in France. During that period, Grover Dale was also in Europe making two films – *The Young Girls of Rochefort* (shot in Rochefort by Jacques Demy) and *Half-A-Sixpence* in England. After his second Parisian sojourn, Tony flew back to the States, and the offer of a television musical and a Broadway play. At least, if his films were not seen, he would be visible in other areas.

19

STAR-SPANGLED TONY

'We're both trying to make the best out of an impossible situation . . . Now I suggest you roll up your lips and smile so we can get to work' – Andy Hobart in *Star-Spangled Girl* (1966–1967)

Among Tony's intimate circle of friends was composer and lyricist Stephen Sondheim. The latter's last big success had been *A Funny Thing Happened on the Way to the Forum* in 1962, and he would have to wait a few years for another. In the meantime, Sondheim had written the music and lyrics for a rare TV musical called *Evening Primrose*, based on a James Collier story. It was to be the first creative collaboration between Sondheim and Tony.

Shot on location in Stern Brothers department store on 42nd Street and 6th Avenue, *Evening Primrose* was broadcast on 16 November 1966 as part of the ABC Stage 67 series.

'It was one of the worst series ever filmed,' Tony explained. 'I think our project suffered somewhat from being a part of it. And it came off a little stiff because they insisted on doing it on tape instead of film.'

The story, a sort of musical *Twilight Zone* episode, takes place in a department store at night. Fleeing from the pressures of the outside world, an unhappy poet (Anthony Perkins) hopes to live and work there after hours. But he finds he is not alone. In his newfound sanctuary he suddenly comes across a group of hermits who have been hiding in the store for years. Among them is a young girl with whom he falls in love (Charmian Carr, who played the eldest daughter in the film *The Sound of Music*).

The piece has rather sinister undertones with the presence of the Dark Men, represented by hulking shadows, who lead alternative lives in the mortuary. In the end, Tony and his sweetheart are turned into shop window dummies, in the form of a bride and groom.

Tony is rather tentative in his dance movements in the opening number, which he sings when alone in the store before he realizes that there are other people around. ('I am free; I am free.') It compels him to perform on the up and down escalators, often with his arms outstretched, so no wonder he keeps giving little awkward sidelong glances, as if asking, 'Where's the camera now?' But both Tony and his partner put over the songs with charm, gently floating along on Sondheim's pleasant but undistinguished melodies.

It looked as though Tony's career was moving in the direction in which he felt most relaxed, that of a light comedian and singer. Putting behind him the angst of many of his films and his two previous Broadway successes, *Tea and Sympathy* and *Look Homeward, Angel*, he had the chance to be in the kind of theatre he liked, and at which his father had excelled – a boulevard comedy, and a Neil Simon one at that. Unfortunately, although *The Star-Spangled Girl* ran from 21 December, 1966 to 5 August, 1967 at the Plymouth Theatre, it was far from one of Simon's best efforts.

Making up the three-hander were former child actor Richard

Benjamin, making his Broadway debut three years before his first adult screen role in *Goodbye Columbus*, and, in the title role, Connie Stevens, ex-teen star and singer of the 50s.

The play concerned two pseudo left-wing San Francisco journalists who fall in love with a right-wing all-American beauty. The playwright describes Andy Hobart (Tony's role) as 'about 26 [he was now 34], but has the worried look of a man twice his age [he looked half his age]. Andy is a dedicated idealistic cynic charged with the energy of an angry generation. He wears an old tan sports jacket over his khaki trousers, a checked shirt and no tie.'

The play came in for a critical whipping. One critic thought it Simon's weakest comedy ('a three-act contrivance that seldom generated anything heartier than an occasional chuckle'), and Walter Kerr in the *New York Times* explained that 'Neil Simon, your friendly neighbourhood gagman, hasn't had an idea for a play this season, but he's gone ahead and written one anyway'. Happily, the actors remained relatively unscathed.

During the run, there were rumours that the three members of the cast were busy trying to upstage one another. When this accusation was put to Tony in a *New York Post* interview, he denied that anyone was deliberately trying to steal scenes, but admitted that he might have drifted too far upstage at times, and that there had been some awkwardness in their relations. (Richard Benjamin, in fact, was a close friend of Tony's, and remained so.) Around the second month, Tony went down with pneumonia and had to go into hospital.

'I read in *Variety* that the grosses were going down and I was sure it was because I was out. I became so determined to do the show the doctor finally agreed and filled me up with antibiotics and let me go on. In this flying-high condition I walked onto the set and suddenly it hit me – the lights, the audience, Oliver Smith's beautiful blue cyclorama outside the window. In my half-stoned state I just wanted to sit down and cry. "This is so wonderful – this is my love!" It was sort of one step past that high magical feeling I always get when I step on stage.'

He was able to prolong this feeling after the Broadway run ended by taking the play on tour, beginning on Boxing Day, 1967, which allowed him to direct for the first time. This came about by accident. George Axelrod, the director on Broadway, had returned to California to write, produce and direct *The Secret Life Of An American Wife*. Tony had wandered in to pick up his mail at the theatre one day, and he saw that the replacement actress, Sheila Wells, was crying.

'When I asked her what was wrong, she said, "They just told me to run on and start screaming!" and I said, "Well, I'm just an actor and I don't want to tell you what to do, but maybe I could help you do it this way . . ." and that's really how it all started.'

He felt that Axelrod's production had been 'a bit on the frantic side', and he planned 'to do it in a much more reasonable way.' Being an actor, he tried to treat his cast, Sheila Wells and Remak Ramsey (Benjamin's replacement) as he would have liked to have been treated when he was starting out. However, he described his method as 'very exacting. I have strong feelings about the play and how it should be done. I tend to interrupt actors. You should tell them more than will be used.'

The road production took in Newark ('Handsome young Perkins, who has an uncanny ability on stage to look as if he is thinking about the problem on hand, also is a director of merit' – *Newark Evening News*), Miami, Fort Lauderdale, Los Angeles ('I cannot imagine the play being played any better than they play it' – *Los Angeles Times*), San Francisco, Denver and St Louis.

The play's success gave Tony the confidence to direct a further eight plays, and two films. Unfortunately, when Paramount made the film version of *The Star-Spangled Girl* three years later, Tony was passed over both as actor (Tony Roberts was cast instead) and director (it was Jerry Paris, who botched it). This bore out the prejudice of film producers against Tony as a comic actor.

After the Broadway run of *The Star-Spangled Girl*, and before the road show, Tony, for the first time, entered the Actors Studio. There he participated in various workshops, acting and directing. As many critics and audiences over the years had assumed that his acting technique was derived from work at the Actors Studio, he thought he would now have the chance to prove them right.

Part IV

THE LATENT HETEROSEXUAL

20

CURIOUSER AND CURIOUSER

'I've learned that people only pay attention to what they discover for themselves' – Dennis Pitts in *Pretty Poison* (1968)

It was thirty-one-year-old Noel Black, a documentary and short-film director, making his first feature, *Pretty Poison*, who presented Tony with his best screen role since *The Trial*.

'We were looking all over for an actor to play the lead,' recalled Noel Black. 'I saw Tony in *The Star-Spangled Girl*, and thought he'd be ideal. I sent him the script, and he wanted to do it but with one reservation. He was unwilling to leave the play. He didn't ask for more money or anything, all he wanted was a delay in the shooting. I then met him for the first time at Joe Allen's after a performance of the Neil Simon play. He had enormous charm and intelligence, the very qualities I wanted to come through in the role he would be playing. I was looking for the young Tony of *Friendly Persuasion* and *Fear Strikes Out*, not *Psycho*, although commentators naturally made the comparison between Norman Bates and the character in *Pretty Poison*.'

The character was that of Dennis Pitts, who had inadvertently killed his aunt when he burned down a house at fifteen, and had been confined as a disturbed juvenile for some years. Now deemed fit to be released, his parole officer tells him, 'Believe me, Dennis, you're going out into a very real and tough world. It's got no place at all for fantasies.'

But fantasies are the only things that keep Dennis going while working at a dead-end factory job at the Sausenfield Chemical Co. There, he spends the time by imagining the bottles passing on the factory line to be the high-school drill team with whom the honey-haired Sue Ann Stepanek (Tuesday Weld) marches after school. The chemical in the bottles is the same shade of red as the skirt which flaps about Sue-Ann's sun-tanned thighs. He has a fascination with red, just as Hitchcock's Marnie was disturbed by it.

Dennis gradually becomes convinced that the chemical waste his employers discharge into a nearby river at a rate of seventy million gallons a year is 'a diabolical substance'.

'I've traced all the stream patterns. By next spring there may not be an unmonstrous fish as far south as New York.'

Deciding to destroy the polluting factory, he enlists the aid of the teenage Sue-Ann, drawing her into his imaginary life as a CIA agent spying on the factory. But he soon discovers she is kinkier than he, and has murder on her mind. She drowns a nightwatchman and eventually shoots her mother (Beverly Garland). Beside her, he is made to seem almost harmless. She is a cold-blooded killer, he is merely a young man with a vivid imagination. After she has shot her mother, he is sick in the bathroom. She is the dominant partner, and takes the initiative in the love scenes, though her view of sex is, 'When grown-ups do it, it's kinda disgusting, because there is no-one to punish them.'

Tuesday (born Susan) Weld had many more psychological problems to overcome than Tony did. At the age of three she was already supporting her widowed mother, older brother and sister on the proceeds of child modelling and TV performances. She suffered her first nervous breakdown at nine, was an alcoholic at ten, and attempted suicide at twelve. She made her screen debut at thirteen, and despite the titters her name and image used to provoke, after fourteen films she had gained a reputation as a talented actress.

'Tuesday and Tony got on professionally, though she probably resented how much more in tune he was with me than she was,' explained Noel Black. 'He was the quintessential professional. Even though he had made twenty or so movies and this was my first, he listened to everything I had to tell him. What he brought was a personal sense of humanity and dignity, which gave the character a sympathetic quality.'

The film does contain one of Tony's most absorbing performances. As a man who carries deep emotional wounds – one of his more subtle variations on Norman Bates – he conveys shifts of mood within a controlled hysteria. Sparks of his singularly off-beat humour leaven the character, as when he is asked what crime he committed to have been put on probation, he replies, 'I performed an abortion on a peach tree.' He was, however, at thirty-five suspended in an adolescence almost as protracted as Jerry Lewis's.

Obviously influenced by the freewheeling style of Jean-Luc Godard's first period – the relationship of the central couple is reminiscent of Jean-Paul Belmondo and Anna Karina in *Pierrot-Le-Fou* – Noel Black shot *Pretty Poison* on a low budget at lush locations around Great Barrington, Massachusetts in the autumn of 1967. This early example of a movie with ecological concerns took thirty days to shoot, with literally one day in a studio for the scenes in the prison and an office.

'While I was looking for the location in four states, I came across a lot of factories expelling worse things into rivers than shown in the film,' remarked the director. The last speech given by Tony sounds almost as a prefiguration of AIDS.

'There was some poison once, but no one recognized it. In fact, that poison was even quite pretty-looking. So the problem was: what to do about it? It took me some time to realize that what to do about it was very simple. Nothing . . . because who would listen to me, known to be no good, but if that poison just stayed there, getting worse and worse like poison always does, spreading until the blindest man could see, until he had to see . . . I've learned that people only pay attention to what they discover for themselves.'

Alas, this bizarre black comedy-melodrama did not inspire Twentieth Century-Fox with any confidence, and they dumped it in a double bill on 42nd Street, after an opening in Los Angeles. Their unwarrantable action was partly explained by it being the year (1968) of the double assassination of Robert Kennedy and Martin Luther King, and a corrosive tale of insidious madness in which a teenage girl shoots her own mother, seemed, to timid studio chiefs, excessive.

Neither star was invited onto the *Tonight Show* (a must for plugging show business wares), and, initially, *Pretty Poison* was not given a press showing. Nevertheless, the distinguished and hypercritical Pauline Kael caught up with it and thought it 'a remarkable first feature . . . which presupposes an attentive, intelligent audience.' She went on to praise Tony who 'develops from a quirky, sneaky funny boy into a decent, sympathetic man (a loner, but not by choice) making us realize that the man was waiting in the character all along. I think it's the most beautifully conceived and the most precise performance Perkins has ever given.'

It remained pretty poisonous at the box-office, even when it shifted to art houses, whose audiences, seeking the non-commercial, resisted a film starring Tony Perkins and Tuesday Weld. Tony himself supported the film all the way, and railed at the distributors. Rex Reed felt that the studio had done their damnedest to ruin an 'offbeat, original, totally irreverent examination of violence, refreshing in its subtlety and intelligent in its delivery,' by changing the title from *She Let Him Continue* (from the Stephen Geller novel) to *Pretty Poison*, opening it in Los Angeles before New York, then at grindhouses before transplanting it to art houses. Reed also thought that Tony's 'energetic and lyrical' performance was his best work in years.

Pity then that so few people saw it. *Pretty Poison* later gained cult status, and ever since buffs have sought out Noel Black's other work vainly hoping to find something as good. Unfortunately, his promise was not fulfilled.

Black continued to see Tony for many years, during which attempts were made to get together on some projects. In 1974, there was a possibility of making a film called *Killer*, written by Richard Malby, for New Line Cinema, but it failed to come to fruition. Towards the end of his life, Tony fought long and hard to get Noel Black to direct *Psycho IV*, but that too was in vain.

Although Tony lived in Los Angeles from time to time during the 50s when under contract to Paramount, he was really only a Hollywood star nominally, because he made a number of films abroad, continued to do stage work and lived in New York. In 1967, he bought a brick town house in Chelsea, where Helen Merrill occupied the ground-floor apartment and he lived in the rest of the house with Grover Dale. But there was friction between Helen and Grover, so she decided to move out after a few months, leaving the two men alone with Murray, their half collie-half German shepherd dog.

Tony's circle of friends had widened somewhat in the past few years, although his social engagements were strictly circumscribed. Among his close friends, some gay, some straight and some bisexual, were Stephen Sondheim, Leonard Bernstein, Herbert Ross, Burt Shevelove (co-librettist of *A Funny Thing Happened on the Way to the Forum*), Mike Nichols, Hal Prince, Richard Benjamin and his wife Paula Prentiss, Tony's agent Sue Mengers, and the entertainer Jack Cassidy (husband of Shirley Jones, and father of David Cassidy).

Most of the group were keen games players, especially Sondheim and Tony. On Halloween night of 1967, the pair of them staged the Eleanor Clark French Memorial Treasure Hunt, named after a long-forgotten political candidate whose campaign posters they had found in Tony's basement. Four teams of five people, mostly celebrities, raced around Manhattan looking for Eleanor Clark French's posters, which marked the site of each new clue. One such was at an East Side brownstone where a little old lady offered them coffee and cake. Those sharp enough to remember an earlier clue – 'you can't have your cake and eat it too' – put their slices of cake back in place untouched, and discovered that the icing on top spelled out the location of the next clue. The little old lady happened to be Mrs Perkins, Tony's mother.

All these games, dinner parties, and a few sexual liaisons outside his relationship with Grover, both distracted from and reminded Tony of a certain dissatisfaction with his life. As a result, he began to be rather prickly socially, though few directors found him difficult to work with. According to the producer Howard Rosenman, who met Tony at Sondheim's house,

'He made a lot of people very, very, uncomfortable. He had a cool detached way of looking at you and letting you know what a schmuck you were.'

There were times when he could be cruel. He once described a friend's wife as having a laugh 'like an Airedale caught in the lawn-mower.' On another occasion Tony, the writer Dodson Rader and a few other friends were in Burt Shevelove's suite at the Algonquin, when Jack Cassidy came in. The first thing Tony said to him was, 'Where's your fucking beard?'

Ironically, Cassidy had a beard and, touching his chin, asked, 'What do you mean, Tony?'

'You know what the fuck I'm talking about. Your wife.'

There was an embarrassed silence, as Cassidy always made a great thing of being straight.

At thirty-five, Tony was still trying 'to find himself', a favourite expression of the 1960s, and one which remained attached to him into the 1970s. Both psychotherapy and drugs were to assist him along that path, but in 1968, when political events were beginning to rattle the foundations of the USA and Western Europe, Tony was still plainly, as Paul Jasmin remarked, 'not comfortable with his celebrity or life.'

'I felt my life was a bit narrow,' commented Tony. 'I felt my ways of dealing with things were very limited. My communication powers were very dim as an actor, and as a person. It just didn't seem enough.'

It is perhaps too simplistic to put this discomfort down merely to his sexuality. There are heterosexuals who are equally uneasy with fame, and feel themselves drifting aimlessly without a stable relationship. It is quite possible that there was something in Tony's nature, regardless of sexuality, that prompted him to feel unhappy with himself, though he never suffered from extreme forms of melancholia or depression. Discontentment is as strong a word as one could use, but strong enough to drive him to start a long series of visits to the analyst Mildred Newman. Dodson Rader, who also went to Newman around the same period, referred to her as 'a quack shrink, who specialized in "curing" gays.'

Mildred Newman had been a student of Theodor Reik, one of Freud's most devoted disciples. Freud claimed that everyone was bisexual and that if exclusive homosexuality was abnormal and neurotic it was involuntary, the result of unconscious forces over which the individual had no control, and that homosexuality was the result of an arrested stage of development. As Tony had already learnt in a painful manner to cope with fame, he was now, in Rosenman's words, 'looking for a heterosexual adaptation'.

Grover Dale also went to sessions with Newman at the same time for the same reason. It is a reflection of the depth of their relationship that they would both wish to 'cure' themselves of it. However offensive the notion may seem to gays who have accepted their sexuality without shame, what attracted Tony and Grover to Mildred Newman was the notion that she could change their leanings, and that consequently life would become easier to cope with. It is important to remember that even during the so-called 'sexual revolution' in the late 1960s, there were no openly gay film stars in America, and rarely anyone else in the public eye in other fields. Therefore, Tony was attracted to the sort of self-help homilies preached by Mildred Newman and her husband, Bernard Berkowitz, found in *How To Be Your Own Best Friend.*

'If you decide you want to help yourself, you can choose to do the things that make you feel good about yourself instead of things that make you feel terrible. Why should you do what gives you pain when it is just as easy to give yourself joy? . . . This is the tragedy of some marvellous performers, who need endless applause to tell them how great they are, but who feel a chill as soon as they enter their dressing rooms. They have never heard it from themselves . . . When you do something that makes you feel bad inside, ask yourself whether that's the way you want to feel. If not, stop doing what makes you feel that way. Instead, do the things that make you feel good about yourself . . . People who do not love themselves can adore others, because adoration is making someone else big and ourselves small. They can desire others, because desire comes out of a sense of inner incompleteness, which demands to be filled. But they cannot love others, because love is an affirmation of the living, growing being in all of us. If you don't have it, you can't give it.'

To the French writer Jean Genet, a homosexual is 'a man who is out of step with the world, who refuses to enter into the system that organizes the entire world. The homosexual rejects that, denies that, shatters that whether he wants to or not. For him romance is only a kind of stupidity or deception – for him only pleasure exists. To live with surprises, changes, to accept risks, to be exposed to insult; it's the opposite of social constraint, of the social comedy. It follows that if the homosexual accepts more or less to play a role in this comedy . . . he's cheating, he's lying; everything he says becomes suspect.'

Genet, who relished being a thief, outcast and revolutionary, and who romanticized non-comformism, was the antithesis of Tony, who wished to play a role in the social comedy without cheating and lying. He desired a state of conformism, which only his sexual orientation prevented him from achieving. However, it would take a few years before there was any substantial change in Tony's interior and exterior life.

Meanwhile, with the taste for directing in his mouth after the road tour of *The Star-Spangled Girl*, Tony directed Peter Ustinov's anti-war play, *The Unknown Soldier and His Wife* (for the first time not acting as well), for a summer stock production at the Playhouse-in-the-Park in Philadelphia in August 1968.

'The first of many qualifications a director must have is that he knows what he wants,' Tony told the *Philadelphia Inquirer* at the time.'Background in the theatre is important. If you've spent your life seeing through the eyes of drama or comedy, it's almost like typing the touch system – you think in those terms. A good imagination is necessary. I was born with that, so I can't pat myself on the back . . . a director needs a middle-brow intellect. Hopefully he should be smart enough to understand the author's intentions and still down to earth enough to know what the public will respond to. Many directors excel in one quality or another.'

In December of the same year, Tony directed one of the few classics he was involved in – Molière's *The Imaginary Invalid* at the Milwaukee Repertory Theatre. (His father had one of his greatest triumphs playing the Molière part in *The School for Husbands*.)

Charles Kimbrough, many years later to appear in *Murphy Brown* on TV, who played the lead, said: 'I was impressed with how Tony immediately made himself part of the company. He was great fun to work with. As a director he is very specific. He loves nailing down the details. Even half an hour before the opening, he came in with notes.'

Kimbrough was directed by Tony again the following year, at the same theatre, in the first American production of Gert Hoffman's *The Burgomaster*. The *Milwaukee Journal* found that 'Under Anthony Perkins's expert and high-spirited direction, *The Burgomaster* moves along swiftly and straightforwardly, taking less than two hours.'

Due to his shyness and lack of ease in the limelight, Tony never appeared at political rallies and was reticent on political matters in public though he was not altogether apolitical. His views tended towards the liberal or what was dubbed 'radical chic' by Tom Wolfe at the time. His next couple of films found him working with many of its members.

WUSA, the curious title of the first, was the fictional name of a

New Orleans radio station on which Paul Newman is an announcer. He hates himself for selling out his liberal principles, but enjoys his lucrative position at the station, used to propagandize a neo-Fascist movement. Opposing him and Pat Hingle, the 'evil fool' behind WUSA, is Tony, a gangling, naively idealistic social worker, whom everyone calls 'Boy' and who is attempting to make a better world, especially among the black poor. When he learns that the project he is engaged in is a vast fraud designed to discredit welfare, he becomes more and more deranged and finally attempts to assassinate right-wing demagogue Hingle with a high-powered rifle.

Although the film retains enough to make it a worthwhile contribution to the short list of American political satires, what power the original novel, *Hall of Mirrors*, possessed became muddied on screen under Stuart Rosenberg's direction and in the script by the novel's author, Robert Stone. However, Tony stood out as an anguished, neurotic liberal – Norman Bates with a political conscience – playing up the comic elements in the earlier scenes. 'A twitching compulsive mass of uncertainty and pain,' in the words of one critic.

WUSA was the first film in which Tony took what could be classified 'a character part', playing a subsidiary role.

In early 1970, Tony joined the large cast of *Catch 22* to play Chaplain Tappman, under the direction of his friend Mike Nichols. Of the director, Tony recalled: 'He is so agreeable and so inspiring to actors that in a way they give their performances to him rather than to the lens. He understands that distinction and it is one that he's had trouble sorting out and it's kept him from making certain films. There is something Mike Nicholsish about the way the actors perform, almost Nichols and Mayish. There were a few laughs in *Catch 22*, but I think we were all rather self-conscious. I know I was trying to please Mike, and I'm not sure how funny some of that stuff was. Plus the fact that it was such a bleak piece it was difficult to know whether to go for all out laughs or just to go for intensity, which was basically what we did.'

Speaking in a slow, formal and clipped manner, Tony gets laughs from his intensity as the withdrawn, nervously self-effacing cleric, who has a slight headcold which he can't seem to shake off.

'I had no idea chaplains looked like that,' Alan Arkin's Yossarian remarks at Tony's boyish appearance. 'I've never seen a chaplain before.'

'It's not necessary to call me father,' Tony insists. 'I'm an anabaptist.'

While reading a prayer at a funeral, he is distracted by a naked man in a tree.

'Oh, its Yossarian,' he mutters, in a throwaway manner, as if it is the most natural thing in the world.

Later, he explains, 'I'm not here to judge.'

'What are you here for?'

'I'm not sure about that either.'

Confused by his identity, he says, 'I even have trouble imagining I'm me.'

Unfortunately, the film also suffered from an identity crisis.

Catch 22 was shot at a cost of $18 million, nine years after the novel by Joseph Heller was published, and failed both commercially and critically (though Vincent Canby raved about it in two articles in the *New York Times*). Orson Welles, who played General Dreedle and had longed to direct it himself, said, 'You can't watch it. It's really dreadful.'

Yet *Catch 22* was another of the sporadic examples of Tony's gift for comedy, a path from which he kept straying. He was extremely keen to do more comedy, but because of the impact of Norman Bates, still potent after a decade, the mark of Cain was upon him. Years later, Tony, regretting that he had not made more film comedies, admitted, half-jokingly, to have had a 'one-sided career'.

It was four years since Tony had appeared on television in the Stephen Sondheim musical drama *Evening Primrose*, and he was keen to take up an offer from ABC to appear in a TV movie called *How Awful About Allan*, to be broadcast in September 1970.

It was directed by Curtis Harrington, who specialized in offbeat, rather campy horror stories. At the time, he had only three features behind him, *Night Tide*, *Queen of Blood* and *Games*, all of which showed a weird imagination, and in all of which Norman Bates would have felt quite at home.

Initially, Harrington was very apprehensive at working with Tony. He knew the star was used to the luxury of time in shooting a feature film, and might not adapt to the strict tightness of TV, although he had done live TV many years before.

'We walked around the RKO lot, and I said, "You know we have to work very fast." He replied, "I'm prepared for that."', recalled Curtis Harrington. 'The shoot took about twelve days, the exteriors being shot on the Warners lot and the interiors at RKO. Tony was a consummate professional. He knew his lines pat on the set every morning. He was extremely charming, but with a very wicked sense of humour. At the sharp end was the producer George Edwards, whom Tony said lived in a time warp; from the way he combed his hair and the suits he wore, he was frozen in the 50s. Edwards changed his hairstyle and mode of dress after Tony's withering remarks.'

As an example of the actor's professionalism and 'almost excessive preparation for the role', Tony, who normally wore contact lenses, went and got opaque ones fitted so that he could more easily get into the role of the semi-blind character.

'He had to be led onto the set, but he had rehearsed so perfectly in his normal lens that he knew where the camera was,' Harrington remembered. 'It was his idea. My only fear was that he would slow things up that way. But it didn't.'

The teleplay of *How Awful About Allan*, written by Henry Farrell, opens with a fire at an old wooden house as the credits appear over Tony's eyes. He is a guilt-ridden, semi-blind mental patient who is released from hospital to stay with his disfigured sister (Julie Harris), who proceeds to torment him. He had burned down the house as a child, and feels guilt about his father's death and sister's disfigurement. His own blindness is psychosomatic. This is demonstrated by a subjective blurred vision, as if produced by a bad projectionist. He is also paranoid, and feels everyone is laughing at him.

Tony, speaking in a clipped monotone, tries to tinge everything he says and does with menace. He cannot walk up or down stairs without being seen in shadow. He makes the gestures of the partially blind, though it is not certain whether he cuts his hands with a large kitchen knife by accident or by design. The film ends, as it begins, with a close-up of his eyes.

The preposterous plot, the sort in which it storms almost every night, might have gripped if it had been written and directed more convincingly. Tony's performance had elements of Joseph K. and Dennis Pitts, the touched arsonist in *Pretty Poison*, but was most reminiscent of that persistent ghost, Norman Bates.

21

GOD AND MAMMON

'He's not my real father. He found me . . . Without him I wouldn't exist' – Charles Van Horn in *Ten Days' Wonder* (1971)

Another opportunity to turn his back on Norman Bates and return to the bright and bouncy world of the Broadway musical presented itself to Tony in 1970. George Furth, an actor friend of Stephen Sondheim, had written eleven one-act plays with eleven different roles for Kim Stanley. Tony, who had pleasant memories of working with the 'Method' actress in *Joey* on TV some fifteen years previously, expressed an interest in directing the plays. However, Sondheim and his friend Harold Prince, the stage director, decided to turn the Furth plays into a musical called *Company*, in which they asked Tony to star.

He initially accepted because it meant that he would be surrounded by close friends, such as Sondheim, Prince and Furth, and would be able to sing on stage once more. But when the first advertisements for *Company* appeared in the *New York Times* giving him top-billing, he began to reconsider, feeling that his name would unbalance what was essentially, as the title suggests, a company show. He also had second thoughts about his role – another innocent sap – which he believed might not give him much satisfaction. So he approached Prince and Sondheim to ask them if he could bow out before rehearsals began.

'I told them that I know I agreed to do their show and I will do it, but what I *really* wish was that I was not acting but directing some other show. And they reacted with such class and with such understanding and let me go.'

He was replaced by the clean-cut Dean Jones – the obverse of the nervy, angular Tony – who made his name in kiddie-oriented Walt Disney features, and had played a college boy in the film of *Tea and Sympathy*.

'For some reason I was the first person to turn up backstage after the opening night performance,' Tony recalled. 'Dean was standing there and he said, "Man, I really tried. I tried to make this part mine, but I couldn't." I sympathized with him. He was good in that role, but the person who plays that part is always unappreciated. And having turned down the role, I thought to myself, not knowing what the part turned out to be, that when I went to the opening I should bring along my gun because at the end of the first act I'm going to put it against my temple and fire. But I didn't. I thought that it was a brilliant show . . . and I was happy I wasn't in it.'

A few weeks after turning down *Company*, Tony was offered the chance to return to the theatre as director of a two-act play by Bruce Jay Friedman called *Steambath*, due to open in April 1970 at the Truck and Warehouse Theatre, Off Broadway, with comedian Dick Shawn in the lead. Tony got Grover Dale to do the choreography for the show.

The play was an allegory set in a seedy New York steambath,

which turns out, literally, to be Purgatory. Tandy, a young Jewish man puzzled to find himself in the steamroom, comes to the realization that he is dead, as are all the others in the room. This makes him annoyed at the untimeliness of it all. He has just been divorced, quit the Police Academy, is writing a novel about Charlemagne, and doing charity work among brain-damaged welders. His sense of fitness is outraged when God turns out to be the bath-attendant, a Puerto Rican (Hector Elizondo) who talks slang and is anything but majestic. The hero's entreaties to return to all the important activities of his life fall on deaf ears. It becomes clear that his life had in fact, been empty and useless.

Preview audiences at this rather whimsical but blackly funny off-beat comedy, reacted unfavorably to Dick Shawn as Tandy, because they seemed to want him 'to be far more serious and emotional than we had originally expected', as Tony told Rex Reed in the *New York Times.* Rip Torn was then brought in to bring more gravitas to the piece, although he was playing the extremely strenuous role of Edgar in Strindberg's *Dance of Death* in Washington D.C. at the time. No wonder Torn was too exhausted to get very far with the part, and he departed. So Charles Grodin stepped in for further previews in May, while Tony was filming *How Awful About Allan* in Hollywood. When he returned, he had to find a replacement for Grodin, and another actor who had gone down with pneumonia, as well as getting a replacement for the stage manager, who had left the show. Eventually, Tony took over the role of Tandy, without a single run-through with the rest of the cast, in a few previews before the opening on 30 June.

As the doubting Jewish steambath client, Tony disturbed many of the critics, who felt he was too much the WASP. 'Friedman's work is deep Jewish and Perkins is WASP enough to start a nest,' wrote one reviewer. (This echoes Orson Welles's unrealized notion of presenting Joseph K. as Jewish, and yet casting Tony in the role. Also, Otto Preminger rejected Tony for his aborted *Joseph and His Brethren* in 1957 because 'we're looking for Old Testament faces. You have a New Testament face'.) Another critic thought Tony had given in to overacting by 'nibbling his nails, twisting his mouth to indicate puzzlement, and other hammy tricks, he would never, as a director, permit.'

Tony later explained, 'Directing and acting in it I couldn't really see what anyone was up to. So when I gave the actors directions and said something like, "Go a little faster," they would have every right to say to me, "Well, how do you know, you can't see it?"'

It was almost three years since Tony had appeared on stage in New York, and his name in the cast helped carry the play for 127 performances until 18 October. It is curious that, given Tony's desire to direct new plays, and appear in them from time to time, that he did not do more Off-Broadway work, but *Steambath* remains his only visit to that area of theatre as an actor. However, four years later, he directed a play called *The Wager* by Mark Medoff at the Eastside Playhouse which ran for three months.

Being in *Steambath* enabled Tony to spend a few months at his three-storey red-brick house on the leafy Chelsea street, which he shared with Grover, and Murray the mongrel. However, most of their weekends were spent at Grover's house in the country, a couple of hours outside Manhattan.

About once a week, when they were in New York, Grover and Tony would hold Monopoly parties. They would invite a few friends round for cocktails, snacks, and a game of Monopoly. One evening, someone turned up with 'a handsome kid from California,' as Dodson Rader described him in the memoirs of his friend Tennessee Williams, *Tennessee, Cry of the Heart*. Rader identifies the 'handsome kid' merely as David, and his lover is referred to anonymously as 'a movie star.'

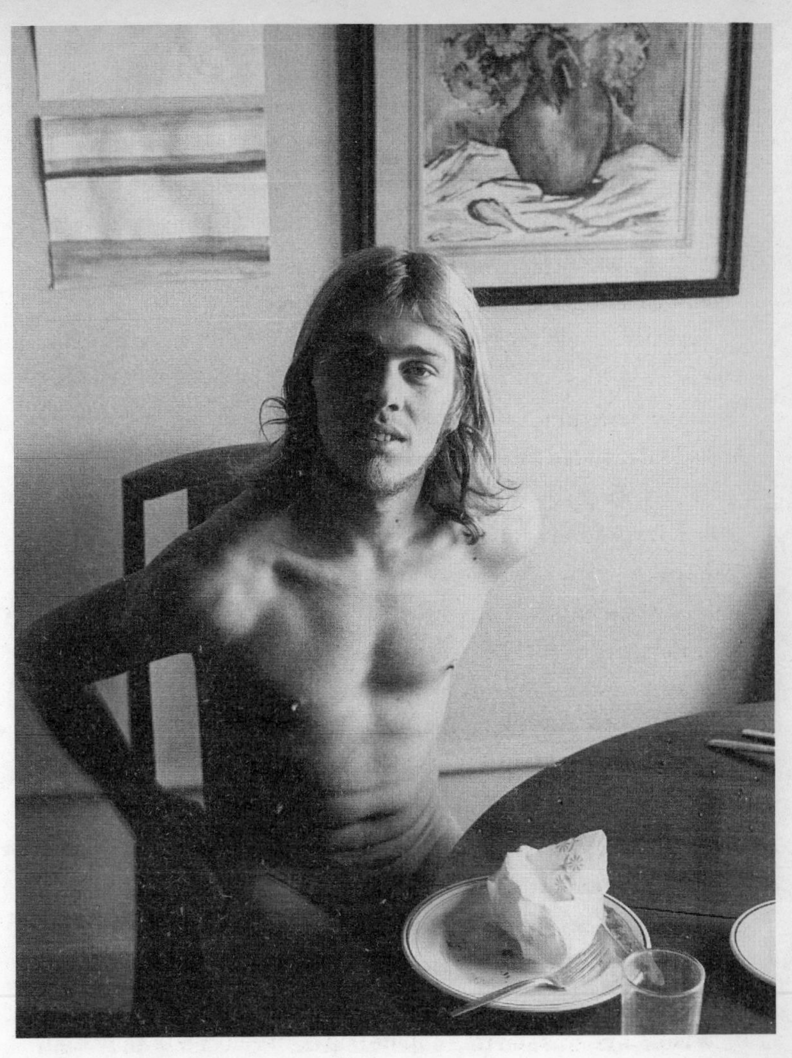

CHRISTOPHER MAKOS IN THE EARLY 1970s
(CHRISTOPHER MAKOS).

He wrote: 'When I met David he was the lover of a movie star, although I didn't know it then, and the three of us lived through a kind of French farce with me hiding in the kitchen when the star arrived – I didn't know who he was, because David wouldn't let me out of the kitchen until his "business meeting" was over, and vice versa.'

Actually, 'David' was a young photographer called Christopher Makos, and 'the movie star' was Tony. The blond 'astonishingly sexy and sex crazy' Christopher Makos, whose family came from Macedonia, was in his early twenties when he met Tony in 1970.

Substituting the real names, Rader later explained: 'We were both lovers of Christopher, at the same time, neither of us aware of the other's romantic involvement. I would go over to Chris's very small apartment, he'd open the door and say you can't come in now, and there were times when I was there, and Tony would arrive and Chris would tell me to go in the kitchen, and close the door.'

In fact, Chris had met Tony before Dodson. It was Tony who gave the rather aimless young man his first camera, thus sparking off his career as a photographer. (Many years later, Makos set himself up in a photographic studio in Greenwich Village, and also ran a TV cable show called Makostyle, in which, so the publicity claimed, the 'world class photographer and artist, also known for his close friendship with artist Andy Warhol and Malcolm Forbes', promised to scrutinize the 'STYLE capitals of the world'.)

When Chris was starting out, he told both Rader and Tony that he was having trouble finding work as a photographer, so they encouraged him, helped him, and got him commissions.

'Finally, Tony approached me at a party and said we should end this "French bedroom farce". He asked me, "Have you been giving Chris money for rent?" "Yes," I replied. "So have I." Neither of us knew about it, and we both laughed.'

But the curtain had some time to fall on the 'farce'. Being attractive and the youngest person at that first meeting with Tony across the Monopoly board, Chris Makos was made a fuss of by the other guests, who included long-time friends Paul Jasmin and Stephen Paley. Tony and Chris then saw each other on a regular basis. As both of them used to cycle around New York, they would go for rides together, often stopping in Central Park.

'I was awestruck hanging around with a star, and he was awestruck that he was hanging around with a young blond from Southern California,' commented Makos. 'So we were both awestruck for different reasons. The only intellectual problems we had occasionally came about only because of cultural and age differences.' Makos felt that Tony's relationship with Grover was winding down at that stage or, at least,

'I was too young and naive to notice any tension there may have been between them because of my presence.'

Although Makos found that Tony liked to keep a very low profile, found it hard to express his feelings, and was conservative about many things, he was 'extremely sexual'.

'He was like everyone else, when they forget who they are, they can do almost anything in bed.'

In March 1971, Tony was busy directing Patrick Hamilton's very successful Victorian thriller, *Angel Street*, for the Playhouse in the Park in Cincinnati. The 1939 play about a husband intent on driving his wife insane had been the basis of *Gaslight*, filmed in Britain in 1940 and by MGM in 1944 starring Ingrid Bergman and Charles Boyer. A few days after it opened on 1 April, Tony was on his way again to Europe (with Chris Makos) to make two pictures that sit awkwardly, even in his oddball filmography.

Claude Chabrol, who had kept in touch with Tony since *Le Scandale*, wanted to cast him with Catherine Deneuve and Orson Welles in an adaptation of an Ellery Queen novel entitled *La*

Décade Prodigieuse, translated as *Ten Days' Wonder*.

'We were going to film in September [1970],' explained Chabrol, 'but Orson wanted to lose weight. He had grown enormous. Tony was busy doing something else [*Steambath*] and Catherine Deneuve couldn't film until March. I modified the shooting around Orson. I asked Tony if he would be free in April. He said there was no problem. Unfortunately, Deneuve went off to make something else and I had to take Marlene Jobert although she didn't correspond to the character I had in mind.'

The location of the novel was shifted from a drab American town to a magnificent private estate in Alsace. Chabrol changed three of the characters' names to those he used most frequently – Charles, Helene and Paul, with Welles playing Theo Van Horn (representing God, no less).

Despite having been extremely close to Welles on *The Trial*, Tony, according to Chabrol, was 'still a little overawed by Orson.' There were few people alive who had met Welles who were not, though Chabrol retained as much control over the great director-actor as he could.

'Orson always wanted his own way as an actor,' Tony recalled. 'There was a long sequence that he had at a dinner table and Chabrol had worked out a zoom shot which refocused through several sets of candelabras. Orson went up to his room and started sulking and refusing to come down, so I acted as go-between and it turned out that he didn't like the candles. He felt that they would take away from the impact of his performance. He had a long speech and he considered that the candles were killing it. I went down and told this reluctantly to Chabrol, because Orson had said that as a director he had always worked with actors in the following way, namely that if an actor felt there was something wrong or there was something about the close-up that he didn't like, he would gladly and easily change it. But Chabrol was feeling a little spiky that day and wouldn't go along with the removal of the candelabras. I think he removed half of them. Orson was grumpy. He kept maintaining that he was willing to change his outlook on a close-up if an actor didn't like it. But this was obviously something that Chabrol was not in the mood to give him.'

Actually, only one unobtrusive candelabra remains. Ironically, Welles used scores of candles to light the advocate's vast rooms in his own scenes in *The Trial*, and Tony filled a room full of them in *Psycho III*, his film directing debut.

Ten Day's Wonder opens with Charles Van Horn (Perkins) waking from a dream of Creation (represented mostly by underwater visions of sea anemones and jelly fish) in a sleazy Parisian hotel to find himself with blood on his hands.

'I woke up with blood all over me,' he tells his friend and former professor Paul (Michel Piccoli), explaining that he is afraid he is going to kill someone. The professor persuades him to go back to the Van Horn country estate to use his 'Logic of Science' in sorting out the family mess.

Theo Van Horn, Charles's adoptive father, is an old patriarch who wishes life to be as it was in the autumn of 1925, which was the best time of his life. To satisfy his whim, he gets his child-bride Helene (Jobert) to wear flapper frocks (courtesy of Karl Lagerfeld), bob her hair and drive an ancient Rolls, while Charles affects knickerbockers, plaid stockings and sweaters, and a stiff-collared tuxedo for dinner. Theo is worshipped by his wife, and has been sculpted as Jupiter by the awed Charles. Theo chooses to play God, creating his own world, dictating the behaviour of those he places in it. But Charles has cuckolded his father (flashback in long shot to a demure sex scene in the bushes), who in turn frames Charles for the murder of his wife. God had not reckoned with his own capacity for imperfection, so he comes to his own grief.

This portentous and enigmatic theological thriller, in which the ten days of the action represent each of the ten commandments, was shot in a virtuoso, high-Gothic style by Chabrol, possibly influenced by Welles's deific presence. The restless, probing camera mirrors Tony's nervous, agitated performance. In the first sequence, when everything is framed at an expressionistic angle, Tony stumbles around giving a convincing interpretation of a man on LSD. Reasonably recovered, he reacts like a volcano about to burst. Offering another example of infantilism, he is made to look rather ridiculous in his knickerbockers, and throws a croquet mallet to the ground in a tantrum.

'You're a child,' his friend tells him.

'I'm what!', he explodes.

As the plot unfolds, his eyes begin to roll around like pinballs. Someone is trying to blackmail the son and daughter by threatening to show their love letters to Theo. The blackmailing voice on the phone sounds like Mrs Bates. Finally, Tony destroys the sculpture of his putative father, screaming, 'I'm free! Free! I'm free!'

That same heart-felt expression which he sings in Sondheim's *Evening Primrose*, and which he repeats at the end of *Psycho IV*, after annihilating Norman Bates once and for all from his life. Here, however, he ends by impaling himself, in a crucified posture.

Chabrol noticed the difference in Tony's personality between *Le Scandale*, shot five years previously, and *Ten Days' Wonder*.

'One thing I saw in this second film that I hadn't seen before was that Tony could turn on the charm. He knew he was a charmer. He had a slightly irreverent attitude, mocking not only others but himself. He was more relaxed and very agreeable to work with. What always astonished him was how we worked in such a more easygoing manner than exists in Hollywood. He was also much more liberated about his homosexuality. He even brought a good-looking young friend [Makos] onto the set from time to time.'

Tony never made another film with Chabrol. Nevertheless, they did continue to see each other when Tony came to France and when Chabrol went to the USA.

A few years after they had worked together, Chabrol met Tony at a party in Los Angeles.

'I think I did him a great service,' explained Chabrol. 'He had been offered the role of a Nazi soldier in a French film version of an awful novel by Simone de Beauvoir called *Le Sang des autres* (*The Blood of Others*). He said it was a question of money, which he had been promised under the table to avoid tax. "I would love to play the German officer, it's very much me," he said. "I'd love to do it." I told him, I didn't think it was right. He later agreed and didn't do it.'

There are those who think that it is a pity that Tony was not dissuaded from making *Someone Behind the Door* (aka *Two Minds for Murder*), which he made in Paris after completing *Ten Days' Wonder.* It was based on a French novel set in Normandy, but transposed to Folkestone in England, to allow the characters to speak English, albeit with an American accent. All the exteriors were shot in Folkestone, though most of it takes place in an elegantly furnished house, owned by a top English neurosurgeon, Laurence Jeffries (played by Tony), filmed in the Boulogne Studios in Paris over eight weeks.

Directed by Nicolas Gessner, the rather ingenious plot of *Someone Behind the Door* tells how the neurosurgeon takes home a homicidal amnesiac (Charles Bronson), and uses him as an instrument to kill his wife Frances (Jill Ireland) and her French journalist lover Paul (Henri Garcin). He does this by trying to convince the man that Frances is, in fact, the amnesiac's wife who is betraying him. The lover is killed by the catatonic man, but before he can kill the wife, after raping her, the doctor intervenes and confesses his whole scheme.

Most of the film is a head to head between the two stars, one thin and one thick. Tony, in a brown polo-neck and checked tweed suit, does not smile much, and has a distracted air during most of the film – the character's only pleasure seems to come from what were called 'executive toys' in the 1970s. He has impeccable taste, owns a Miro, plays the harpsichord, and drives a Jaguar. When the police arrive to question him, Tony nearly knocks over a wedgewood vase in trepidation.

'I'm not Dr Frankenstein,' Tony tells a troubled Bronson, the latter's Zapata moustache making him look even more doleful. Poor man, he has forgotten how many sugars he takes in his tea. When Bronson is trying so hard to remember his past, he looks like a constipated man on the pot, while Tony looks on in distaste. At the climax, his distaste becomes disgust, when berated by his wife after his confession. He sweats, vomits in the kitchen sink, and then opens all the doors and windows, while the autumn leaves blow in.

Originally, *Someone Behind the Door* was to have been an Anglo-French co-production, but the English unions refused to accept American stars in the leads. As the film could not have been made without the money that was available only because of the casting of Charles Bronson, the joint arrangement had to be abandoned. Robert Shaw was first approached to take the role of the neurosurgeon, but he objected to playing opposite a 'guy from Spaghetti Westerns', and Bronson refused to work with Shaw, who he considered a 'has-been'. That left the door open for Tony.

Nicolas Gessner went up to Alsace to see Tony during the filming of *Ten Day's Wonder.* When he handed the script over to Tony in the restaurant set up for the cast and crew on the estate where the film was being made, Orson Welles, whom Gessner had directed the year before in *Twelve Plus One*, stood up and yelled loudly across the place, 'Nicolas, why did you bring him a script? Why didn't you bring me one?', at which Tony blushed deeply.

Gessner described the difference between Charles Bronson and Tony as 'an aristocrat and a nouveau riche'; Tony, who had been a star for most of his life, and Bronson who had suddenly emerged after playing supporting roles for twenty years. Tony realized, though, that he had the reputation of being box-office poison, while Bronson had attracted the money for the picture. It was Bronson who had the Rolls Royce (Tony drives a Jaguar in the film), the best accommodation and the biggest dressing-room. Tony made ironic remarks about the differences in status, while implying it did not really matter to him.

Tony knew he had the better role, and enjoyed acting Bronson off the screen. The relationship of the fictional characters on the set was reproduced off the set by Tony and Bronson.

'Tony and I understood each other with a wink of an eye, without talking,' recalled Nicolas Gessner. 'Bronson felt as left out and confused as he is in the story. He would say things like, "I must be very careful that you two quick-thinking wise guys don't get me to do things I would regret." This slight tension between them enhanced their performances.'

The contrast between the two actors' personalities and life style was so marked that there were far-fetched jokes among the crew, who knew of Tony's sexuality, that the very macho and very married Bronson was falling for his male co-star. (Tony and Chris Makos were staying together at the trés chic L'Hôtel in St Germain dés Prés, in the same room in which Oscar Wilde died.)

There was only one scene Tony needed a lot of persuading to do. After performing an operation, he comes out of the operating theatre with a nurse, who proceeds to strip him to the waist and erotically fondle his torso. He explained that he felt rather embarrassed at his age (thirty-eight) about playing a sex object.

During the shooting, Tony's passion for games and puzzles was satisfied because there was an enormous jigsaw puzzle laid out on the floor of the studio, and everyone took part in piecing it together.

'I never had to yell, "Silence!" Tony especially worked on the puzzle when he was not required,' commented Gessner.

Someone Behind the Door was the last of the nine films Tony had made in France between 1961 and 1971, although he was to appear in a few further pictures in Europe in the future. He returned to the USA, where his life was to take a different though parallel direction.

22

DUMP THE FAGS

'*Women are so different from men*' – Cornelius Hackel in *The Matchmaker* (1958)

Shot in Mexico in 1971, *The Life and Times of Judge Roy Bean*, directed by John Huston, was an episodic tale of the famous 'hanging judge' (Paul Newman) obsessed with actress Lily Langtry (Ava Gardner). The same story had been told with more vigour and style by William Wyler as *The Westerner* in 1940. John Milius, who wrote the screenplay and had hoped to direct it as his debut feature, imagined a much grittier film. But John Huston told him, rather insultingly, that he hoped to 'make a turd [the screenplay] smell sweet'.

In a cameo role as the Reverend LaSalle, an itinerant preacher, Tony appears in one of the earliest sequences. Although he soon vanishes from the film, his disquieting semi-comic presence creates an impact that lingers on throughout the less gripping, somewhat lethargic events that follow.

He rides into view resembling a scrawny crow, dressed in a

black bowler over long black hair, sombre black suit, cloak and black gloves. In a southern drawl, he expresses himself in Biblical language.

'Vengeance is mine, sayeth the Lord,' he croaks, as he buries all of Bean's victims. 'Let their teeth be broken in their mouths.'

Speaking Spanish to the Mexican Indians, he brings out Maria Elena, a Mexican girl who saved Bean's life. He suggests that, as Bean's mistress, she should live in a little shack on the side.

He then departs, saying, 'I'll pray for you, Bean.'

As he rides off, he narrates, 'It was the first and last time I saw Judge Roy Bean. I haven't seen him since so he probably went to Hell!'

Also in the cast, though they never appeared together on screen, were two of Tony's friends, Tab Hunter and Roddy McDowall. In the role of Maria Elena was Victoria Principal, some years later to become renowned on television as Pam Ewing in *Dallas*. It was not only her first film, but her first professional engagement.

She was living in Mexico at the time and, in order to get the part, she dyed her hair jet black and came to the interview with Huston barefoot and speaking Spanish.

John Milius remarked, 'Everybody wanted to fuck her. But she was aloof and was supposedly going off on weekends with Frank Sinatra. She was very ambitious.'

John Huston had just married for the fifth time, which kept him from making a play for the debutante actress, though he also found her attractive. At first, Victoria felt alienated and intimidated.

'I didn't talk unless spoken to. I was so nervous I was non-existent. As soon as I was off-camera, I'd go back to my room and hide out.'

She was, therefore, drawn to confide in Tony, whom she found unthreatening. One night after a day's shooting, she inducted the forty-year-old 'virgin' into the 'joys' of heterosexuality, a situation that recalled the end of *Tea and Sympathy*. The irony was that with all those macho men around, she chose Tony to go to bed with. ('Years from now, when you talk about this – and you will – be kind' – *Tea and Sympathy*)

For Tony, it was proof that he could overcome his hitherto exclusively gay sex life and, as he believed, a fear of women. There was also, at the back of his mind, the desire to marry and have children. This experience was an undress rehearsal for a longer relationship with a woman.

Now that Tony had slept with a woman, and ungallantly told as many people as possible, he felt he could permit himself to play an overt homosexual for the first but not the last time. After all, what had he to fear? He no longer had a screen image to sustain, even though he came on like Joe Stud in life.

The role, which again had certain indirect parallels to his own life, was that of BZ, a suicidal homosexual with a penchant for sado-masochistic sex. *Play It As It Lays*, directed by Frank Perry, based on Joan Didion's novel, and adapted by Didion and her husband, John Gregory Dunne, was shot in Malibu, Las Vegas, Hollywood and the Mojave Desert in the summer of 1972. It reunited Tony with Tuesday Weld four years after *Pretty Poison*. Despite the disagreements they had had on that picture, Tuesday actually asked for Tony to be her co-star on it.

'The greatest thing for Tony is that for the first time in his life he's playing a fully grown man, he's not that tall shit-kicking boy anymore,' observed Frank Perry.

Play It As It Lays attempted (and failed) to anatomize a breakdown suffered by a young Hollywood actress called Maria Wyeth (Tuesday Weld). BZ is a nihilistic producer of motorcycle movies, and the only man who understands her. He is married in name only to Helene (Tammy Grimes), because his domineering mother (Ruth Ford) paid her to stay with him.

When he visits Maria during one of her depressive moods, he asks,'Did I catch you in the middle of an overdose, Maria, or what?'

When Maria is unable to tell him the meaning of life, BZ takes an overdose of seconal, and dies in her arms. The main trouble with the film is that its cheerless message is transmitted in so chic a manner (Roy Lichtenstein was employed as 'visual adviser') that the bleakness at the heart of the novel has become transformed into a series of flashy visual images, intended to convey despair but only creating it in the audience. As a result, the tale is unable to elicit compassion for the leading characters, although the friendship between the screwed-up actress and the morose gay (a tautology meets an oxymoron) is touchingly portrayed.

Pauline Kael commented: 'Anthony Perkins uses his contrasting skinny tightness, in his supporting role, very well; when his lines are dry, he's the best thing in the picture. But who would deliver lines like, "We've been out there where nothing is?"'

Gay author Arthur Bell, writing in the *New York Times* in April 1973, just after the film's release, criticized the stance which it took towards BZ.

'Homosexuality is the secondary theme . . . A handsome stud tells Tuesday Weld to "dump the fags". A couple of reels later, one of the "fags", Tony Perkins, noshes a couple of handfuls of seconals and dies in Tuesday Weld's arms, because that's the way it is when you're depressed and talented and suppressed and suffering from an overpossessive mother, a mockery of a marriage to Tammy Grimes, and too much money. Homosexuals have to end up unhappily or, better still, dead.'

According to Tony's therapist Mildred Newman, and her husband Bernard Berkovitz: 'Analysts once thought that they had little chance of changing homosexuals' preferences and had little success in that direction. But some refused to accept that and kept working with them, and we've found that a homosexual who really wants to change has a very good chance of doing so. Now we're hearing all kinds of success stories. The nature of homosexuality hasn't changed, but the way of looking at it has.'

Dodson Rader remembered a farcical occasion when Newman and her husband gave a party in their large duplex Manhattan apartment for all the gay men they believed to have cured.

'The place was filled with about thirty couples, some of them very famous. Every one of them had a wife or girlfriend and they were all trying to prove to their shrink how happy they were in their new straight roles. About an hour and a half into the party, in walked the handsome young actor [Barry Bostwick] who was starring in *Grease*, which had just opened on Broadway. Everybody stopped talking and stared at the door. It was astonishing. As the kid walked around the apartment, I noticed one guy after another would go over to him and slip him their phone numbers. Their sense of self-delusion was laughable.'

During his therapy, Newman asked Tony what sort of woman attracted him. He flipped through a copy of *Vogue* until he pointed to a spread on twenty-two-year-old Berinthia 'Berry' Berenson. She was the sister of model-actress Marisa Berenson, granddaughter of fashion designer Elsa Schiaparelli, grand-niece of the great art critic Bernard Berenson, and daughter of the late Robert L. Berenson, a former US Foreign Service officer and shipping executive from Boston, and the Marchesa Gina Cicciapouti di Guilliano of Ischia, the former Gogo Schiaparelli Berenson. Berry, who went to school in Switzerland, Italy, France and England was a member of the international jet set if ever there was.

Coincidentally, Berry Berenson claimed: 'When I was twelve I fell in love with Anthony Perkins in *Phaedra*.'

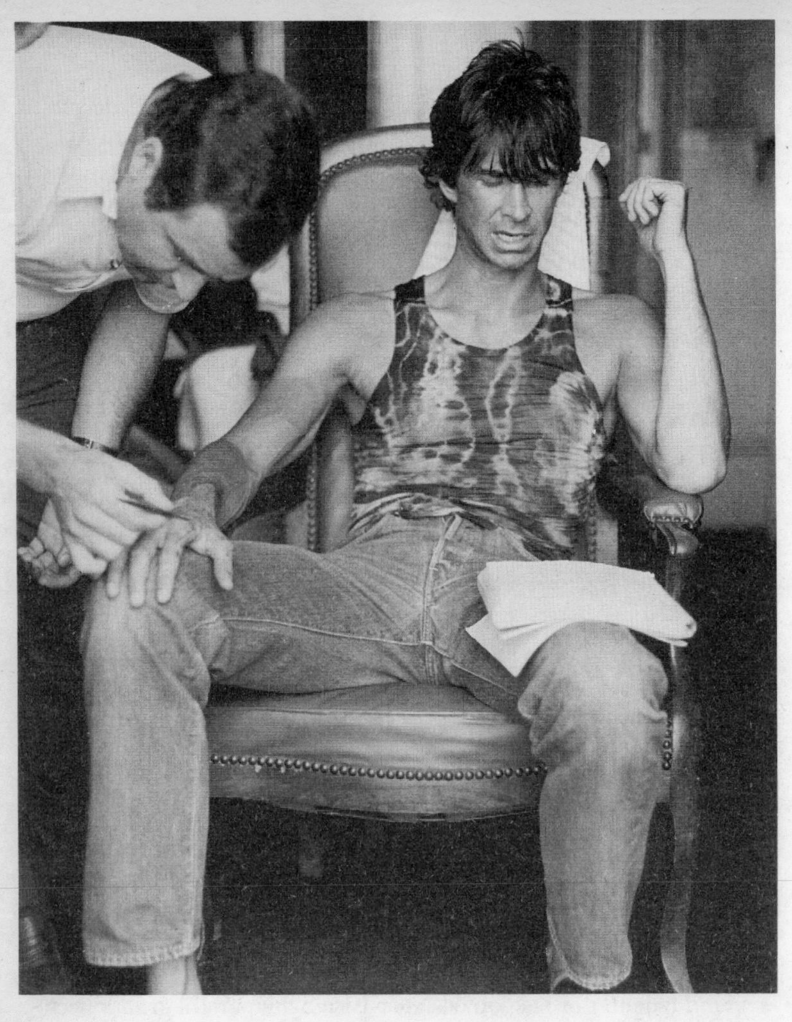

ANTHONY PERKINS BEING MADE UP FOR A SCENE IN *PLAY IT AS IT LAYS*, 1972 (CHRISTOPHER MAKOS).

Since her first glimpse of Tony on screen, she had kept a scrapbook on him, and when she and her older sister Marisa were in Paris, and heard he was living there, they went through the phone books vainly trying to find him. Ten years later, now a fashion photographer – she would usually turn up in blue jeans and pearls for a photo assignment – a protégée of *Vogue* editor Diana Vreeland, with connections in the movie business, she came face to face with Tony.

After *Play It As It Lays* completed shooting, Ruth Ford held a wrap party for the cast and crew. Joel Schumacher, later a director but then a costume designer on the film, arrived with Tony, who hated parties and was standing in a corner complaining, when Berry walked in. Schumacher, who happened to be a friend of Berry's, introduced them.

'I really didn't want to meet him,' said Berry. 'It was one of those things I preferred to keep a fantasy. But I remember walking into the dining room, and I knew he was standing behind me because he was very intense, and I turned around and there he was. I practically fainted.'

She did not, and confessed her adolescent crush to him. A few days later, they met again at the writer Dodson Rader's thirtieth birthday party held at the Dakota. As was their habit, Tony and Grover arrived separately. Despite the presence at the party of such luminaries as Mick Jagger, Andy Warhol, Liza Minnelli, Maureen Stapleton, Truman Capote and Tennessee Williams, Tony and Berry sat side by side on a sofa for most of the evening talking to each other in an animated manner.

A short while later, Berry called Tony to ask if she could talk to him for Andy Warhol's magazine *Interview*, for which she had done some articles. He agreed reluctantly.

'I thought she was cute and pretty but a little frantic,' Tony recalled. 'I forgot her until she phoned me and reminded me. She came over and the whole thing was so unorganized. She really didn't know what she was doing, but it was so innocent it didn't put me off.'

In November 1972, Berry arrived at the Chelsea townhouse, and was greeted on the fourth floor by Tony clad in a black T-shirt and threadbare jeans. She got him to talk to her rather openly, although much of what he said was a variation on the insecurities he had previously expressed more guardedly to other journalists.

'Being a private person sounds wonderful on paper, but it hides a lot of ego things, anxieties and fears,' he told her. He also described an experience that could almost be read as a metaphor of his sexual life.

'I was at this guy's house. The phone rang, he answered. When he hung up he said, so and so's coming over, you've just got to meet them.'

But Tony was shy and hid in the closet of the bedroom. He peered through the panel at what was going on.

'It turned me on, but then it wasn't watching that turned me on; I wanted to be out there in the room with them or just with one of them. So I cleared up the closet instead.'

As the interview progressed, Tony and Berry found that they both cried easily in movies.

'The movie I cried most in was *Marriage Italian Style*. When I saw *Ballad of a Soldier* the tears came out of my eyes so violently, they didn't run down my cheeks but sprang out like I had a water pistol,' he admitted.

It is understandable that Tony would have been moved to tears by *Ballad of a Soldier*, a touching Soviet film about a young soldier on four days leave from the front attempting to visit his mother. But it remains a puzzle as to what he found to weep about in *Marriage Italian Style*, Vittorio De Sica's broad erotic comedy, which starred Tony's erstwhile co-star Sophia Loren.

After the interview, during which they sunned themselves on the balcony, Berry found excuses for other meetings – to go over the transcript, to go over the edited transcript, to look at the photographs, to look at the photographs again. Finally, she ran out of reasons to see him.

'We were sitting there, and I had a feeling it was like the last time I would ever see him, because I was beginning to feel a bit ridiculous. He put on this Italian record, and it touched a chord in me and I started to cry – hysterically! He didn't know what to do with this weeping woman, so he said, "Well, would you like to go to the movies?" And I made him dinner and we never went to the movies and that was it.'

Tony gave another version, saying it was Berry who asked him to the movies, promising to cook him dinner first. Uncharacteristically, he accepted, though he thought, 'What have I done? What on earth have I got myself into?'

23

THE MATING GAME

'I want to get rid of the past' – Norman Bates in *Psycho IV* (1990)

Stephen Sondheim had the walls of the lower level of his Manhattan home covered with 19th-century game boards, slot machines, and puzzles. As a way of relaxation, he would throw mystery game parties, in which Tony was one of the keenest and most inventive of the participants. (The 1967 Halloween treasure hunt, which sent several teams of celebrities searching thirteen locations all over New York, was still talked about by those that took part.)

On one occasion, former choreographer Herbert Ross, with three undistinguished films behind him as director, was so exhilarated by winning a game, that he suggested it might make a good basis for a movie whodunnit. It eventually became *The Last of Sheila*, that diverting but far too clever picturalization of one of these labyrinthine intellectual diversions that occupied Sondheim and co. during much of their leisure time.

Tony explained how his collaboration with Sondheim on the

screenplay came about.

'Steve started work on it, but at one point he decided he didn't want to do it all himself. He called me and said, "Now I know this is ridiculous but would you like to collaborate with me on this project?" I had never written a word but he said, "Look, it's not as though we have to do this. It's not as though we've accepted any money or anything. If you don't like what I write and I don't like what you write, we'll just forget it." So I said okay and then we circled it and circled it for three months and Steve finally said, "I think we've got to start writing something. How should we start? And I said," Let's take the first sequence, I'll write one part and you write the other. So I went home, put a piece of paper in the typewriter and typed "Fade In" and just started writing.'

While Tony was shooting *Play It As It Lays* in Hollywood and Sondheim was working on *A Little Night Music* in New York, they would send each other scenes and then edit them on the phone. As Sondheim was more interested in the puzzle, he handled more of the plot, and Tony, who was more interested in the atmosphere, dealt with 'the scary stuff.' There were only two scenes in the entire screenplay that they wrote in the same room at the same time.

'The writing took over a year, the composition of the story took over a year, and the writing of the screenplay another six months. That's proof positive that we didn't really know what we were doing,' Tony commented. 'We wrote a script that was something like two hundred and thirty pages long. We actually gave it to Warner Bros. and said, "Well, you know we can shorten it a little, but how did you like it?" Of course no studio ever likes a long script; it doesn't matter what's inside.'

They ended up with about a hundred pages that were never used, but being an intricate puzzle with clues all the way through, it was extremely difficult to cut.

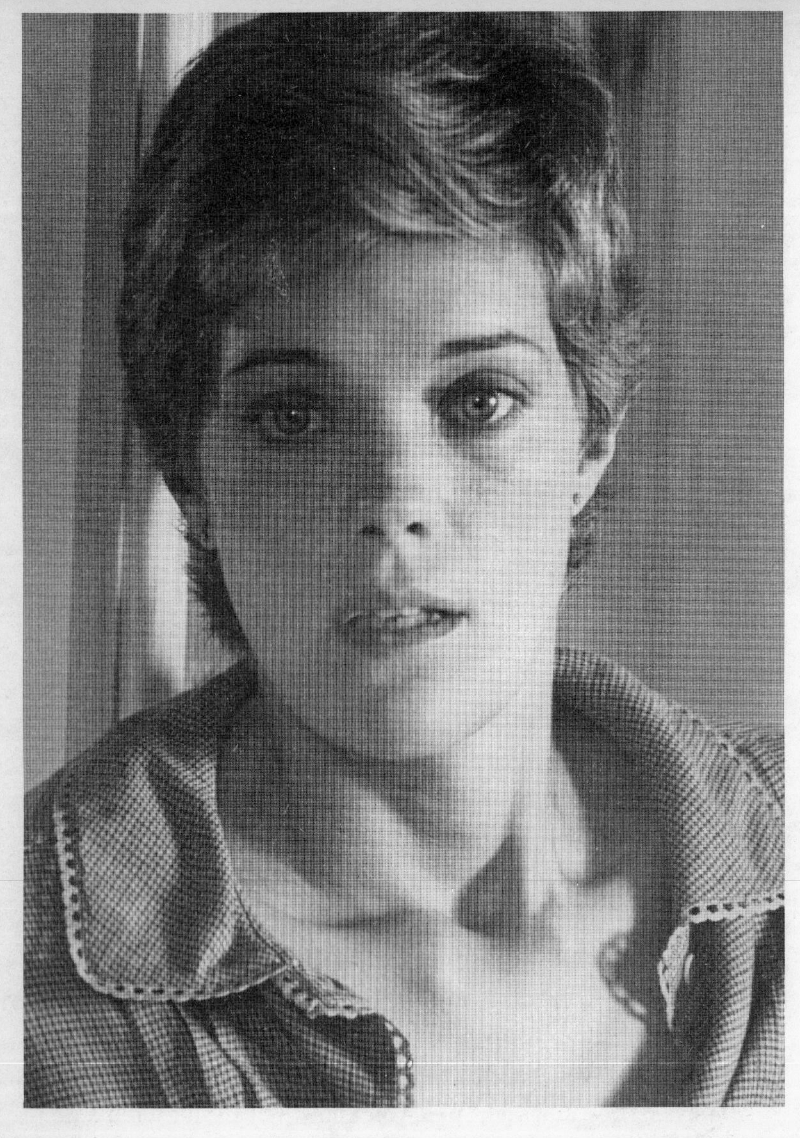

Berry Berenson at the time of her marrage to Anthony (Photofest).

Initially *The Last of Sheila* was set on a snowbound weekend in Long Island, but the locale was shifted, hedonistically, to an island in the Aegean. Unfortunately, two weeks before rehearsals were to begin on board the *Marala*, a luxury yacht moored near Mykonos, it capsized, and they had to find new locations on the French Riviera.

The starry cast was made up of a bunch of mutual friends – Richard Benjamin, Dyan Cannon, James Coburn, Joan Hackett, James Mason, Ian McShane and Raquel Welch, and the film was directed by Herbert Ross.

'One of the things I enjoyed most was spending time on the movie set watching Steve take pictures of the stars – that's a side of him that one might not expect to see. It really turned him on and it was beautiful!' Tony exclaimed.

The core of the plot concerned Clinton (James Coburn), a movie producer, on the first anniversary of his wife Sheila's mysterious hit-and-run death, inviting six friends to his yacht on a week's cruise off the south coast of France. The yacht is named after his wife. His plan is to expose one of the guests as the driver of the car that killed his wife, through a kind of treasure hunt which he calls The Sheila Greene Memorial Game. (An in-jokey allusion to the Eleanor Clark French Memorial Treasure Hunt of 1967.)

Each guest has been given a name with a guilty secret written on it, a secret that applies to one of the guests, though not the one holding the paper – Shoplifter, Homosexual, Ex-convict, Informer, Little-Child Molester and Alcoholic. The instigator of the game is murdered while in drag, impersonating a nun. The clue to whodunnit is in the title, the answer being sparked off by the redundant 'Little' in Child Molester.

'Is this game only a game?' asks Joan Hackett at one stage. Most audiences have no choice other than to take it as such, but it was considered by those within the incestuous Sondheim clique, and those hovering on the edges, as a *film à clé*. The more knowing among them believed that the lines about secrets referred to the two screenwriters and one or two other participants:

'The longer you try to keep a secret, the more it wants to get out.'

'The thing about secrets – we all know things about people but we don't know the same stuff.'

Others thought that the film reflected Tony's feelings about Hollywood.

'Tony had the Olympian contempt of a really smart person for the skulduggery and nightmarish obviousness of the business,' observed producer Howard Rosenman. 'I think they both [Sondheim and Tony] had a delicious time satirizing Hollywood.'

The Last of Sheila was filled with recognizable Hollywood types – sadistic producer, down-and-out director, bitchy agent, unsure sex symbol, pushy manager and ambitious screenwriter. Dyan Cannon as the gossipy agent was said to be modelled on Tony's agent Sue Mengers. The married screenwriter Richard Benjamin, who claims to be homosexual, has elements of Tony in him. ('I had a thing with Clinton. It's in the past now.'); his wealthy, eccentric wife (Joan Hackett), the movie sex-queen (Raquel Welch) and Anthony, her husband-manager (Ian McShane), and the bullying producer (James Coburn) were thinly disguised amalgams of people Tony had worked with recently. James Mason as the failing director with a penchant for very young girls, was a sly reference to *Lolita*. All the characters are witty, but selfish and vicious, yet they believe themselves charming.

Some of the lines reminded those who knew Tony of his camp and caustic humour, Dyan Cannon's character being the best cypher for this. She says things like, 'I hate my luggage more than life itself.'

She also wonders how Benjamin can afford Vuitton bags by writing Spaghetti Westerns. Tony had a thing about Vuitton lug-

Thursday, 9 August 1973, that the wedding of Tony 'never will I marry' Perkins and Berinthia 'Berry' Berenson took place in a garden at the house of the Reverend Ernest Davis Vanderburgh, an Episcopal clergyman and social worker at Wellfleet, near Tony's house at Cape Cod. It was a highly informal, almost hippy, ceremony in the presence of a few friends. Lucy Saroyan and Mrs Osgood Perkins were the couple's witnesses.

Berry, barefoot, wore a pink, blue and green English silk granny dress, American Indian jewellery, and a double strand of pearls given to her for her birthday by her new mother-in-law. She carried a bouquet of wild flowers. The groom wore white slacks, a white shirt and fifteen year-old boots. He gave his bride a ring of Indian turquoise set in silver with little arrows along the sides. The wedding party included a couple of Tony's friends, Michael O'Hara and Stephen Paley, and neighbours, Mr and Mrs Joseph Schoonjongen, and Mr and Mrs Benjamin Algase, who brought a picnic lunch. After everyone had feasted on seafood salad, cake and champagne, they all went to the beach.

Soon after, Tony told an interviewer that marriage had put an end to what he called 'my couch years,' his nine years under analysis.

'Gay, bisexual, heterosexual. If you want the label for a lot of my fe, it's none of those – try confused or scared. But it's all straight ow,' he said, chuckling at the unintended pun on the penultimate ord.

'Tony was undoubtedly sexually attracted to Berry', stated Ben gley, something which the newly-married man was happy to ast about to friends.

Tony always talked about getting married and having children en he was in his forties,' said Chris Makos. 'The funny thing is Berry Berenson and I looked similar, not only because we had short fair hair, but similar features. This was noticed

gage, because in the later *Winter Kills*, he exclaims, 'What will you do? Stab me through my Vuitton luggage?'

When Coburn asks about Benjamin's bad back, and the latter starts telling him, Coburn cuts him off by saying, 'I don't wish this topic to degenerate into the discussion stage.'

There is even an echo of the last line from *Tea and Sympathy*.

'When Clinton talks about this – and he will – be confused.'

And was there not another wink in the audience's direction when James Coburn is murdered dressed in drag as a nun?

The picture was not a success, though the *New York Times* found the script 'a dazzling technical achievement. No loose ends, no red herrings, the logic is impeccable. They play fair with the audience. It is heartless, but it has a brain.' About a decade later, Sondheim and Tony teamed up again to create a mystery story called *Crime and Variations*. It was to be developed by Motown productions for potential presentation on Home Box Office. They wrote a seventy-five page treatment with all the scenes, stories and clues laid out, although the scripts themselves were written by another writer.

'It's a fairly intricate murder investigation,' said Tony, who had also written the unproduced film treatment with Sondheim of *The Chorus Girl Murder Case*. 'We follow the same crime puzzle through the eyes of different people investigating it, and it's set in the New York socialite world. I'm a sort of catalyst. And it is fun, although you have to be prepared to have your ideas looked at sceptically and sometimes with a bit of impatience.'

Tony had taken Chris Makos with him to the French Riviera for the shooting of *The Last of Sheila*. One day, after they had returned to New York, Dodson Rader, who had a date with Chris, went to fetch him. While Chris was taking a shower, Rader wandered into his darkroom. What he saw there shocked him.

'I found a number of photographs taken by Tony in the south of France of Chris in the nude in sado-masochistic bondage poses against rocks. I loved Chris and I was deeply angered by what I saw. I no longer liked Tony much after that.'

It is not clear how interested Tony was in S/M sex, but he may have enjoyed it vicariously from time to time. ('Why, she wouldn't even harm a fly' – *Psycho*.) Chris Makos considered that 'all actors look for lovers or friends who can be good directors, because a good director can get you to do what they tell you. I felt I was too young to direct him. I think he would have liked to have been directed by me.'

According to Andy Warhol's gossipy diaries: 'Tony used to hire hustlers to come in through the window and pretend to be robbers. I wonder if Chris had to do that. I guess maybe he did. Chris did get wild.'

'Tony was very crazy sexually,' observed Makos. 'Not in a bad sense or anything. He made love in a healthy, all-encompassing way. Those pictures Dodson mentioned are not sado-masochistic. Dodson has taken a writer's licence. I've published pictures taken by me of a friend tied up with ropes. It was all for fun. We were just goofing around, and everybody said how kinky I was. I even took a photo of Tony, stripped to the waist, wearing a studded dog collar, but it doesn't mean that Tony was into anything sado-masochistic in contemporary terms. I wouldn't put Tony in that category.'

The photo Markos refers to is, in fact, a series of pictures in which Tony is seen talking in a relaxed manner on the telephone, while playing with the cord. He is wearing spectacles and a tight little sleeveless jumper, which stops just above his navel. Shadows create ambiguity as to what he is or is not wearing below the waist. Around his neck is indeed the dog collar mentioned, but he

is hardly in a sado-masochist pose.

However, one of Tony's exclusive set did relish S/M
Well-dressed guests would often go over to dinner at t
house, when suddenly his boyfriend would show up i
torn T-shirt and jeans, and order the host about. If
wanted to go to the toilet, he would raise his hand to ask
permission.

Chacun a son gout . . . but Ben Bagley believed that 'T
always looking for a tender experience, while some of
friends went for rough trade.'

Tony had found it in Grover and a few others, but the
his strongest commitment towards another person hap
be a woman.

The last work Tony undertook before his marriage was a
the theatre in 1973 to direct Neil Simon's 1970 comedy, *Th
bread Lady*, for summer stock which toured the New En
cuit. The play, which contains a pathetic, bitchy h
actor and a vain aging beauty, starred Maureen Stapl
recovering alcoholic Evy Meara. As it was the role she
on Broadway, Tony did not have very much to teach h

The reviews for his direction in the local press were
datory. One critic mentioned that the 'package sho
that 'still seems to be working on the admonitions la
rector Anthony Perkins some time ago.' Yet the p
the Straw Hat Award (given to summer stock com
director, best actress (Stapleton) and best newco
yan, the daughter of the playwright William Sa
ton's daughter).

With Berry three months pregnant, she
decided to get married, although they had pr
their disdain for matrimonial contracts. It w

when we were both part of the Andy Warhol crowd, and some people joked around that he substituted Berry for me.'

'A lot of people looked at the two of us and said, "Who are they kidding? This is never going to work,"' commented Berry. 'I was so naive I couldn't figure what they were talking about. I'd say, "Why not?" And it did, much to everyone's amazement.'

When Tony told her he had been a 'virgin' until he was forty, Berry remarked,

'It just didn't register. I had been very sheltered. I hadn't had a boyfriend until I was nineteen, so it didn't seem so strange that he hadn't had that many. I mean, this was literally my thinking.'

'She was very innocent,' said Howard Rosenman. 'He married her so I guess he had an innocent side too. I think that's what he was going for.'

Berry's 'innocence' was both natural and studied. She had been very close to her flamboyant couturiere grandmother Elsa Schiaparelli, who had made 'shocking pink' famous and whose autobiography was called *Shocking Life.* (Schiaparelli died in November 1973, a few months after the marriage.) Berry had moved in elevated circles as well as Bohemian ones; she had hung around with members of Andy Warhol's factory, and had lived abroad for some time. Berry seemed a bundle of contradictions.

For film writer Frank Rose, 'Berry had moved with a racy crowd, yet she was still fresh out of boarding school. She was an odd mixture of innocence and protectiveness. There is unanimous agreement among their circle of friends that Berry didn't know about his sexual adventures. It is more likely that she preferred not to know or, in fact, care.'

For Noel Black, 'Berry and he were like the lovers in *Le Grand Meaulnes.* She was his Earth mother, sister, lover, wife. I was delighted to see him so happily married. His shrink certainly helped him change his life style.'

For Dodson Rader, 'Berry had great compassion and charm. She had a tomboyish quality and yet could be very shy, feminine and maternal. Although pretty, she was always overshadowed by her sister in looks.'

Much of their relationship was expressed in the Lorenz Hart lyrics for 'You're Just The Mother Type', a song Tony recorded (with Nancy Andrews) some years later.

At the same time, Grover Dale, who had followed Tony into psychotherapy, imitated his lover by getting married to singer-dancer Anita Morris. She was the star of the Broadway musical *Seesaw*, for which Grover choreographed the opening number. There was a bizarre set-up during the first few years of the marriage – while Tony and Berry lived upstairs, Grover and Anita lived downstairs in the same house in Chelsea. Those that knew Tony and Grover well, considered Grover to be the more devoted, the more in love. He also had a more pleasant disposition, and wanted to please Tony. Despite their simultaneous marriages, by living in the same house, there was a certain continuity in their relationship, though the sexual side had dwindled. Grover was kept active with his dancing, and made a six-and-a-half minute film called *This Is My Body* for a programme of shorts called *Ciné Dance*.

To all appearances, neither Berry nor Anita performed the superficial function of 'beards' (a whisker or two, maybe), and both Tony and Grover – unlike some closeted gay men who made unhappy marriages – were fortunate to have fulfilled themselves as husbands and fathers. (Tragically, Anita Morris died aged fifty, in March 1994. She and Grover had one son.)

The two couples entertained often and lavishly – Tony, Grover and Anita's show business crowd, and Berry's *haute couture* and photographic friends. An essential element at these gatherings was drugs – hashish, amphetamines, cocaine and various potent 'cocktails'. Howard Rosenman told of how Tony offered him a 'fabulous' new drug at a Christmas party.

'Will it make me paranoid?' Rosenman asked.

'Oh, no, doll! It'll make you the life of the party.'

It was an animal tranquilizer and sent Rosenman into a zombie-like trance for three hours. But every time Tony walked past Rosenman, he patted his head and said,

'Doll, you're the life of the party.'

'Tony and Berry were like the wild, crazy people who found each other and proved that it could happen,' recalled Joel Schumacher. 'Their marriage became a true source of hope for all the misfits and exotics, because they were us and we were them.'

Then it was back to film business as usual – after all, Tony now had a wife to support, and a child on the way. Both his next two screen appearances were under the direction of the respected but very erratic Sidney Lumet. The first, *Lovin' Molly* (the dropped 'g' gives a clue to its being a redneck drama) was a dreadful flop, and the second, *Murder on the Orient Express*, was a dreadful success.

Lovin' Molly (aka *The Wild and the Sweet*) was set and shot in Texas, and covered forty years (1925–1964) in the lives of its three protagonists. They were Molly (Blythe Danner), a life-affirming, salty farm woman; Gid (Tony Perkins), a withdrawn uptight farmer, and Johnny (Beau Bridges), a placid footloose cowboy. She shares her bountiful love between the two men, but refuses to marry either of them. At the end, Gid obligingly has a heart attack and dies.

Blythe Danner gamely attempted to make of Molly a livin', breathin' liberated woman, but Lumet's direction and the lines she had to utter ('my menfolk began rising with the moon . . .') defeated her. It was all as phony as the ageing make-up worn by all three participants in the *ménage à trois* towards the end of the saga. A slow and rambling replay of themes from *The Last Picture Show*, it betrayed Larry McMurtrey's novel, *Leaving Cheyenne*, on which it was based. In fact, the author objected to what was done to his work.

According to one critic,'Mr Lumet took a piece that was awful to begin with, but authentically awful, at least, and he antiqued and rinky-dinked around with it until whatever bleak dignity it could claim was coated in a sticky, sugary, falsity . . .'

Tony, now pushing forty-two, struggled to convince as the young man in his early twenties that he is supposed to be at the beginning, and who 'then ages in the stiff-faced manner of a person who's had too many facelifts.' A line Tony delivers in *Mahogany*, his next film but one, encapsulates much of his life and career.

'Well, you're only young once, but you can be immature forever.'

In a sense, it had always been convenient for Tony to pretend to be naive and boyish, mainly because people do not expect you to give opinions on serious matters, and they do not demand them from you. Male Hollywood sex symbols from the previous generation like Clark Gable, James Stewart, Robert Taylor, Cary Grant, Alan Ladd, Robert Mitchum, Henry Fonda and Gregory Peck moved easily from youth to maturity, more often than not improving with age. Among Tony's near contemporaries, Marlon Brando and Paul Newman were among the survivors, but there was a group of pretty-boy actors, which included Tony, whose careers withered with middle-age – Tab Hunter, Farley Granger, Troy Donahue, Jeffrey Hunter, Sal Mineo, John Derek and Richard Beymer. James Dean, of course, had the good sense to die young.

No longer able to exploit his boyish charm and the youthful

uncertainty that was his stock-in-trade, Tony was beginning to flail around to find roles in keeping with his new image. The problem was that neither Tony nor anybody else knew how to define it.

24

HIGH AND LOW

'*Well, you're only young once, but you can be immature forever*' – Sean McAvoy in *Mahogany* (1975)

In the spring of 1974, after his last two pictures had failed miserably, Tony was invited to Pinewood Studios outside London to play one of the suspected killers of millionaire Mr Ratchett (Richard Widmark) in *Murder on the Orient Express*, the first of the Agatha Christie all-star films. Sidney Lumet was the surprising but able choice as director.

According to Tony, 'Lumet wisely refused and disdained to become interested in or involved with the actors' personal gripes with each other and with the script. He wouldn't listen to it. He'd say "look I'm far too busy, go to lunch together and work it out." There were personality conflicts. The actors had to fend for themselves and they did.'

Set in the 1930s, it was all as smooth and plush as the eponymous train, much of it consisting of interviews of the suspects by an over-the-top Albert Finney as Hercule Poirot, sporting a ridiculous waxed moustache and speaking in what was supposed to be a Belgian accent. Among the star cameos were Lauren Bacall (nouveau riche widow), Sean Connery (irascible British colonel), John Gielgud (English butler), Ingrid Bergman (shy Swedish spinster), Wendy Hiller (termagant aristocrat) and Tony as McQueen, Widmark's prissy secretary.

Pale-faced and nervous, he bites his nails, speaks in stuttering spurts, mutters under his breath, gulps, shakes his head and flutters like a startled bird. He exudes guilt far more flagrantly than his Joseph K. ever did.

Of course, as is traditional in the conventional whodunnit, he is not the only one who had reason to kill Mr Ratchett, who treats him like dirt. Joining his boss for breakfast, he happens to mention that he slept badly.

'The Belgian in the upper berth snored.'

Ratchett tells him to go back to his compartment immediately and catch up on his sleep, before the wretched secretary can take a mouthful of his breakfast.

After the murder, McQueen fidgets uneasily as he faces the Belgian detective.

'Forgive a Freudian question,' says Poirot, 'Do you love your mother?'

'I did. She died when I was eight. An impressionable age. Why do you ask?'

'You cried out mother twice in your sleep.'

'Did I? I still dream about her.'

McQueen then stands up indignantly, 'Tell me I'm emotionally retarded. Tell me that's why I never married.'

The suggestions of an Oedipus complex, and murderous intentions, if not actions, echo another of his homicidal characters – Norman Bates. If his performance were not so wittily self-knowing, Tony could have been accused of facile repetition.

During the shoot, Lord Snowdon had been commissioned by the *Sunday Times* to take a picture of the whole cast and crew. After the camera had been set up, it was noticed that the only one who had not appeared for the group photograph was Tony. While all the rest of the company patiently waited, a call went out for him. Eventually he was found hiding in a closet and refusing to come out.

Finally he was cajoled out by the make-up man. Rumours flew about the set – he was stoned, he was having a nervous breakdown, he had been spurned by the make-up man – all of which might have had some truth in them.

One of the crew remarked that Tony's temperamental behaviour reminded him of Monty Clift's during the making of *Freud* in 1962, when the actor used to hide in his limo, refusing to emerge.

Despite the end of his 'couch years' and the respectability that marriage is supposed to bestow, stories were still rampant that Tony was a drug addict, emotionally unstable, and was having affairs all over the place. However, the birth of his first child, Osgood, on 2 February, 1974, had a sobering effect. He had become a father at exactly the same age as his own father. It seemed to fulfil a deep need in Tony, and instilled in him a new sense of responsibility. Joseph Stefano, the *Psycho* screenwriter, ventured an analogy with the mentality of a serial killer like Norman Bates, whose own childhood was screwed up.

'They try to get it right. They go back to where it hurts; they do it over and over. In making a family he was going back to where it hurt, making it right.'

As film parts were only coming his way in fits and starts, Tony continued to direct for the theatre, though his next stage project was as unsuccessful as some of his last pictures. It was a summer stock pre-Broadway tryout of *Don't Call Back*, a play by Russell

O'Neil, which opened on 8 July 1974 at the Falmouth Summer Playhouse on Cape Cod. It starred Arlene Francis as a popular TV personality with a rebellious teenage son, who brings his criminal friends home and threatens his mother with a gun.

A short time after Berry had given birth to Osgood, another Berry (male) entered Tony's life.

Berry Gordy was the Detroit music executive mogul who created Motown records and helped make Diana Ross into a star. He had recently had a success with the production of *Lady Sings The Blues*, a biopic in which Ross played Billie Holliday. Gordy had now found another vehicle, entitled *Mahogany*, for his lover Diana.

It was a story about a poor black girl from Chicago who becomes the toast of the international fashion world with the help of a celebrated photographer, who dubs the model 'Mahogany' because, in his eyes, she is 'rich, dark, beautiful and rare'. However, she renounces her high life for the love of a poor but honest black politician (Billy Dee Williams).

In order to choose an actor to play the photographer, the producer Rob Cohen, screenwriter John Byrum, Diana Ross and Berry Gordy, the executive producer, met one afternoon in Gordy's office. Gordy handed Ross a copy of The Academy Player's Directory.

'Okay, Diana, you pick who you want to work with.'

'I want him. Can we have him?' she said pointing to Jack Nicholson.

Gordy replied that he cost too much. Ditto for her second choice, Warren Beatty. Finally they settled on Tony. As the photographer is a psychotic homosexual, one wonders, with typecasting so prevalent in Hollywood, why his name did not come up immediately

Tony told *Cue* magazine: 'I play a successful photographer, a Richard Avedon figure. I went to Avedon himself to do research, and I found myself getting really involved in photography. In fact, they're using some of my pictures in the ads.'

Tony also gained advice from his photographer wife.

Mahogany began shooting on 12 November, 1974 in a tough Chicago neighbourhood, under the direction of the rather effete English director Tony Richardson – a curious choice for this essentially black Motown story.

According to Richardson: 'The atmosphere on the set was tense, I thought. There was quite a lot of drugs there. One of Diana's co-stars was certainly on the stuff at the time and, as a result, his timing was off. Naturally, he would throw off the people who were not on drugs. Diana, who was never on anything, didn't realize how strongly this co-star was on the stuff.'

Why Richardson was so coy about naming Tony as the co-star is not clear. Perhaps he felt that it would defame the actor he had wanted to work with a decade earlier on the Tennessee Williams play, *The Milk Train Doesn't Stop Here Anymore.* Tony, though always the professional, usually needed something to help him gain confidence during the first few days of a shoot.

Richardson, whose persona was that of a white, upperclass English gentleman, minced onto the set in expensive fur coats. There was a feeling among the cast and crew, whether justified or not, that he could not relate to black people, and would perceive the film from a racist perspective. As a result, Gordy and Richardson clashed practically every day. The final straw was a dispute about the casting of a bit part, which led to Gordy sacking Richardson, and telling the press that the director did not 'understand the black experience'. Gordy immediately took over the direction himself in the USA before location work in Rome in January 1975.

Unlike Tony Richardson, Tony Perkins had no trouble at all being accepted by the black performers in the film, and got on very well with Ross, with whom he kept in touch. He seemed to give out the right signals, which dope certainly facilitated. Because of the nature of Hollywood, and the few roles offered blacks until fairly recently, Tony had not acted before with a black star, except for the short, effective scene with Diahann Carroll in *Goodbye Again*, when she sings 'Love Is Just A Word' to him.

Mahogany was a couple of pegs down even from that soap opera, but more enjoyable in a perverse way. *Time* thought: 'Movies as frantically bad as *Mahogany* can be enjoyed on at least one level; the spectacle of a lot of people making fools of themselves.'

It would be unfair to say that about Tony's performance. Sean McAvoy, the waspish fashion photographer, was the sort of flamboyant sarcastic role at which he was adept.

'Try saying "shit", instead of "cheese"', he advises potential models. 'My saints are a camera and a gun, they're both fiercely trivial.'

Aside from being 'fiercely trivial', he is mentally unbalanced and impotent, and sees his models as inanimate objects. In the end his morbid possessiveness towards Diana Ross, his Galatea, leads him to attempt to kill them both in a car but only he dies, repeating a death scene from *Phaedra.*

'From Perkins druggie-male-hustler mannerisms we can tell he's trying to do something completely ghastly with the role, but really the picture would be better off if he didn't,' wrote Pauline Kael. Another critic thought Tony had contributed 'the most memorable performance, with a kind of spinsterish acidity, looking disdainfully around him as though he knew he had trodden on something but, really, it wasn't worth while bothering about.'

The moral of *Mahogany*, delivered by the politico to the model was 'success is nothing without someone you love to share it with you.'

If that went for failure as well, Tony now had someone he loved to share it with, or, as a friend of his put it, 'if his career was going down the toilet, at least he had someone to wipe his arse for him.'

25

HORSE FEATHERS

'I'll erase the welts cut into his mind by flying manes' – Dr Martin Dysart in *Equus* (1975–1977)

'We go to the opening of *Equus* with Tony Perkins and his wife Berry Berenson. I think it is a crock of faggot shit. Me and Tony get into a pretty heavy argument about it over snacks at Sardi's after. When we say goodnight, and kiss air, he feels me up. High school high school high school. Six months later he takes over Anthony Hopkins's part in *Equus.*' So wrote Julia Phillips in her brash book *You'll Never Eat Lunch In This Town Again.*

'When I saw Anthony Hopkins in the play last fall, I loved it because I knew this was something I could never do,' Tony told *Newsweek*, when he was a month into the part.

It was the waspish British director John Dexter who urged him to take the role.

'I told him every reason why I couldn't,' Tony explained. 'I looked too young. I couldn't play a classical part. The role was one hundred per cent beyond my acting muscle. He said those were precisely the reasons I should do it. After the first day [of rehearsal], he said, "Off to the vocal coach and breath coach." Many American actors don't think of such things – I never had.' And whenever I began to revert to my old mannerisms,' Dexter would say, "Not that, Luv. We've seen it before." Now when I twitch I know it's there.'

Tony took over from Anthony Hopkins as the psychiatrist Martin Dysart in *Equus* at the Plymouth Theatre on Broadway on 30 June 1975, playing it on and off until 13 June 1977, a two-year period which Tony described as 'probably the most exciting of my life, as far as acting is concerned.'

Equus exposes much of Peter Shaffer's woolly thinking, but the imaginative use of actors in masks to represent horses strengthens the ritualistic elements, and makes for reasonably vibrant non-naturalistic theatre. Shaffer sets up a phony conflict between the intellectual values of psychiatrist Martin Dysart and the instinctual actions of seventeen-year-old stable boy Alan Strang. The latter is given to riding barebacked and bare at night, and also prays to a picture of a horse above his bed. Confused by his hysterically religious mother and anti-religious father, he blinds six horses with a metal hook because they have witnessed his failure to rise to the occasion in the hay with his girlfriend.

Treating the boy creates a crisis in the analyst, and the play moves towards an outburst from him in which he declares his envy of the Dionysiac freedom his patient has arrogated, and his disbelief in the methods he is using to 'cure' him. Despite the play's weaknesses as thesis drama, it did attempt to redefine normality and postulate Jung's assertion that 'Neurosis is an escape from legitimate pain,' all of which was familiar to Tony both intellectually and emotionally.

The boy, Alan Strang (played by Thomas – later Tom – Hulce), was the sort of role Tony might have played in his younger days when he was on the receiving end of a psychiatrist in *Fear Strikes Out* and *Psycho.* Now he was required to understand a very misunderstood boy.

'Some people assumed I was taking the part of the boy,' said Tony, 'but I looked at some of the pictures in front of the theatre and I looked at least a hundred. I was so happy!'

For the *Newsweek* reviewer: 'Tony Perkins became Anthony Perkins this summer. Although he has always used his full name in stage and screen credits, the tall, gangling actor had never really outgrown his image as the twitchy, misunderstood "Tony" . . . but six weeks ago, at the age of forty-three, he stepped into one of the most grown-up roles on the contemporary stage.'

John Dexter, who had made an important contribution to the play's creation, was able to guide Tony towards an interpretation which naturally differed greatly from his predecessors, Anthony Hopkins, Richard Burton and Alec McCowen (the originator of the part in London). Both Hopkins and Burton had fine rolling Welsh voices, but their interpretations were rather too external, though each gave a fiery display. Both McCowen and Tony came closer to portraying the complexity and ambiguity of the man. It is feasible that as homosexuals, like the author and director, they were able to mine certain depths in themselves to bring out the ambiguous attitude to the boy in the character of the psychiatrist.

Instead of the Brooks Brothers suits worn by the other Martin Dysarts, Tony chose a ninety-dollar off-the-rack affair from Macy's second floor.

'I sit on it every night before the show so that it's nice and wrinkled . . . And since I've been playing the role for a year, I've got a hole in the sole of my shoe that I won't let them touch. My tie is frayed, and that's the way I want it. The character is a man who isn't concerned with what he's got on . . . on my third night, I went out with my fly open. When I finally noticed it, I gulped and then, with enormous dignity, zipped myself up.'

Tony admitted to having the cold sweats every night, and going up to the stage manager after each performance and saying. 'Was I okay?'

For one critic, Tony held the stage 'with a febrile alertness to everything around him, an expansive urgency that erases recollections of the withdrawn misfit . . . head forward like a swiveling desk lamp, arms dangling vestigially except to smoke or scribble notes, voice spitting out the interrogations and self-loathing monologues in an accent that settles for a mid-Atlantic compromise.'

Tony handled the intense demands of the part, which included eight monologues, with force and subtlety. Dysart (the name echoes Dysfunction, Dionysiac Art, Dies, Dry heart, and Dis, the Roman God of the Underworld) is supposed to be a normal person representing the audience, but he is sicker than the patient he is required to heal, his intellectual detachment disguising sterility. It was as if Tony was confronting his younger self every night, or his divided self, between that part that wanted to be normal and that part that was not.

On 12 February 1976, Sal Mineo was murdered, aged thirty-seven. He was stabbed to death as he returned to his Hollywood home from a rehearsal for the play *P. S. Your Cat Is Dead.* A mystery still surrounds the killing, but it might have been either drug- or sex-related. Mineo, best remembered for his role as Plato, the boy with a crush on James Dean in *Rebel Without a Cause*, was a lonely figure who took drugs and was homosexual, despite once boasting to a fan magazine that 'My hobby is girls.'

Mineo was only one of a number of stars of the 1950s who died prematurely. The tragic toll of what seemed a blighted generation already included Pier Angeli and Marilyn Monroe by suicide;

James Dean, Jayne Mansfield and Audie Murphy in accidents; Jeff Chandler by blood-poisoning; Monty Clift by heart attack, brought on by drink and drugs; cancer victims included Laurence Harvey, Jack Hawkins, Susan Hayward, Judy Holliday and Kay Kendall (leukemia). Some years hence there would be the deaths of Vera-Ellen and Audrey Hepburn (cancer); William Holden, Richard Burton and Peter Sellers (heart attacks); Grace Kelly, Jeffrey Hunter and Natalie Wood (accidents), and Rock Hudson and Anthony Perkins (AIDS).

But in the late 70s, the forty-four-year-old Tony was relatively happy and healthy, and seemed immune from disaster. Marriage and fatherhood created an enchanted carapace around him. He ate wholesome food and never touched alcohol. He did, however, indulge in drugs, though never enough to make him an addict. After all, cocaine, which cost around fifty dollars a gram at the time, was Hollywood's favourite narcotic and a status symbol. Success was measured by the quality and quantity of the expensive drugs handed around at social gatherings.

On 9 February 1976, Berry gave birth to a second son whom they called Elvis, a name Tony insisted was not related to the rock singer, but meant 'fair of face'. (In what language, he never specified.) It was either his peculiar sense of humour or his naivety that made him think that people would not automatically assume he named his second son after Presley. The derivation of the name is obscure, but some think it comes from the Irish saints Elli, Elly, and the feminine Elva. There is a place called St Elvis in Dyffed in Wales.

Tony, who had sought meaning and redemption through acting, fame, psychotherapy, spiritual gurus and drugs, now gained most satisfaction from his wife and sons.

'Talk about family values,' commented his friend Paul Jasmin. 'That family is Tony's one great legacy.'

Certainly, the work he was taking on at the time, did not make much impact. According to Sue Mengers, 'He wanted to take care of his family, so if a piece of garbage came up, he would do it rather than wait and see if something better came along.'

Tony also made stipulations, however, that unless there was an offer he could not refuse, he preferred not to work during the summer so he could be with Berry and the children.

'My brother and I had a magical childhood with exceptional, caring parents who knew how to guide us so we wouldn't become bigheaded because they were famous,' recalled Tony's son, Osgood. He recounts an early memory of his father.

'I must have been five years old. We were in Toronto and he had taken me to see the city from the top of an immense skyscraper. Down below, for miles around, there were lights. I remember my father holding me around the drop. I thought I could have fallen if he had not held me back, but I trusted him and I knew that he would not let go of me . . . Evidently, this was not the case as the top of the tower was protected by glass.'

Tony was in Toronto for the making of *Winter Kills*, in which John Huston meets his death by falling from a skyscraper.

This black and witty conspiracy thriller, the first feature directed by William Richert, and based on the Richard Condon novel, was set fifteen years after the assassination of a popular young American president. His half-brother (Jeff Bridges), in searching for the real murderer, stumbles across pieces of a jigsaw that refuse to be completed. In an attempt to uncover the truth, he finds himself up against his megalomaniac father, played with relish by Huston, who runs a large commercial empire. Tony, in more than a cameo and less than a substantial part, played John Cerutti, a disturbed computer expert who keeps the information bank for Huston. At one point, when threatened by Bridges, he says, 'What will you do? Stab me through my Vuitton luggage' the sort of camp line that usually crept into his roles from the mid-70s. (Berry had a walk-on as a nurse in the morgue.)

While taking a break from *Equus*, Tony appeared as a guest on the zany *Saturday Night Live* show on 14 March 1976.

'We were watching the show one night and I turned to Berry and said, "Would you like to see me do that?" and she said, 'Yeah, that would be fun." So I called them about it. It was a whim. I was on vacation from *Equus* and wasn't doing anything else so I thought – why not?'

Tony appears in several sketches, most of which spoofed his career. The most memorable piece was a spot for the Norman Bates School of Motel Management.

'I felt I was taking my revenge on *Psycho*, exorcising it somehow. Afterwards, I was tremendously relieved,' he explained. But it was only a provisional exorcism.

When Tony's long run in *Equus* ended on 13 June 1977, he and Berry decided to move to Hollywood because they thought California would be a better place than New York to bring up the two kids. Now that he was a married man and a father, he felt he had less to fear from the small, narrow-minded community than when he had been there previously as an eligible and vulnerable bachelor. He also felt that living in what was still the movie capital of the world, he would be on the spot to take more acting jobs, the better to play his latest role as breadwinner for a growing family.

26

MR, MRS AND MIZ

'Listen, I got problems in my life, sure, but they're not you' – Neil Curry *in Remember My Name (1978)*

Despite having a long and successful run in *Equus* on Broadway, as far as film-makers and the film-going public were concerned, Tony had disappeared into the ether. Because *Mahogany* was a box-office flop, and the release of *Winter Kills* was delayed for three years until 1979, Tony had last been seen widely on the big screen in *Murder on the Orient Express* four years earlier. Thus, the title of his next film, *Remember My Name,* seemed appropriate.

Remember My Name, produced by Robert Altman and directed by his protégé Alan Rudolph, was a step up from Tony's last efforts. He played a man caught between two women – his hell-hath-no-fury first wife (effectively played by Geraldine Chaplin) and his conventional suburban second wife, played by Berry Berenson. Tony explained how Berry got the part.

'I had an appointment with Altman and she happened to come

along, because we were taking one of our children up to the pediatrician and she just happened to be there. In fact, both children were with us, and they were running around the suite and Berry was trying to catch them. She was not there for any other reason than for convenience sake and Altman literally handed her the part just on the strength of the way she was chasing the kids around the apartment.'

There is nothing in the role to suggest what Altman must have seen in Berry's behaviour with Osgood and Elvis that day, because the woman in the film is childless. Perhaps he saw something of the suburban wife in her. Nevertheless, he had confidence in Rudolph's ability to get a performance out of her.

'Considering Berry had never acted before I thought she did a very good job. She always astonishes me with her naturalness,' Tony told the National Film Theatre audience some years later, having forgotten that they had performed together before on stage in *The Voice of the Turtle* in summer stock in Cape Cod in 1977. She had also done a bit of acting previous to that. Her older sister, Marisa, had already featured in four films, though her impact had been minimal. From the evidence of both sisters' film appearances, acting was not their forte, whereas their grand-uncle Bernard Berenson and maternal grandmother Elsa Schiaparelli were renowned performers in life.

The thirty-four-year-old Alan Rudolph had made his directorial debut the previous year with *Welcome To LA*, whose aimless characters and plotless screenplay appealed neither to critics nor the public. In contrast, *Remember My Name* had a more constructed screenplay, being an updated psychological version of a 1940s Joan Crawford-type vehicle about a wronged woman bent on revenge, though Rudolph chose a method that is more anecdotal than melodramatic.

Berry Berenson and Anthony Perkins in *Remember My Name*, 1978 (Photofest).

The plot: Emily (Geraldine Chaplin) had been imprisoned for twelve years for having run over and killed one of her husband's girlfriends. On her release, she tracks him down to California, where he has got himself married again. Emily's object is to make his life a misery, so she pulls up the flower bed of his home, rams into his car, throws a rock through the window and threatens Barbara (Berry Berenson), wife number two.

When Emily breaks into the house while her ex-hubby is at work, she confronts Barbara, the suburban wife. 'Are you a good fuck?' she asks.

It is doubtful whether Barbara is, because her hard-hat husband goes drinking with his buddies till late every night. He gets more aroused by his unstable first wife (who calls him 'spider monkey') and, after a long drinking session, they go to bed together. Emily has succeeded in doing what she wanted, and leaves. End of story.

Tony told the *New York Times* during the shooting: 'We don't know which wife I end up with. That will be decided in the cutting room, which is characteristic of the way Altman and Rudolph work. They want the story to tell itself.'

The short-haired, boyish, snub-nosed, flat-chested Berry does what she can with the role, although she seems listless at first, then expressionless, and gradually emotes like a trapped animal as the tension builds up slowly. Tony, straining to convince as a bluecollar construction worker, watches her rather anxiously.

When Geraldine Chaplin sees Tony for the first time in twelve years, she says, 'Look at your hair, it's grey . . . and your face. I bet you've been through it.'

This was the sentiment some audiences, who had not seen Tony in a film for some time, might well have shared.

Following *Remember My Name*, which was a box-office disaster,

Tony appeared in two TV productions – one set in contemporary New York and the other in 19th-century France.

The former was a well-meaning redemption-through-affliction soap opera called *First You Cry*, adapted from Betty Rollin's book about her mastectomy, with Mary Tyler Moore as the TV reporter author. Tony played her unsolicitous husband, Arthur Herzog, who is 'not exactly eager to deal with the fact that I'm mangled,' as she puts it.

He is embarrassed to kiss his wife in public, talks slightingly about marriage at literary cocktail parties, and does not wish to hear her troubles while he is busy writing a book on earthquakes. When Moore leaves him to live with old flame Richard Crenna (as sickeningly warm, loving and understanding as Tony is cool, selfish, and confused), Mary Tyler Moore says, 'I miss his lack of charm sometimes,' though charm was a quality which Tony still had in abundance.

Although it is Mary Tyler Moore's film, Tony was well cast as someone who does not wish to get deeply involved in another person's problems, but eventually misses his wife when she is not there. At the ending, which manages to skate around sentimentality, the couple finally take leave of each other at that over-used film locale, the Rockefeller Center rink. He just leaves, saying 'See you around', before turning back. Remembering he once rebuffed her kiss on this very spot, he kisses her, and mutters, 'I'm so very proud of you,' and retreats without a backward glance, stifling his emotions.

A lack of charm and a stifling of emotions were essential for the role of Inspector Javert in *Les Misérables*, a scrupulously-made three-hour television film shot in France and England in 1978. Although Richard Jordan as Jean Valjean was far too lightweight both physically and histrionically, Tony as his nemesis turned in a mesmeric performance. As a satanic Javert, he is straight-backed, sour-faced and cadaverous. With long sideburns under a tricorne, arms folded across his chest, and his mouth turned down at the edges, he is an unsmiling dry man without warmth, a rare character in Tony's repertoire. Yet, under this harsh exterior, Tony allows a grudging respect for Valjean to enter Javert's piercing eyes.

This stickler for rules and laws, explains to Valjean:

'There are two kinds of person. Those who attack society and those that guard it. We are guardians.'

Javert's character, in a screenplay that strays too often from the Victor Hugo novel, has been given a further psychological twist in that he admits that his father was a convict and he was born in prison, whereas in the book he is the son of a prison guard. His suicide, therefore, becomes a tragic moment.

27

EVIL DAYS

'*You can't tear out my soul, because I've already done that myself*' – Neil Curry in *Remember My Name* (1978)

'I think, Dr Durand, that you are a man who longs for a sense of his own greatness, but has not yet found his true direction,' says megalomaniac scientist Dr Hans Reinhardt (Maximilian Schell) addressing Tony Perkins as Alex Durand, an unwelcome visitor to his spaceship in *The Black Hole*.

This remark has some bearing on the wayward direction in which Tony's career was heading. In this forty-million-dollar Walt Disney production, loosely based on *20,000 Leagues Under The Sea*, Tony could have echoed a comment made at one stage by fellow astronaut Joseph Bottoms.

'When I signed up for this job I never thought I'd end up playing straight man to a tin can.'

The tin can is an overcute robot called Vincent with the voice of Roddy McDowall, who speaks in homilies.

Tony hero-worships the Captain Nemo-like Schell.

'You will be remembered as one of the greatest space scientists of all time,' he says.

'Are you interested in black holes?' asks Schell.

Resisting the need to guffaw at this question, Tony replies, 'How can one not be overwhelmed by the deadliest force in the universe.'

Tony's eyes take on a Stephen Hawking-like gleam, as he exclaims that he wants to go, 'on a pilgrimage straight into what may be the mind of God!'

On first seeing all Dr Reinhardt's hardware, he exclaims, 'In . . . Credible'.

Despite the in . . . credible special effects, spectacular settings and holograms, *The Black Hole* was Hollywood at its most mimetic, and was not much of an advance on the old Flash Gordon serials. There must be something wrong with the characterization of the humans (Yvette Mimieux looks and acts like a wax fruit) when the most touching moment is the death of an old battered robot (with the voice of Slim Pickens).

Tony, in a high-collared designer space suit and snazzy coloured polo-neck sweater, seems to have taken his cue from the mindless human slaves and robots that Schell has on board his space ship, by playing the role robotically.

'Most of the acting was done in front of one of those incandescent blue screens, and after a while you do feel a bit foolish,' explained Tony. 'Until you see it, when you say "Gee, I remember when I was doing that my vision of that was quite different." But how was I to know? They don't exactly say, "It's going to look like this; it's going to look like that." '

Tony exits about halfway through the film, when he is killed by the rotary blades of Max, a homicidal robot. Although his death is bloodless, a spinning claw bores right through him.

After being skewered by a robot in a space epic, Tony was catapulted into a triangular drama called *Twice a Woman* (*Twee Vrauen*). It was shot in English in Holland in 1978 by George Sluizer, the Dutch director, born in Paris in 1932, who would only gain international fame nine years later with *The Vanishing*. *Twice a Woman* was shown at the 1979 Cannes Festival, but made little impression.

It told of Laura (Bibi Andersson), a lonely forty-one-year-old divorcee and a curator of an icon museum, who invites Sylvia (Sandra Dumas), a girl she meets at the museum, to her home. They go to bed together, though neither has slept with a woman before, and their relationship develops into an affair. Tony played Alfred, Laura's ex-husband, who has remarried and has two children by his second wife. He is a cold, analytical theatre critic 'given to pontificating on sexual theory in a manner calculated to drive feminists up the wall,' in Laura Kay Palmer's words.

Alfred, who was married to Laura for seven years, confronts her and warns of the consequences of her lesbian relationship. When he meets Sylvia, he determines to steal the girl away. Ditching Laura cruelly, Sylvia takes up with Alfred, and they shack up together in a decrepit hotel. She only wants to get pregnant. Once pregnant, she leaves Alfred and returns to Laura. The film reaches a bloody conclusion.

One of the film's principal interests lay in the rarity value of its picture of female homosexuality (although out of the three love scenes the film contains, one is between the women and two are between Tony and Sandra Dumas). Tony delivers a speech which touches again on the theme of the outsider. In fact, it could be Norman Bates talking.

'I believe . . . we all have the feeling that we don't belong, and we have nothing to do with this world. That we're only guests. But we don't want the others to notice. I think everyone has that feeling.'

After the large salary he received from Walt Disney Pictures for *The Black Hole*, Tony had another good payday for his role in *ffolks* aka *North Sea Hijack* aka *Assault Force*, which was shot in Ireland.

Ffolks is the strange name of Roger Moore, a super-frogman trying to save a British oil rig from destruction. Tony played Lou Kramer, a sarcastic, vindictive, short-fused, deranged villain, who has stolen the ship, the *Esther*, and is demanding a ransom of twenty five million pounds in five different currencies from the British government, or he will use the stolen ship to blow up an oil rig and a production platform. Moore and his frogmen must capture the *Esther* and bring Perkins to justice.

The film, made by action director Andrew McLaglen, and derived from the Jack Davis novel *Esther, Ruth and Jennifer*, was fair enough thick-ear entertainment, the equivalent of a paperback thriller one reads in a day on a beach and throws away.

'As a fiendishly clever international criminal, who turns into a babbling psychopath, he becomes monotonously mannered long before the picture is over,' was one critic's comment on Tony's performance.

With *ffolks*, Tony was now set in the inexorable direction of the irredeemable homicidal maniac, in which he suppressed his asset of charm. 'Have smirk will travel' might have been his motto, and from Ireland it took him to Toronto, where eight weeks shooting began on the Canadian thriller, *Double Negative* aka *Deadly Companion*, in January 1979. (Usually an aka title denotes trouble.)

In an apparent variation, the mental patient in the film was not Tony but Michael Sarrazin, a photo-journalist who has been placed in an institution following the strain of being tortured in a Middle East prison, coupled with the discovery on his return home to Canada of the brutal rape-murder of his wife. He sets out to track down the culprit.

Tony is Lawrence Miles, the prime suspect, a nasty blackmailer given to perverse games, who had been the lover of Sarrazin's wife. His only distinguishing characteristic is that he happens to have a good classical record collection. Again, he meets his end before that of the film, shot by security guards. The art of dying was something Tony was now doing 'exceptionally well.'

Double Negative, whose title could describe most critics reaction to it, had static direction, absence of logic, and unconvincing characters. It was inexplicably shown at the Cannes Festival in 1980.

It was really only because of his association with *Psycho*, and a few allied parts, that Tony was asked to play host on *The Horror Show: Creatures of the Night*, a compilation documentary of horror movie clips written by Richard Schickel and broadcast on 6 February 1979.

At this period, according to Frank Rose, Tony 'seemed unable to establish a screen identity that could carry him past the anxious young man he had played in the 50s and early 60s. As a middle-aged father, acting ceased to be a route to stardom and became a way to make a buck instead.'

'It was almost like the Tony of *Fear Strikes Out* and *Phaedra* was already dead,' commented Denis Christopher, 'and now there was this fake Tony, this caricature Tony.'

In 1980, Tony bought the rambling house in Seattle Drive that clings to one of the Hollywood hills. It opened onto an immense pinewood deck overlooking the near vertical backyard of the family's secluded unpretentious hacienda. Because of the slope of the terrain, the house looks as if it is suspended in the trees. Stairs lead to a garden down below, which resembles a rain forest, and on the right there is a swimming pool.

Anthony Perkins and Berry Berenson (Photofest).

The deck was the gathering place for all family occasions such as birthday parties. 'Where the good times happened,' according to Osgood II.

Although they continued to entertain friends, in terms of the social whirl the Perkins couple virtually disappeared. Berry, especially, was a homebody.

'It was as if she had been kidnapped and hidden away by Norman Bates,' commented Dodson Rader.

28

LIGHT RELIEF

'I'm an insecure middle-aged man who made a complete ass of himself' – Jason Carmichael in *Romantic Comedy* (1979)

Since 1968, the year of *Rosemary's Baby*, Tony was part of an uncamp group that included Mia Farrow, Roman Polanski, Mike Nichols, and set designer Richard Sylbert, who would meet for dinner parties at each other's homes from time to time.

Eleven years on, Tony and Mia – still known and billed as 'the victim in *Rosemary's Baby* and the killer from *Psycho*' – got together for a Broadway play by Bernard Slade called *Romantic Comedy*. It opened on 8 November 1979 and ran almost a year at the Ethel Barrymore, the scene of Tony's first Broadway success, *Tea and Sympathy*. At the time, Mia Farrow had just divorced André Previn, a marriage which had kept her mainly in England (he was conductor of the London Symphony Orchestra) during most of the 70s. The films she had made during that period had created as little impression as Tony's in that decade.

Tony's role of Jason Carmichael, a successful playwright, is described in the text as 'in his mid-thirties, not conventionally handsome but, despite his crumpled face, possesses a mixture of arrogance, charm and sophistication that gives him a certain magnetism.'

The action of the play takes place in the study of Jason Carmichael's New York townhouse (the usual setting for this kind of commercial Broadway comedy) and moves from the mid-60s to 1979. It was the sort of conventional piece in which Tony had started his career in summer stock, and he was delighted to return to his theatrical roots, as well as to the world in which his father had made his name. In fact, the producer Morton Gottlieb had this in mind when he suggested Tony to Bernard Slade.

'If this were 1935, Osgood Perkins would play this part. Why not get Tony?'

The only difference being that if it were 1935, Osgood would not have been called upon to play a nude scene as Tony was. Reacting to her naked co-star became one of Mia's favourite scenes.

'I'm the only one who hardly sees him, because I'm looking away portraying embarrassment,' she explained.

The scene comes about because Tony is in his apartment expecting his masseur. In walks Farrow as prudish New England schoolteacher and would-be playwright Phoebe Craddock. Slade's directions read:

'Jason enters from the dressing room. He is totally nude. Oblivious to Phoebe, who is in a frozen state of shock, Jason carries a portable massage table which partially shields his body from the audience. His back is three-quarters to the audience, she is behind the desk facing the audience, staring fixedly at Jason's hairline, trying to appear unruffled . . .

'You're younger looking than your photos. Of course most of those were head shots. Ha, ha. What a dumb thing to say.'

She asks if he is naked.

'You're just a white blob to me. I'm not wearing my glasses.'

'I rarely receive guests in the buff,' he assures her.

They soon become a successful playwriting duo. The two of them hover on the edge of an affair though each is married to another. Finally, they learn to live as workmates instead of playmates.

'*Romantic Comedy* was good boulevard theatre which is exactly the kind of thing I like to do,' commented Tony. 'I think one sharpens one's mind a little by appearing on the stage. Long runs are what really appeal to me. I'm probably unusual in that respect. I feel once you've gone to the trouble of learning it and rehearsing it and all that agony, by the time the requisite four months are over you're just getting it. We had a disastrous opening, and it wasn't until the third or fourth month that we really started to get rolling with it.'

But by the time the film version of *Romantic Comedy* was made in 1983, neither star was considered hot enough for the picture, and Dudley Moore and Mary Steenburgen took the roles. Farrow's screen career had picked up a little because of her relationship with Woody Allen, but Tony's was decidely lacklustre.

During his stay in New York for *Romantic Comedy*, Tony was asked by Ben Bagley to record a few numbers for his Rodgers and Hart album *Too Many Girls*. Tony turned up at the recording studio with seven-year-old Osgood and five-year-old Elvis. When he was about to enter the recording booth, they clung to his knees and refused to let go. Tony, therefore, asked Bagley if they could come into the booth with him while he recorded the song 'I Didn't Know What Time It Was', promising that the boys would not make a sound. Bagley reluctantly agreed. The boys were dead silent, and Tony recorded the number without a hitch.

When *Romantic Comedy* ended its run in October 1980, Tony began one of his leanest periods in terms of work.

'He was angry because he spent long stretches of time not working,' Berry commented. 'At one point he went two years without working, but he was such a stoic he never talked about it. He never complained. He learned to play the piano. He made phone calls. He would sit by the phone and wait for agents to call. Most of our friends didn't know. Now people say, "Oh, if only I'd known, I'd have given him work." I'm not sure I buy that.'

Adding to his depression, was the recent death of his mother. The woman who had played such a dominant role in his formative years, but whose direct influence, like that of most parents, had waned with time, had now gone from Tony's life. He had gained immense satisfaction from having been able to marry and supply his mother with grandchildren before her death, proving that he was the sort of son she always believed him to be. Her explanation for his prolonged bachelorhood, was that he had simply waited for the right girl to come along. But Berry was worth waiting for, the ideal daughter-in-law in Mrs Perkins's eyes; not only would she take care of her son, but she was upper class and wealthy as well. Tony waited only a few years after her death before he was prompted to dump most of the blame for his psychological hangups on his ever-loving mother, using some of the language of Norman Bates. ('Matricide is probably the most unbearable crime of all' – Dr Richman in *Psycho*.)

As consolation for his loss and his enforced idleness, Tony did have time, however, to be close to his children, and watch them grow up. 'My greatest pleasure is observing my children's development as human beings and understanding how much we may miss, those of us who are not actors, because the life of children, because the development of a personality is so close to what an actor deals with in a commonplace way. It's fascinating to be able to observe that in children, and adapt it to my own work. I want for them perhaps the independence I didn't have as a child. At the moment [1983], they've expressed a heated desire to become professional ice hockey players and I figure it takes a bit of acting to really have a career in ice hockey playing.'

In 1982, Tony also took part in an all-star charity show called *Best of Broadway*, in which his contribution was to sing 'Never Will I Marry' from *Greenwillow*, his hit from a flop show. All the others, including Mary Martin, Ethel Merman, Robert Morse, Chita Rivera and Alexis Smith performed hits from their hit shows. (It had to wait three years before it was shown on national TV.) The only other offers he got during this period were for two inferior television films.

It was over twenty years since Tony had filmed *On The Beach* in Australia. Despite that film's pessimistic message, both the world and Tony were still extant. It was a much older and somewhat wiser Tony who went off to Australia for a TV mini-series called *For the Term of His Natural Life*, based on an 1874 novel by Marcus Clarke. He played the Reverend James North, a compassionate chaplain in an Australian penal colony in the 19th century, a sensitive portrayal of a man tormented by the daily outrages of prison life, his inability to prevent them, and by the secret vice to which he retreats . . . alcoholism.

Not since his role as Algernon Moncrief in *The Importance of Being Earnest* in his college days had Tony played Oscar Wilde. There was a period in the 60s and 70s when his indiscernibly aging face put one in mind of Dorian Gray's diabolical bargain and the sin-laden senescent portrait in the attic. By 1982, however, though still remarkably youthful-looking for a fifty-year-old, he was lined enough to discount the portrait theory.

In a TV play called *The Sins of Dorian Gray*, a perverse updating to the era between 1950 and 1980 of Wilde's novel, the days when Tony might have been considered for Dorian were well and truly gone. This time the title role was taken by a woman, a beautiful fashion model (Belinda Bauer) whose screen test ages. However, the modernization and heterosexualisation of the decadent *fin-de-siècle* parable sapped the story of its allure, delivering a work by a certain Oscar Tame. Tony, who played Henry Lord, a mysterious, heartless fashion mogul, only makes one regret that he never had the chance to play Wilde's Lord Henry and demonstrate his talent for delivering witty, ironic epigrams. Meanwhile, driving along the bumpy road that symbolized his career, Tony came across a sign that read Bates Motel – Vacancies.

Part V

O, HORRIBLE! O, HORRIBLE! MOST HORRIBLE!

29

THE BATES MOTEL REVISITED

'*Memories are more likely to occur here*' – Norman Bates in *Psycho II* (1983)

'I spent about ten years of bitterness about the typecasting and also resistance to people coming up and talking about *Psycho*,' complained Tony. 'It was painful really until Berry said, "Why don't you get into this instead of resisting it? Then people will see that you have other qualities that are not Norman Batesish, that you're not remote and suspicious and shy and hard to get to know."'

It seems that Berry not only helped him overcome his fear of women, but also his resentment towards Norman Bates. This acceptance, and the lure of a fat pay-packet, led him to confront his alter-ego again in the Hitchcock-less sequel *Psycho II*. It was also a chance to capitalize on the fact that however wayward his career had become, he was still identified with one of the most famous characters in movie culture. At this stage, he knew he would not get another role like it.

For many, the idea of making a sequel to a masterpiece was

anathema. When Robert Bloch, who had signed away the film rights, sequels included, heard about *Psycho II*, he said,'I have no idea what their movie is about. I imagine Norman goes back home, hires a plumber and builds a new shower.'

But Tony found many excuses for embarking on the project. Alma Hitchcock, the director's widow, told Tony she saw no reason why a sequel to *Psycho* should not be made, and Hitchcock's daughter Pat, who had appeared in the original, was supportive. Tony rationalized: 'I wanted to return to Norman after all these years because he wasn't the same person. He's learned certain social skills, and he has realized his potential for anti-social behaviour. It showed a developed person. Those developments seemed good inducements indeed. There were many things about Norman that we never knew at all from the first film. I would suggest we know more about him. I felt he had always been an interesting character, given the wealth of information that the author has given him. I was sure it would be interesting to see more of his story . . . We have dealt with the survivors and characters and tried to put together a story, which I felt was strong enough to support the film. I decided I'd have to put myself on the line as the world class authority on Norman Bates. It didn't seem fair to be shrinking and reserved about it. I was very outspoken about anything in the script that I felt was uncharacteristic. I rarely use my authority or weight. I don't usually follow the pattern of the actor who likes to interfere with the side issues of film-making. I'd rather leave it to whoever is doing it, without undermining his or her authority.

The director was the thirty-four-year-old Australian Richard Franklin who, as a twelve-year-old, had sneaked into a cinema to watch *Psycho.*

'I liked his point of view. I liked his affability,' Tony explained. 'He moved around in a slow, absent-minded sort of way. In many ways he reminded me of a young Hitchcock. He also knew when to stop studying Hitchcock's films. He had worked with Hitchcock. I didn't see his previous films. I didn't want to prejudice myself.'

Just as well, as Franklin's previous films, all Australian, included *The True Story of Eskimo Nell* (1975), a vulgar unfunny comedy; *Patrick* (1978), a dreadful thriller about a comatose patient with telekinetic powers; and *Roadgames* (1981), an attempt at a Hitchcockian thriller, which starred Jamie Lee Curtis, Janet Leigh's daughter. In the 1970s, a number of young directors went in for empty excercises in Hitchcockiana, more likely to create dizziness than *Vertigo*. All they proved was that it was almost impossible to imitate the Master. Even Mel Brooks's parody, *High Anxiety* (1977), showed he had virtually no feeling or understanding for Hitchcock, whose work is used as a basis for low comedy. Naturally, it contained the inevitable shower scene, with Brooks being attacked by a bellhop (Barry Levinson) with a rolled-up newspaper.

But Tony continued to make out the case for *Psycho II*, while conceding that 'none could excel the original story line of the first *Psycho*, its originality was virtually unparalleled at that time. We haven't quite found something as original. It's very hard to find . . . but we felt it wouldn't be honorable and dignified to make a sequel to *Psycho* unless we observed the rules of discretion and reserve that I think would be necessary to come up with. I really firmly believe that the violence in our film in no way keeps up with the commonplace that one is likely to see today. So we won't be measuring it against that. We were really measuring it against what we felt the demands of the violence in the story needed, and we realized that shooting in colour gave us perhaps an edge. But the light levels are very low. It's shot in a lovely gloom.'

'Lovely gloom' was an odd way of describing the not particularly distinguished colour photography, and if the violence observed more 'discretion and reserve' than other thrillers around in the early 80s, it still had its fair share: Lila Loomis (Vera Miles) meets her end with a carving knife shoved down her throat; the doctor (Robert Loggia) is stabbed through the chest before tumbling over the bannister; Norman Bates has the palms of his hands slashed by a knife, only to have them cut deeper when he tries to grab hold of the blade; and an elderly woman has her head bashed in with a shovel.

To open the film with the famous shower scene from Hitchcock's *Psycho* was audacious but self-defeating, because it is the best directed sequence in the entire picture.

'We needed something to enable us to refer to the first film. That's why we started with the bold move of the shower scene. Everything was replicated beautifully. Lots of the members of the crew were the original members. There were many familiar faces on the set. The house had been moved to an even more lonely bluff. The producer had been first assistant. I hadn't seen Vera Miles for twenty-three years. It was even more agreeable than the first time. I think we were both ready for it. We just fell into each other's arms.'

Certainly the Gothic house on the hill, with its musty, old-fashioned rooms and furniture is all there – the stuffed birds, the jagged stairway leading down to the decrepit motel. Tom Holland's screenplay for *Psycho II*, 'based on characters created by Robert Bloch', took the story forward twenty-two years, to the day Bates is released from the mental hospital. He ill-advisedly returns to live in the same house of murder, where 'memories are more likely to reoccur'. He is soon getting notes and telephone calls for his 'dead' mother, and sees her from time to time, first in flashback, in which he catches a glimpse of himself as a child (eight-year-old Osgood Perkins, making his screen debut).

Tony, who claimed not to have seen *Psycho* for many years, and purposely avoided watching it while preparing for the role, is convincing as a rehabilitated early middle-aged Norman Bates. At first, Tony plays Norman as ill-at-ease as much in his clothes as in his body. He stammers on the word 'cutlery', and cannot say 'bathroom', when he invites a young girl (Meg Tilly) to stay. She is actually Mary Loomis, the daughter of Lila Loomis, the sister of Marion Crane, the shower victim. They are there to confuse Norman into imagining he has reverted to his crazy condition, so that he will be recommitted to the mental institution.

However, he tells Mary, grinning warmly, 'I don't kill people anymore, remember?'

He plays Mozart and Beethoven on the piano to perfection, and sometimes has the air of someone who has spent the last twenty-two years in Manhattan, rather than in a mental institution. But, when he gradually becomes confused, and believes himself to be as unstable as previously, and that his mother is alive and killing, his voice takes on a deep monotone and his eyes stare unblinking at something beyond the material world. Blood spills out of the toilet bowl and shower plug, someone is spying on Mary undressing, an old woman is seen in the house.

The often cleverly contrived plot twists and turns itself into a hernia, and then haemorrhages towards the end when it moves into a grotesque caricature of the original. At the coda, Mother's voice is heard saying, 'Remember Norman, I'm the only one who loves you, only your mother truly loves you.'

The sign is switched on again with a buzz – Bates Motel: Vacancies. In other words, it is open for business for two further scenarios. The fact that Norman Bates is exculpated from four murders committed during the course of the film, and he seems to get away with another, implies that the makers were looking towards the possibility of a third *Psycho*. The last iconographical shot is of

Family Portrait – Berry and Anthony with Osgood and Elvis (Sygma).

Norman in silhouette standing outside the house at the top of the steps, looking up at a lowering sky.

For *Psycho II*, Tony really put himself on the line. He did more publicity for the film than he had ever done. Concurrent with its opening in Europe, he went on the grand tour, going to Italy, France and England. On 3 August 1983, Tony was interviewed by British film critic Ian Johnstone on the stage of the National Film Theatre in London. Before the interview, extracts from *Psycho* were shown. Tony, at the back of the cinema, sat laughing loudly during the shower scene. He later explained, 'Hitchcock called *Psycho* a comedy. Richard Franklin said he didn't know what Hitchcock meant by that statement until he had finished editing and previewing *Psycho II* to an unsuspecting audience, and the amount of agreeable and vociferous laughter was extraordinary. Just as it was when *Psycho* was shown.'

Because of the vast number of interviews he had given over the previous few weeks and on the same day, and his customary grass puffing, Tony found it difficult to remember which anecdotes he had related or not to the NFT audience. As he started a story, which he had told in exact detail many many times before, he stopped for reassurance that he was not repeating himself. When told he was not, he became plainly disoriented, though he managed to emerge through the haze as charming, enlightening and amusing. Johnstone, however, felt Tony was holding back a bit, because 'he had had trouble with his sexual identity.'

As Tony was there principally to plug *Psycho II*, Johnstone had to use sleight of hand because 'no-one really liked the film,' and also because an interview in *People* magazine had appeared two months previously in which Tony had revealed more about his private life than ever before. Johnstone trod warily when referring to the *People* article.

'There's an article in *People* magazine which implies [a few blushes from those in the know] that . . . Brigitte Bardot, Ava Gardner, Jane Fonda and Ingrid Bergman at various times tried to seduce you. Would you like to tell us about that?'

'If you like. It was one of the few things I resented in that *People* magazine piece because I was describing to the writer [Brad Darrach], who is a charming fellow by the way, the sadness and the inconvenience and awkwardness of an actor who would perhaps be able to inveigle a beautiful actress into an affair or into an entanglement of some kind. I was describing myself. And the author chose to put my reflections into the minds of the actresses and I didn't think that was too classy. I have to refute that statement that was printed in that magazine. In fact, he actually quoted me as saying that Ingrid Bergman would have welcomed an affair with me and frankly I don't know how I could have possibly have known that unless the lady and I were actually having one. We didn't discuss it and I thought it was an impetuous remark and it certainly wasn't a quotation of mine.'

Andy Warhol in a diary entry, after reading the magazine article, wrote: 'I love seeing the new *People* magazine with Tony Perkins on the cover, and it talked about him being gay, as if it were all in the past. Isn't it funny? And it talked about Brigitte Bardot and Ingrid Bergman and Jane Fonda trying to make him. Left out Tab Hunter and Chris Makos . . .'

A few days previously, Warhol noted: 'And Chris [Makos] said that he visited Tony Perkins and Berry. I guess *Psycho II* will make a lot of money this summer. He said that when Berry went into the other room Tony started pointing to Chris's crotch and saying, "I'd like to see you," and all Chris could say was, "All right, Norman." I never really liked Tony because he treated me badly once when he was with Tab Hunter.'

Leaving aside the feline nature of Warhol's jottings, Tony could not have been expected to throw off his old life and friends on the instant he became a family man. Of course he had curtailed his gay activities, and his circle of friends had contracted, but being a loving husband and father, which nobody has any doubts about, did not completely quench his sexual nature.

30

JUDGEMENT DAYS

'How can any man be called guilty?' – Joseph K. in *The Trial* (1962)

Tony's re-embracing of Norman Bates set him on a downward spiral or thorny psycho path to the inner regions of video hell. The debased version of Bates and his variants would now take over Tony's screen persona almost entirely – a depraved character who would be completely at home in the lurid world of Ken Russell, the British 'adult terrible'.

In Russell's *Crimes of Passion*, Tony, as the bespectacled Reverend Peter Shayne, is first seen twitching and reciting from the scriptures, while peering through a hatch at a nude woman gyrating to music. ('I'm a kind of voyeur in this film – which, naturally, is far from my own personality.') After getting his vicarious sexual kicks, he goes out into the street and fulminates against the sinners of the world.

'They fuck, they shit and they piss like the scum they are,' he shrieks, curiously attacking a set of natural functions unrelated to morality.

The prurient priest then moves through the sordid red neon-light district salivating salvation, his particular mission being to save a blonde hooker (Kathleen Turner). When confronting her for the first time, he asks if she knows who he is.

'I never forget a face especially when I've sat on it,' she tells him. 'The last Reverend who tried to reform me, I chased him all around the church until I caught him by the organ.'

She is actually Joanna, a smart brunette sportswear designer by day and blonde-wigged China Blue, catering to men's sexual fantasies, by night – the reverse situation of Luis Buñuel's incomparably superior *Belle de Jour*.

'This is a fantasy business, Reverend. You can have any truth you want,' she says, a reasonable comment on American-made films like this.

The Reverend, who 'makes up in diction what he lacks in dick', and who would naturally assume the missionary position, carries around with him a nasty phallic-looking ice pick, and a large bag full of rubber devices. For his torture and delight, Joanna/China dresses as a nun and sings 'Onward Christian Soldiers', while bouncing on the bed.

'What are you going to do? Fuck someone to death?'

'Only with the right woman.'

But any attempt at off-beat scatological humour or satire on sexual mores goes down the toilet with the heavy-handed Russell pulling the chain. With the psychology of the woman's double life left unexplored, the scenario introduces an opaque notion that the Reverend is Joanna/China Blue's alter ego.

'If you're a minister, I'm Snow White . . . Who are you? You're not a reverend. Who are you?'

'I'm you,' he says.

At the dénouement, he threatens her with the ice pick, pinning her to a drawing board. She spits in his face and he swallows it.

After dementedly singing 'Get Happy' at the piano (one of Tony's most flagrant misuses of his singing talent), he stabs her in the back with the ice pick. But for those who suspect that the casting of Tony in films at this period was contingent on his doing his debased Bates imitation, it would come as no surprise that the murderer is in fact the victim. The reverend has disguised himself in China Blue's blonde wig and dress. So the transference tranvestite trick is played on audiences once more by the master/mistress of the split personality.

Variety called Tony's role as the Rev. Peter Shayne a 'homicidal wacko who would like to be like China Blue if only he had the right hormones'.

According to Tony, *Crimes of Passion* was done 'very sensitively, very erotically, very straightforwardly, and the thing I like about the film, it doesn't stare at its sexual subjects. It glances, but you don't feel that they're kind of getting a cheap thrill out of it. The lens is not . . . licking its lips . . . It's observing the scenes, but it's not wallowing in it.'

The Motion Picture Association of America ratings board disagreed and threatened it with an X-rating, which persuaded Russell to edit the film to an R-rating. Later he concluded, 'It was terrible . . . It was just dreadful. Thank God they released it in a complete version on video.' But when it was shown in movie theatres, few people wanted to see the bowdlerized version.

Brian Sandler, who produced and wrote *Crimes of Passion*, cast Tony after he had seen him in *Equus*.

'I hadn't thought of the demonic characters. I thought of him more as an intellectual actor, who could play the cerebral mind games with Kathleen Turner. But it was Tony who made the character more extreme than was written. Originally, I wrote him as a ladies' shoe salesman, who posed as a psychiatrist at night in order to pick up hookers. Tony suggested he be a man of the cloth rather than a shrink. The film was made at the height of the evangelical Christian movement, led by people like Jimmy Swaggart. Ken Russell was delighted with the switch and saw it as a way of attacking religious hypocrisy.'

At one point Tony came up with the idea that the Reverend should carry a monkey around on his shoulder. Russell was happy about the idea, but Sandler objected, considering the character was already way over the top. He was unconvinced even when Tony brought a monkey onto the set, and had test shots made of him with the animal, but the producer prevailed.

Ken Russell, in his autobiography *A British Picture*, wrote that Tony was 'a real prince of a man . . . Perkins turned out to be one of the most dedicated actors I've ever worked with and took his role more seriously than anyone I know, to the extent of taking it home to bed with him. Knowing that a minister of the gutter would inevitably sleep rough, Perkins kipped in his costume and even made and decorated his own props, including a small folding ladder he used as a sidewalk pulpit which he painstakingly covered in pictures of saints and angels and pornographic cutouts from girlie mags. Over the six weeks we worked on that non-union film with its endearing crew of drop-outs, druggies, has-beens and hope-to-bes, we struck up a close friendship, discussing everything from Mahler to my forthcoming marriage.'

There is a strange parallel story to *Crimes of Passion*. During the shooting, Ken Russell, who was about to get married a second time, decided that Tony would be the ideal man to bless the union. As the Reverend Peter Shayne was mere fiction, Tony wrote off to the Universal Life Church Inc. enclosing ten dollars (vide Russell) or twenty-five dollars (vide Perkins) with an application form. He immediately received by return a certificate proclaiming his ordination as a bona fide minister of the said church, with powers to solemnise births, marriages and deaths. According to

Russell, 'The diploma he received was blank. He was left to fill in his name personally. There's trust for you!'

In Tony's version, 'The people from this theological school came down to quiz me, but I think maybe they just wanted to meet Kathleen Turner.'

Whatever the truth, it resulted in Tony's getting the diploma and, dressed in shining white, actually marrying Ken and Vivian Russell on the *Queen Mary*.

'But was he really qualified for such a responsibility?' Ken Russell asked. 'Well he certainly knew Vivian and myself better than the priest who married Shirley and me knew either of us. And he was more than qualified to read the extracts from the works of Thomas Hardy and Wordsworth which made up the bulk of the ceremony. The remainder was worked out by the three of us together and contained no rash promises or dogmatic "I wills" that only saints and angels could live up to but less ambitious aspirations, mindful of human frailty, such as "I'll try."'

After a year, Tony's ordination ran out, and he never renewed it.

While Tony was spending a few months publicizing *Psycho II* around Europe, Yorkshire TV in England was conducting an experiment into Anglo-American co-operation, an attempt to hit the market on both sides of the Atlantic. Their first production would be called *The Glory Boys*, based on a thriller by Gerald Seymour, transmitted in three one-hour episodes. As it was essential that it had two American stars, what started as a small English production had to be slanted for the US market, and a lot of rewriting took place.

Rod Steiger, whose career was as much in the doldrums as Tony's, jumped at the chance of playing an Israeli nuclear scientist on a visit to London, who is the target of Palestinian terrorists. He was especially grateful because he had recently had a heart bypass operation, and was an insurance risk.

The second star part was more difficult to cast, because it was, ironically, that of a maverick English policeman referred to as 'Jimmy'. Although the director Mike Ferguson would have preferred Donald Sutherland, or a British actor such as John Thaw, he and the producers had to choose from a list of American actors available for the right price.

'When Tony's name came up, I wasn't going to say no,' remarked Ferguson. 'The idea of working with Steiger and Perkins appealed to me. But I insisted he play it English. I felt that enough was enough. To impose an American policeman into the Met would have been too unrealistic. Tony was happy to give it a go. He had a dialect coach, and he worked very hard on it. He told me after we had finished shooting that he had actually modelled his accent on mine, since I was the one who was going to be with him all the time we were shooting. I think he was moderately successful.'

Actually, Tony used quite an effective clipped British accent, only occasionally lapsing into American.

'We're all with ye,' he says at one point, his idea of cockney, perhaps.

The first time Tony met Ferguson, at breakfast at the Atheneum Hotel in London, he expressed his anxiety, not about the accent, but about not being able to post-synch all the dialogue. He said he had never expected the dialogue he spoke to appear on the screen, and was very surprised and nervous about that.

Tony had done mostly post-synching in his career, the most blatant example being in *The Trial*. Welles claimed that there wasn't one line of original track in the film, with the director himself having dubbed ten lines of Tony's dialogue, which he defies anybody to find.

'I hated dubbing until I did *The Trial*, then I realized the possibilities of it. Orson's theory, and it's one I subscribe to, is that the very least you can expect in dubbing is that it be as good as the original.'

Tony came to England alone, and told Ferguson that he felt guilty at not having written to his wife for several months. But he kept telling everyone how much he adored her and his two sons, and was always handing round pictures of them, and talking about them and his home. Tony, who was faithful to many of the people he worked with, would regularly send them Christmas cards with pictures of Berry and the kids on them as if to say, 'Remember me, the guy who sang "Never Will I Marry", and who everybody thought was gay?'

'What surprised me was that Steiger and Perkins didn't get on with each other,' commented Mike Ferguson. 'I would have thought that two American stars would have come close to each other, but they displayed a certain professional rivalry. They were playing all the Hollywood tricks. Once I got to know them they took direction, but at the beginning they would say things like, "I don't know what you're talking about . . . Show me that again." Steiger wrote some of his own lines, and would sometimes say, "I want a close-up here." Tony came from another angle. This vastly experienced actor said, "I want to learn, I want to get this right." He was always very charming to work with, and was never the prima donna. He knew what he was doing internally, but he had very little idea of what had gone into the camera. He was almost the first person to shoot and the last. He never wanted retakes or concerned himself with that side of it. He was very involved with what he was doing himself. He always talked about the character as "our Jimmy", that's what "our Jimmy" would do. He wanted to talk quietly about things. He kept the script with him all the time. "This is my Bible," he would say. "I take this to bed with me every night." He was enormously well prepared. I wish I'd had a chance to work with him on something to which he was better suited. But he was quite enjoying doing something that was totally inappropriate.'

Ferguson contrasted the two stars.

'Tony was very much a loner and kept a great deal to himself, while Steiger was gregarious. After the day's work, Rod would say "Where are we going to eat?" Tony ate his lunch with the crew. They liked him for being so co-operative. He integrated with them better than Steiger. They were both as highly-strung as the other. Rod was aggressive and tense; Tony withdrawn and tense. Though he was very sensitive and nervy, a kind of mischievousness and watchfulness lurked in the eyes. He seemed to be amused by almost everything. The look in *Psycho* when he's watching the car going down, appeared at various times during *The Glory Boys.* If you take away the sinister quality of Norman Bates, you have a human being that finds life difficult and funny as well.'

Part of Steiger's contract was that his lover Paula would be accommodated, so he had an enormous trailer – the biggest in the range, whereas Tony had the smallest.

'Why is it that R-Rod's got a queenbago but I've only g-got a m-minibago?' he protested.

Certainly in the star game that was being played between them, Tony lost hands down every time – in front of the camera and off. He was always complaining that Steiger was stepping on the ends of his lines, and was worried that Steiger was grabbing scenes from him. They kept each other at arm's length.

When he meets Steiger in the film, he says, 'I will be with you for most of your stay. I hope we get along.'

Luckily they did not have to play that many scenes together.

'They both came and whispered in my ears,' said Ferguson. 'Rod was saying, "That guy's on drugs, you'd better watch him."

Tony was indeed on amphetamines, which he swallowed just before a take to give him a brief high. When asked why he took them, he explained it was to improve his sexual prowess. However, he had asked the director's permission.

'Do you think it'll be a good idea?'

Ferguson did not object because 'the drugs produced a kind of nervous tension which Tony recognized as being his trademark; part of the package, part of what he was selling.'

Tony returned to the USA to spend Christmas 1983 in California with his family. On his return to Britain on Sunday 29 January, he was arrested and charged with drug possession at Heathrow. When he walked through the Nothing to Declare exit, he was stopped and searched. Traces of cannabis were found in a pipe and a small piece of paper impregnated with LSD was discovered in a bottle of vitamins. Yorkshire TV rolled out as many big guns as they could to get Tony off, but he was fined £100 by magistrates at Uxbridge court for trying to smuggle cannabis and LSD through customs. Giving his address as Brown's Hotel, Mayfair, Tony claimed to have forty pounds in cash and nineteen hundred dollars in travellers cheques. His earnings for 1981–1982 were given as three hundred and fifty thousand dollars.

Mr Michael Caplan for the defence said: 'Mr Perkins is a star of forty films and half a dozen Broadway productions and has given pleasure to millions of people throughout the world.'

He went on to explain that the rigours of the shooting of *The Glory Boys* had put the actor under immense pressure. The magistrate, Mr Bert Tyrell, told Tony, 'It is a pity you have spoilt your hitherto good character.'

This to Norman Bates!! After the hearing, Tony returned to the location during the shooting of a scene. When everyone looked around, he shrugged his shoulders and gave them a broad grin. He was ready to start work again.

Despite the drugs, Tony seldom touched alcohol and ate a fairly healthy diet. On the set, he would eat apples and cheese to keep himself going, which he recommended to others. Tony, who was constitutionally thin, was conscious of his figure. In one scene, when he was on a bed with a gun tucked inside his trouser belt, he was intrigued and proud that he could get it between the belt and the trousers so easily.

Tony's appearance in *The Glory Boys* is delayed until Part Two. Grey-haired and lined, but otherwise lean and healthy looking, the character is never without a cigarette and drinks heavily, usually from a flask in his pocket. The slightly seedy man in a raincoat and an old school tie is a security expert hired to protect Steiger and find those that threaten him. He drifts around on the periphery of the plot, bringing a welcome calm and humour to the hectic and serious proceedings, constantly smiling as at some private joke, and giving little winks and nods. He makes the character more complex and interesting than any of the others, while not being wholly likeable.

In the hospital in order to get information from the IRA man, he plays sadistically with his wound.

'I'm tired. You're dying. Your wog friend is dead.'

The 'terrorists' are, in fact, more sympathetic than the 'goodies'.

At the ironic finale, before lighting up again, he laughs spontaneously when he hears Steiger has died of a heart attack on the plane back to Israel. The role revealed the width of Tony's range when relieved momentarily of the psychopathic strait-jacket in which he was being confined.

31

WEIRD DIRECTIONS

'*The past is never really past. It stays with me all the time. . .*' – Norman Bates in *Psycho III* (1986)

'People have asked the inevitable question, will there be a *Psycho III*, and I've come to the realization or I've been able to formulate it in my mind. It is a tragic story. It's a truly melancholy story, so perhaps it wouldn't be discreet or fair to disturb the ghosts there too often, and maybe it'll be a feeling like that will make *Psycho III* a very difficult thing for me to even think of.'

Thus did Tony tell the audience at the National Film Theatre in London in 1983. But *Psycho II* had done very well at the box-office, a success for an Anthony Perkins film unequalled since *Goodbye Again* twenty-two years previously. By stepping back into Norman Bates's skin, Tony had overcome, for the moment, his pretty poisonous effect on the takings of the films he had appeared in.

Although he had a percentage of the profits, according to Tony, 'I've never seen a dime out of *Psycho II* . . . Actually, I think it's astonishing . . . Now I'm more sympathetic to actors who ask for big bucks up front. They know they're never going to get it any other way.'

Tony was never mercenary, or very good in business deals. When Universal asked him to appear in *Psycho III*, he offered them more for their money.

'We were discussing financial terms for the acting and I said, "By the way, I'll throw the directing in for free. You can have me for X dollars as an actor or as a director and actor for the same amount. There are too many meetings, too many deals, too many pages in a contract in the movie business. I thought, "This is easy. You can put it in one sentence." '

So Tony embarked on his first film as director, emulating Orson Welles by appearing in front of, as well as behind the camera. He sent a card to Chabrol saying, 'I will try to place Psycho III between Psycho I and II.' In fact, Tony had had a hankering to direct a film ever since the late sixties, when he started directing plays. For years, he had the habit of asking directors if he could direct himself in one shot, and most of them obliged.

Norman Bates, having just killed his real mother in *Psycho II*, is still running The Bates Motel, where he has installed an ice machine. Along comes a handsome guitar-strumming drifter (Jeff Fahey), whom he takes on as assistant and handy man; a disturbed young runaway nun (Diana Scarwid), who has lost her faith; and a reporter (Roberta Maxwell), doing a story on insanity defences in murder cases. The locals all consider Norman completely rehabilitated, but his 'mother' is still murderously active.

One girl is stabbed in a phone booth – the hanging mouthpiece on the receiver replacing Janet Leigh's eye – another has her throat slit while sitting on the toilet. At first, she gives a slight shriek because she had forgotten to put the seat down, one of several clever touches in Tony's direction. He has 'mother' find time

First-time director Anthony Perkins on the set of *Psycho III* in a photo taken by his wife, 1985 (Photofest)

to straighten a picture on the stairs, while pursuing a victim, and makes macabrely comic use of the ice machine, in which a corpse is buried. After extracting the rigid body from the ice, with difficulty, Norman kisses the frozen girl – a potent emblem of frigidity and the most emphatic necrophiliac moment in the *Psycho* cycle.

For the first time, Norman is allowed to have a reciprocal affectionate and erotic relationship with a woman. He and the runaway nun go out to dinner, dance intimately, kiss and almost have sex. She, Maureen Coyle, has the same initials as Marion Crane (Janet Leigh), whom she is supposed to resemble. But with her close-cropped blonde hair, she bears a physical likeness to Tony's own wife, Berry. She is killed accidentally by falling backwards down the stairs and being stabbed in the back by a cupid's arrow – an audacious visual pun.

With the help of excellent camerawork by Bruce Surtees, the director-star, though no Luis Buñuel, utilizes his off-beat humour and strong sense of the surreal. While he is occupied in his ornithological taxidermy, he sees a paper bag move along the table (it actually contains a small bird trying to get out) and he imagines he is sewing up a severed hand. After Maureen has cut her wrists, and while she is lying in a literal blood bath, she sees 'mother' as the Virgin Mary, and the knife as a shining crucifix. After her death, a shrine is created for her by filling the parlour with candles – pictorially not dissimilar to the multiple candle-lit scenes in *The Trial.* When Norman escapes from a car that has gone down in the swamp, he utters a 'loud' silent subterranean scream.

Far superior to *Psycho II*, which took itself more seriously, it probably failed to attract as many people because it came too soon after the earlier film – familiarity with the locale and theme bred contempt – or because it veered somewhat jerkily from parody to melodrama, and was too self-allusory.

Norman jokes with Maureen in hospital after her suicide attempt in the bathroom of Cabin One.

'I can't have that sort of thing going on in my motel. It gives the place a bad name.'

'I'm sorry about the mess,' Maureen comments.

'I've seen worse,' replies Norman.

When the drifter takes on the job, he tells Norman, 'I won't be staying long.'

Woody Woodpecker, on television, is seen hitting someone over the head with a shovel (like Norman's killing at the end of *Psycho II*), and when the cartoon character delivers his celebrated mocking laugh, Norman imagines it to be his mother.

While remaining within the confines of the horror picture, making use of the obligatory significant close-ups, and eerie pans, Tony revealed himself to be a more than competent tyro film director. At the climax, when Norman destroys his mother's corpse and is taken back to the mental institution, it seemed as though a final line was being drawn under the *Psycho* story, and that Tony could move into different territory. But as Norman says, 'The past is never really past – it stays with me all the time and no matter how hard I try, I can't really escape. It's always there throbbing inside you, colouring your perceptions of the world and sometimes controlling them.'

Tony himself was unhappy with how *Psycho III* turned out. He later admitted, in a far too self-deprecatory manner, that he thought the film was 'a very amateurish job,' and was 'discouraged by the enormous amount of opportunities missed.'

'It was really an excellent script, but for some reason the studio [Universal] was far more interested in getting the picture on time than it was in examining the quality of the rushes. So I was unable to get anyone to confer with me and tell me that I might be doing certain things differently or better. I was frustrated. I was very short of technical information. Very short of the technique of directing. I figured people would help me with that. They were willing to help if I said what shall we do now, but no-one came up with ideas and with things that were truly nuts and bolts. I remember on *Friendly Persuasion*, on days when Wyler had a thorny problem, he called in his idea men. He would install his idea men in his trailer and they would pepper Wyler's imagination with ideas. I didn't have any idea men. I begged for people to come and tell me that what I was doing wasn't good enough. I couldn't get anyone to do that.'

In order to publicize his first directorial achievement, Tony did the grand tour again. In the autumn of 1986, he was invited to the Ghent Festival of Film Fantastique, where he was interviewed by Patrick Duynslaegher, a Belgian film critic. Once again, freed from what he perceived was the restrictive atmosphere of America, and at a distance from the responsible family man, Tony once again played the bad boy in Europe.

First, he kept interrupting the interview by demanding that a hairdresser be called immediately to cut his hair.

'Why can't I have a haircut?' he inquired querulously of his minder, a man from Universal, who had once worked with Jimmy Stewart.

The man clapped his hands like a medieval courtier for a hairdresser to be brought to the king. After a time, while Tony fretted, a hairdresser was found.

'He was putting on an act. He seemed tense, temperamental and neurotic,' Duynslaeger recalled.

He persisted with his interview, noticing that Tony was defiantly wearing different coloured socks, just as James Dean had once done. After the haircut and the interview were over, Tony asked Duynslaeger if he knew Ghent, and which were the good places to go to, clubs, restaurants . . . The question hung in the air, and he left without waiting for the answer.

That evening, Duynslaeger and Brian Baxter, an English film historian, turned up at The Paradox, a smart gay bar and disco. In the narrow street, ostentatiously parked directly outside the club, was a vast black stretch limousine, totally unsuited to a small town like Ghent. It had been supplied to Tony, complete with chauffeur, by the organizers of the Festival. He was the biggest star in town and he had the biggest car. It was there for all to see in front of The Paradox.

According to Baxter, Tony, dressed in black, 'was standing downstairs in a typical huddled Perkins style, against a wall. You could see that he felt vulnerable, and always had his back in a corner so that nobody could get behind him or touch him. He was with this American guy. They didn't speak to anyone and left together.'

Echoing the story of Tony locking himself in the closet over a make-up man during the photo call on *Murder On The Orient Express*, a rumour circulated from the Festival press office that Tony fancied the young chauffeur of the car, and that he had not only asked for that particular car to be provided, but for the driver to be sent to his hotel room. The man refused, and the Festival organizers were terribly embarrassed about the whole affair.

Back in the USA, Tony was transformed back into Ken Russell's 'Real prince of a man'. An example of his generosity is cited by Ben Bagley. The record producer owed Tony money for his recordings, but Tony told Bagley not to worry. He then presented Bagley with an amethyst ring set in gold which he had got the jeweller to make from his own design.

Tony also agreed to record a number for a new Ben Bagley compilation, entitled Contemporary Broadway Revisited. It was 'All My Friends Have Gone To California', from an unproduced show by John Kander and Fred Ebb, the authors of *Cabaret.* The lyrics conjure up a picture of a 'midnight cowboy' hustling for money in New York to get enough to join his friends in Los Angeles, the penultimate line giving it a gay slant.

> They're surfing up at Malibu I know,
> Or walking down the Strip to see what gives.
> They're lining up to see a TV show,
> Or driving by where John Travolta lives.
> So, mister can you help me on my way?
> I gotta score me fifty bucks a day.
> I'm willing to do anything you say.
> All my friends have gone to California.

The fifty-three-year-old Tony sings it sexily with a Western twang, in a voice that sounds exactly like a street kid. It was the last record he made.

After the cool reception of *Psycho III*, Tony moved back in time to 18th-century France with the role of Talleyrand in a three-part TV movie called *Napoleon and Josephine: A Love Story*, broadcast on ABC in November 1987. Armand Assante and Jacqueline Bisset played the title roles. As a variation on his Inspector Javert, with his deliberate diction, Tony played the wily opportunistic French diplomat who claims that his frequent changes of policy were dictated by the interests of France; similar to Tony justifying his choice of roles, dictated by the interests of his family.

One of these roles was as replacement for an ill Roddy McDowall (the voice of Vincent the cute robot in *The Black Hole*) in *Destroyer.* It gave Tony the chance to place his experience as a film director at the services of the role of a director of a film within a film, a sexploitative women's prison picture called 'Death House Dolls'.

Tony is the highly-strung, sarcastic director, charming only as long as it serves his purposes, and saddled with a laid-back crew half his age. He instals a live current into the electric chair for the female star's death scene, so she will act more realistically. Naturally, she is shocked, both literally and figuratively, and storms off the set.

'All right. That's lunch. Everybody back in an hour. We'll do the shower scene.'

This self-referential remark was meant to provoke knowing laughter among the sparse audiences that saw it. 'The shower scene' in this instance, concerned a brawl among naked girls in the prison shower.

In September 1988, Laura Kay Palmer contacted Tony to co-operate with her on her book *Osgood and Tony Perkins.* His reply was a typically evasive but courteous one, the gist being that he had no desire to see a book on his career and, therefore, could not assist her in any way.

Leaving aside some of the idiosyncratic syntax, semantics, punctuation and vocabulary, the calligraphy was equally singular. The letter was submitted to the scrutiny of the British graphologist Sheila Davidson, without her being supplied with any information whatsoever about the anonymous writer, nor even the person's gender. Below is Davidson's analysis, which will only have significance if taken on trust by the reader:

> Analysis on the writing of A. P. Sex and age unknown. This person is extremely disturbed, neurotic and schizophrenic. There are numerous signs of dishonesty. He has gross problems with his sexuality. I specifically say *he* because I feel that it is a man. There are many signs of religious leanings; it may be that he was brought up in a strict religious family or that he turned to religion. I think this is a very disturbed and sad person. On

the one hand, he wants to be friendly and sociable and reach out to others, but then he withdraws within himself. Money and possessions are very important to him and he will be very thrifty. His most serious problem is his sexuality. There are many signs of homosexuality, but he fights it all the time and denies his feelings. This causes him enormous anguish. His whole life has been one long fight against his homosexuality. It is probably in this that he is so dishonest. He feels very insecure. However, in spite of the chaotic turbulence in his mind, he is able to carry out a task or job through till the end. He is articulate and intelligent, is artistic and has an appreciation of music. He could be quite sadistic.

Whatever the use of such an exercise as another piece in the biographical jigsaw – and sceptics might well argue against its validity – the eerie accuracy of the analysis connotes that Tony's handwriting obviously disclosed a great deal of his psychology and personality to this particular expert. But the graphologist picking her way through the undergrowth of tangled alphabetic symbols, has only brought into the clearing what is already known, except for one detail that seems to ring a false note. 'There are signs of religious leanings,' she writes. In 1988, despite Tony's quest for meaning, he had never manifested a strong religious belief. However, the handwriting acted as a crystal ball, because circumstances would soon intensify those quiescent feelings, unconventional as they would be.

Playing once more on his ghoulish renown, Tony starred in *The Ghost Writer*, which started off as a pilot for a TV sitcom and crash landed. Performed in front of a live audience, it had Tony spoofing his Norman Bates persona, in which he played an author of horror stories who brings his work home with him in more ways than one.

Osgood Perkins II, aged nineteen, in 1993 (Sygma).

In reality, Tony tried to leave his work at the studios when he got home. In spite, or because, of his reputation, both on screen and off, he was determined to make sure that his sons were brought up in as natural a way as possible. Osgood II described the manner in which they lived.

'For us, Anthony Perkins was, in the first place, our father. When other children met us for the first time they were a bit impressed, but it didn't last because we immediately set things straight. My father was an actor, that was his profession. He could have had a different one and that would have changed nothing in our relationship with each other. He didn't see himself as a star and, what is more, I'm not sure he knew that he was a star. That term of reference didn't exist in our home. We really lived in a very simple fashion. Dinners at home, even with the most famous people, were always dinners with friends, never Hollywood events. We attended perfectly normal schools, not those private courses for spoilt rich brats. Our friends were not necessarily the children of celebrities. My father came to cheer us on during football games like the fathers of all our pals. I believe that, indeed, we didn't really much know what it meant to be the sons of Anthony Perkins.'

Osgood – forthright, intelligent and balanced – went on to attend the University of Southern California, taking courses in film-making techniques, before becoming assistant to Mike Nichols on *Wolf* and continued the Perkins acting dynasty by appearing in Fred Schepisi's *Six Degrees of Separation.*

For Tony's second attempt at film directing – aside from playing a director in *Destroyer* – he decided not to act at the same time. He chose a script by Pat Proft called *Lucky Stiff*, about an overweight chump (Joe Alaskey), who has always been unlucky in love. Jilted by his bride-to-be and staying at a ski lodge for singles, he meets a ravishing girl who takes an interest in him. Too good to be true. Cynthia (Donna Dixon) is a member of a clandestine incestuous group of cannibals, and her taste for fat men is purely culinary.

With his already proven ability to create bizarre effects and offbeat gags, Tony succeeded to a certain degree in creating a light comedy out of the gruesome elements, again evidence that he had misplaced his forte. As an actor, no matter how grisly the content of his films, Tony always tempered them with wry humour, and was doing the same as a director. In the end, however, though entertaining, this sort of darkly comic subject had been done campier and with more individual flair before by directors such as Paul Bartel and John Waters. In retrospect, as with *Psycho III*, Tony was less than happy with the results.

'My first attempt at directing *Psycho III* was so discouraging that I thought I'm going to try this again. I again came up short. Everyone did everything I asked. It was my fault. I exuded such an air of confidence and articulateness [sic] and enthusiasm, that they thought I was doing it right.'

Before completion of *Lucky Stiff*, Tony declared his aims thus: 'Cannibalism and incest are taboo subjects. To combine them with violent attitudes was an inescapable no. I not only wanted to mute and remove the violence; I really wanted to play down these subjects. I think that if there's a trend in horror films right now, it's that the gross-out film has had it. They went too far. There's a numbing quotient that comes in when people can sit and watch decapitations while chewing popcorn in a way they are unmoved. There's something definitely wrong. I'm hoping the more suggestive elements of the genre will be on the rise in the next decade and the explicit violence and horror will be on the wane.'

Ironic as the statement appears when spoken by the man with

more blood (or ketchup) on his hands than most, and who was to follow *Lucky Stiff* with more 'explicit violence and horror', therein lies an expression of Tony's genuine volition. But no matter how much he did protest, he was to be led once more down the ghastly path.

32

DR PERKINS AND MR BATES

'You and I really fucked each other's lives up real good' – Neil Curry in *Remember My Name* (1978)

It had to come. The specialist in schizophrenic roles took on the most famous split personality in literature. Filmed mostly in Hungary, but also in Wales, *Edge of Sanity* was another version of the classic *Dr Jekyll and Mr Hyde* story, although Robert Louis Stevenson remained unacknowledged in the credits and unrespected in the screenplay. It turned out to be a tawdry slasher picture which attempted to cash in on 1988's Jack the Ripper centenary.

According to this travesty, Dr Jekyll is not only Mr Hyde but Jack the Ripper as well. The good doctor has become transformed into Mr Hyde after inhaling the fumes from a substance, mixed with cocaine, he has been using on a lab monkey. It was Tony's suggestion that they use cocaine in order to give the double character a contemporary twist, although opium would have been more accurate for the epoch.

In any case, Tony gave the sort of scenery-eating performance that makes it difficult to judge how much was due to real cocaine on the set, and how much to just plain ham acting. Tony played the baser alter ego with demented facial expressions rather than relying on heavy make-up. Glynis Barber (from TV's *Dempsey and Makepeace*) was cast as Mrs Jekyll who accompanies Mr Hyde on some of his debauched jaunts around Victorian London, but, mainly, he stalks the dark streets and lurid brothels alone in search of sensual pleasure and potential victims.

Tony must have known what he was getting into, because the previous credits of the producer Edward Simons had been *The Stud*, *The Bitch* and *Howling III*, and the director, Gerard Kikoine, had just graduated from porn pics, both soft and hard core, and still retained old predilections, dwelling lasciviously on kinky sex scenes.

The original title of the movie was *Dr Jekyll and Mr Hyde: A Journey into Fear*, disregarding the fact that Orson Welles had once made a picture called *Journey into Fear*. Not only was the title changed, but major cuts were made in the screenplay and some scenes were toned down. It still contained flagellation, drug-induced hallucinations, excessive violence, and prostitutes dressed as nuns (a familiar habit from *Crimes of Passion*) and wearing fetishistic underwear.

But, as diligent as ever, Tony approached the role with the professionalism many colleagues have noted over the years.

'I got them to find me a theatre that wasn't being used in downtown Budapest. I would rehearse by myself, trying to fill the theatre with a performance. I spent a couple of days there doing the show as if it were a play. Then I did the same thing in a very small room, even if it were a walk-in closet. I would perform it as if the doorknob were the lens.'

Some of the exteriors were to be shot in Wales, and Tony, after a short visit back to the United States, returned to Great Britain in June 1989, only to find himself once again charged with drug possession, as he had been five years earlier. Yet nobody would have known that he had got cannabis into Wales had it not been for a strange coincidence.

Tony, who had grown the cannabis at his Los Angeles home, thought to avoid the customs by posting it to the hotel in Cardiff where he was due to stay. But in a severe case of mistiming, or just underestimating the efficiency of the postal service, the package arrived five days before he did. It was opened in error by another Mr Perkins who was staying at the same hotel, and he passed it on to the police. This echoes the plot of Tony's last feature, *A Demon in My View*, when he is convinced his namesake is interfering with his post. They were ready and waiting for the actor when he arrived at the hotel. Tony pleaded guilty to evading a duty charge, and was fined two hundred pounds by Cardiff magistrates for smuggling 1.32 grammes of cannabis. The court heard how he intended to use the drug for his own use only to help him relax while filming in South Wales. The cannabis was worth only four pounds and fifty pence and would never have made more than six cigarettes.

'He used cannabis infrequently and always discreetly,' pleaded his solicitor.

Also filmed in Budapest was a TV movie called *Daughter of Darkness*, although the story took place in Bucharest. Naturally, being set in Romania, it had to be about vampires.

Cathy Thatcher (Mia Sara) arrives in Bucharest from Chicago on 11 August 1989 on a quest for her Romanian father who she has not seen for twenty years, just after her American mother has died. She meets a glass-blower called Anton (Tony Perkins) who used to know her father but says he was killed in a car accident in 1966. But it turns out that Anton is in fact her father, Constantin Cyprian, Prince of Transylvania and a vampire to boot.

His fellow blood-suckers, who could have stepped from the pages of Charles Addams, kidnap Cathy and take her to the castle where they gather. They keep plasma in a fridge, which is stolen from the hospital by a woman in love with a young man who is one of the undead. However, he wishes to mate with Cathy and turn her into a vampire. Her father, however, helps her escape, and is therefore subjected to torture by his nocturnal associates. They leave him tied up in a cellar where the sun can get to him. Half his face gets burned before he is rescued by his daughter and a young American diplomat.

There are attempts at humour and an analogy with Ceausescu's regime – the movie manages to recreate the atmosphere of a police state, but the film relies more on stock shocks. Tony, complete with Bela Lugosi black eyebrows and thick accent, did the best he could in the ludicrous circumstances, bringing a certain anguish and poignancy to the character.

'We can't change what we are,' he shouts to the other vampires, and explains to his daughter about the marriage to her mother, before bidding her a tender farewell.

'My love for her was always at war with my real nature. I could never be with her when the hunger [for blood] was upon me.'

At this period of his career, it seemed that Norman Bates seeped into everything he did. There is a scene in which Cathy digs up her father's grave only to find the skeleton of a woman, who, in as much as skeletons differ, is the image of Mrs Bates.

Daughter of Darkness was followed by *I'm Dangerous Tonight*, another supernatural TV drama, this time closer to home. It was directed fairly competently by Tobe Hooper, he of *The Texas Chainsaw Massacre*.

Tony played the seemingly benign Professor Gordon

Buchanan, who is giving a lecture at the department of psychology on animism, the power of inanimate objects to inhabit humans with certain forces outside themselves.

Amy (Madchen Amick), one of his students, buys a trunk at a flea market for use in a college production of *Romeo and Juliet.* In the trunk, however, is a blood-red Aztec sacrificial robe that brings out homicidal tendencies in everyone who touches it, or releases sexual repression.

After Amy has made it into a dress, havoc is wrought. One woman who works at the morgue gets it off a corpse and wears it. Her name is Wanda Thatcher. (Was it merely a coincidence or a political in-joke that in two of Tony's TV movies in a row, there are leading female characters called Thatcher?) Another woman in the red dress gets a cord and strangles her strong football-playing boyfriend while he is . . . wait for it . . . taking a shower. Then she takes a blade and cuts his throat.

Tony's character has nothing to do with the shower murder, but he is keen to get his hands on the robe for some unstated reason. Probably for the power it may give him. When he comes wandering out of the mist with an evil-looking black dog, one can guess that he has hidden desires. But as he explains to Amy, some people who wear the garment might be 'torn between their own natural decency and the forces of the id.'

The last scene has Tony digging up a grave (as he had done in *Psycho II* and *Daughter of Darkness*) in which the shredded robe has been thrown. What he is going to do with it, is anybody's guess.

He had previously quoted Nietzsche (which he pronounces Nietchie): 'Whoever fights monsters should take care that in the process he does not become a monster and that when you look long into an abyss, the abyss also looks into you.'

Ignoring the above prescription, Tony gave in to the blandishments of his monster doppelganger. Although there was a finality about *Psycho III*, and it was also a literal demonstration of diminishing returns at the box-office, Norman Bates refused to be put away for ever, never to reappear in public again.

Psycho IV could have been more accurately titled *Psycho Minus I*, because it is, in the vernacular, a prequel. It sets out to investigate, in a more explicit manner, Norman's childhood and adolescence. Tony portrayed Norman Bates in 1990 (then fifty-eight years old), telling his story to a radio call-in show host (C. C. H. Pounder) while on parole. At the same time, Henry Thomas (*ET*'s buddy eight years before) played the teenage Norman rather blankly, with none of the intensity or humour of the young Tony Perkins. Why Norman should want to reveal all to a radio host, when he must have told his story ad nauseum to psychiatrists over the years, and especially the latest one (Donna Mitchell), whom he has married, can only be explained by the film-makers' need for a more public and dramatic device than a patient on a couch.

Believing his homicidal nature to be genetic, Norman threatens to kill his wife because she is pregnant and he wants to prevent the birth of another monster like himself.

Directed by Mick Garris, and written by Joseph Stefano, the man who wrote the original *Psycho* screenplay thirty years previously, the film, by visualizing Norman's childhood traumas and his relationship with his mother (living), makes it much clearer how and why he became a killer.

A young and attractive Mrs Bates (Olivia Hussey) torments and, unknowingly, sexually arouses the boy. She gets him to massage her and climb into bed beside her, and yet is shocked when she finds a lingerie catalogue in his room, and when he gets an erection while they are romping on the floor together. As punishment, she puts him in a dress, smears lipstick on him, calls him

Norma, and locks him in a dark closet.

'I should have killed you in my womb. You sure as hell nearly killed me getting out of it,' she tells her son.

A short time later, when she takes up with a boorish bartender, Norman poisons them both with strychnine, causing them to take their time in dying painfully as in a Jacobean tragedy.

'How did you kill your mother?' the radio host asks.

'Slowly,' Norman replies.

From then on, young Norman starts on his serial killing spree in drag.

For those whose fascination with the Bates story is endless, the film entertainingly completes the jigsaw, though Laura Kay Palmer noted a number of errors: 'Norman was five years old, not six, as he says in *Psycho IV*. Mother's wig, brown here, was grey in all the previous pictures. Are we supposed to imagine that it turned grey from the stress of all those murders? Norman couldn't very well have spied on his mother and her new boyfriend in Cabin One. The Bates family didn't go into the motel business until Mother's lover talked her into building the motel. ("He could have talked her into anything.") When the couple was later found dead from strychnine poisoning in Mother's bed, the authorities closed the case as a murder-suicide. They would hardly have been fooled if Norman had dragged the bodies back to bed after tumbling all over the house with them . . .'

These details may be only of interest to *Psycho*-philes, but it does look like carelessness on the part of the so-called world authorities on Norman Bates – Stefano and Tony.

Psycho IV was the only one of the cycle with a happy ending. After almost knifing his wife, Norman agrees that they should have the child.

'I want to get rid of the past,' he declares, and proceeds to burn down the old house and all the ghosts within it and himself. How

ANTHONY PERKINS INCOGNITO (CHRISTOPHER MAKOS).

ineffably sad then that Tony had so little time to enjoy his liberation from Norman Bates. 'I'm free!' are his last words.

However, the ominous cry of a baby is heard over the end titles as an open invitation for someone, ten or twenty years hence, to follow the fate of Norman Bates's child in further *Psychos* stretching to eternity.

Tony was in Brussels in June 1992 for the Festival de Fantastiques to introduce a number of his films. He looked very ill, but he made a short, humorous speech, his words only slightly slurred. Among the films shown was his last feature, *A Demon in My View.* The film was a pitiable illustration of the 'eternal return' of Norman Bates. A German production set in London, it was based on a crime novel by Ruth Rendell about . . . a mother-obsessed serial killer with a doppelganger. How predictable of the producers to think of Tony, and like an alcoholic with demon drink put before him, he involuntarily accepted.

'I immediately thought that Anthony Perkins was the only actor who could bring a sense of a man hiding from his past, which he cannot come to terms with,' commented Petra Haffter, the director, whose second feature this was.

Tony played Arthur Johnson, a bachelor who seems to live an irreproachable life. He doesn't hang around pubs, nor does he get involved with women. But he gets his kicks, in his cellar, by making love to a mannequin dressed up as his mother. His life is disrupted, however, when his namesake, a young German student called Anton Johnson (Uwe Bohm) takes up residence in the same apartment house. Arthur believes Anton is intercepting his mail and is spying on him. Things come to a nasty head when Anton gives Arthur's mannequin away to a group of kids for a Guy Fawkes bonfire.

In this sluggishly directed film, shot in Hamburg (interiors) and

London (exteriors), Tony, skinny and spikey, with a brogue-tinged English accent, goes through the motions, struggling manfully to uncover the black abyss in the character's soul. Was this the note on which Tony's film career would end?

Unhappily the agony was prolonged, at least for erstwhile admirers of the talented actor, when there followed *In The Deep Woods*. Made for television, it has a conscious though tenuous connection with the Stephen Sondheim musical *Into The Woods*. But whereas the musical attempted to find Freud in nursery rhymes, the film used nursery rhymes (superficially) to explain the psychopathic acts of a serial killer. Apart from the inane psychological denouement, even more simplistic than in *Psycho*, it has a reasonably ingenious whodunnit plot, with enough red herrings to stock a fish market. But it was directed by numbers (by Charles Correll), using all the cliches of the genre – a subjective camera following a victim; lone women in empty, dark streets and car parks, quirky policemen etc.

Who is the serial killer who only murders successful young 'career women' in their early thirties in the woods? The killer is described as a sociopath – 'a person who does bad things but doesn't feel bad about it,' unlike Norman Bates. Tony, looking rather tired and listless, and more cadaverous than ever, yet still a disturbing, watchable presence, and wearing the same raincoat throughout, pursues children's book author and designer Rosanna Arquette wherever she goes. If he's the killer then he is an extremely indiscreet one.

He claims to be a private investigator, then the father of a murdered girl, and then the fiance of one of the victims. With pain in his eyes, and in a quavering voice, he pleads with Arquette, whose brother he believes to be the killer.

'Thirteen years I've been on this case. My whole life has been finding this guy. You've got to help me.'

At the end, Tony is exonerated of all suspicion and the real murderer, whom he had suspected, is exposed. The last shot of Tony's film career is a large close-up in which he gives a great sigh of relief; a sigh shared by many who had watched his vicissitudinous career since the sanguine days of his glowing youth.

'There was a sense of sadness about him. It was a cosmic melancholy; a disillusionment born of a search for something he could not seem to find but which pity and compassion had sent him questing for. His face was a fusion of the Tragic and Comic masks.'

Appropriate as this passage is when applied to Tony's last performances (and especially his final one), the above was written in 1938 to describe Osgood Perkins, his actor father, whom he did not know, and whose name lives on in his son.

Part VI

END GAME

'And now was acknowledged the presence of the Red Death. He had come like a thief in the night. And one by one dropped the revellers in the blood-bedewed halls of their revel, and died each in the despairing posture of his fall. And the life of the ebony clock went out with that of the last of the gay. And the flames of the tripods expired. And Darkness and Decay and the Red Death held illimitable dominion over all.' – Edgar Allan Poe (*The Masque of the Red Death*)

'What's happening to me is of no great importance, but I think it's representative of what's happening to a great many other people as well' – Joseph K. in *The Trial* (1962)

Someone must have been telling lies about Anthony P. In 1990, Tony went to see his doctor about Bell's palsy, a facial disorder which had been worrying him, especially as it could affect his acting. A few weeks later, emblazoned across the sensationalist pages of the *National Enquirer* was the headline 'Psycho Star Battling AIDS Virus'. In prurient prose was the news that Anthony Perkins, aka Norman Bates, had been found to be HIV positive. Although most readers of the *Enquirer* absorb a fair amount of salt while perusing its pages, and those people that matter take scant notice of the tabloid's scandal-mongering, that most meretricious of proverbs – 'there is no smoke without fire' – forces itself into the consciousness.

Tony and Berry were shocked to the core when they heard about the story from well-meaning friends, and they bought a copy of the *Enquirer* in order to read about something they knew nothing about as Tony had never even been tested for AIDS. The source of the article came from a laboratory technician at the doctor's surgery, who had apparently analyzed Tony's blood on the sly. Since he had become a movie star in 1956, Tony had conscientiously guarded the secret of his sexuality, but now he was being stigmatized for far worse a 'sin'.

By the mid-1980s, as more became known about AIDS, and the disease claimed an ever-increasing number of victims, it gradually dawned on homosexuals that the 'insane times' of the 1960s and 1970s were at an end. The party was over. Responsible members of what is called the gay community, spoke out against promiscuity. They were not killjoys, but they were saying that it was joy itself that was killing. When Rock Hudson became the first world-famous movie star known to have died of AIDS, a pall of fear crept over Hollywood. Actresses refused to play intimate scenes with actors who were known as, or even suspected of, being gay. Insurance was very difficult to come by. Truly, if it were revealed that an actor had AIDS, he would not only 'never eat lunch in this town again', but would never work there either.

Tony was determined to sue the *National Enquirer* for libel, when Berry suggested he have a blood test in order to make his case irrefutable. The world crumbled around them when the results came back. Tony had tested positive for HIV, the virus that causes AIDS.

'I was devastated,' recalled Berry. 'I couldn't believe it, and then I immediately thought, what about me? what about the children?'

The trauma was slightly allayed when both Berry and the boys tested negative. Then began the painful process of facing up to the situation. The title of the 1978 TV drama, *First You Cry*, in which Tony played the husband of a breast cancer victim, comes to mind. The heroine explains how she felt on hearing the news.

'First you cry, then you go crazy, and then you learn to accept it.'

But though he cried at first, Tony did not go crazy, nor did he learn to accept it. What Jean Genet said about homosexuality, could be applied to the AIDS victim.

'The sentence passed against thieves and assassins can be revoked. But not our sentence.'

Tony decided that he wanted the knowledge kept a secret even from his closest friends, which heaped a tremendous burden upon Berry.

'He simply never wanted anyone to know. He figured if anyone knew they'd never give him work again. He went twice to stay at the hospital, and once as an out-patient, and we went under another name. I literally asked myself, "Who am I today?" It was weird. You lose your sense of reality. You can't even be yourself in a situation like this. You're signing "Mrs Smith" [Mrs Bates?] or whatever. You think that this man has spent his entire life giving people so much pleasure in show business and this is his reward. He can't even be himself in the end.'

When former co-star Shirley MacLaine learnt much later of Tony's illness, she commented: 'This is so terrible that people who are sick have to keep it to themselves. And the suffering that goes on in isolation, that's as tragic as anything else.'

'Anthony Perkins's reticence to come forward while alive was unfortunate but understandable . . . I wouldn't reveal it either if I was in his shoes,' said Jeff Yarbrough, editor-in-chief of *The Advocate*, a gay and lesbian magazine. 'There's just no reason for a man like that to take that kind of a risk. What is it going to accomplish? Nothing. I think this role model stuff is nonsense.'

In contrast, Larry Kramer's dramatic alter ego says in his play *The Normal Heart*: 'Every gay man who refuses to come forward now and fight to save his own life is truly helping to kill the rest of us. How many of us have to die before you get scared off your ass and into action.'

'When Tony heard about Brad Davis [the actor who died of AIDS aged 41 on 8 September 1991], I'm sure he was concerned,' said Berry. 'I knew Brad well. We were acting at school together . . . It broke my heart that he [Tony] wasn't able to share it, this poor guy, and maybe he was right. Maybe they wouldn't have given him work.'

Hollywood Supports was set up by Richard Jennings to combat AIDS phobia and make HIV positive or HIV negative not a condition of film and TV employment. As a result, there is no blood test for cast insurance on most productions. Just five months before he died, Tony qualified for medical insurance to appear in his last movie, *In The Deep Woods*, although it was virtually impossible for AIDS carriers to get insurance.

'Apparently Tony passed the physical without qualifications and there was not one moment of time lost to any condition that he manifested on the set,' said Len Hill, one of the producers of *In the Deep Woods*, whose business partner Phil Mandelker died of AIDS in 1984.

The film took twelve to fourteen days to shoot in San Diego in April 1992, often requiring the team to work through the night.

'Tony worked without complaining or requesting special treatment or extra rest,' remarked Len Hill. 'The only comment he made to me was one night when we had hoped to complete a twelve-hour day by two a.m., and it looked like we'd be going fourteen hours and not finishing until four a.m., he said, "I must warn you. I lose my charm after three a.m."'

Despondent and racked with guilt – although he had never been promiscuous – Tony asked his friend Dennis Christopher to investigate doctors and therapies on his behalf. Christopher suggested he see Marianne Williamson, Hollywood's resident New Age guru of the moment.

An attractive, charismatic, thirty-nine-year-old Jewish ex-nightclub singer from Texas, she had captivated a glitzy clientele with her blend of new-time religion and self-help. Tommy Tune, Lesley Ann Warren, Cher and Roy Scheider were among those who went to her lectures; David Geffen sought her assistance, and she had officiated at the wedding of Elizabeth Taylor and Larry Fortensky. Mike Nichols, Stephen Sondheim and others were part of her Manhattan branch, but they became disaffected with what they saw as the increasingly dictatorial behaviour of the self-styled 'Bitch of God', and set up a rival organization called Friends In Deed.

Williamson's message was what is called 'spiritual psychotherapy', a mixture of meditation, prayer and heart-to-heart conversation, which, to the outsider, comes across as a platitudinous feel-good philosophy derived from the agony aunt pages of women's magazines and day-time TV chat shows.

Many of her followers were gay, not only because she had organized Angel Food, a service delivering three hundred hot meals a day to housebound AIDS patients in Los Angeles, but she preached love and forgiveness to those who felt excluded from established religions with their emphasis on sin and their intolerance of homosexuality.

'Your soul is not sick,' she would tell them. ('I knew a pain I can only call soul cancer' – Norman Bates in *Psycho III*.) She counselled those with 'life-challenging illnesses' – the words fatal and death were never uttered – and each week led ninety-minute support sessions for people with the AIDS virus, which she claimed would prolong the participants' lives.

Although Tony knew her well, and consulted her several times, he refused to be seen at the support sessions for fear he would lose work. While Berry tried to keep his weight up, and hoped for a cure, the whispers became louder, forcing Tony to make a public denial. He claimed 'perfect health', and tried to brush off his emaciated figure with the remark, 'I just don't eat fattening foods.'

Fortunately, Tony's celebrated thinness allayed suspicion in many quarters, and his face, though leaner, did not show as marked a change as, say, Rock Hudson's had done.

Nevertheless, there was an indication that Tony had a desire to tell his story, because he called an editor of a publishing house to say that he wanted to write his autobiography. He explained that he was prepared to tell everything, much of which would be drawn from the private black diary he had kept for years. The fact that he knew he was dying prompted him to make this suggestion. But later, when the editor tried to contact him, and left messages, Tony never called back.

'He became very depressed and very unlike himself,' Berry explained. 'He felt like he had messed up our lives, and we kept telling him it was okay. I mean, it would have messed up our lives if he had had a heart attack, like his dad did, which was what he'd always prayed for. At least we got a chance to say goodbye . . . I don't understand this disease at all. I don't know how he got it.'

Osgood's reaction when the press first spoke of his father's illness was: 'Anthony Perkins was a star and evidently his "case" interested the press, especially the tabloid press. But the press had very little to sink its teeth into, only rumours which were neither confirmed nor denied. My father had taught us enough for us to take the judgement of others at its true worth. As for what was said or written at that moment, I didn't care. When people asked me questions which were too specific, I lied, saying it was all rubbish. But I lied for my own convenience because I was unable to explain things I myself didn't understand. It was not a case of hiding the truth. In any case, telling the truth would have done nothing except attract pity for myself from people who couldn't understand. [They couldn't understand] both our helplessness and our infinite complicity that united all four of us. That belonged to us alone. And still belongs to us. Those intense and dramatic moments bonded us even more.'

Osgood, who had been living away from home while attending college, returned to Seattle Drive when he heard the truth from his mother.

'I simply returned home because I felt it was my place to be there. I knew why. He did, too, no doubt, but we never spoke of it . . . Our relationship was composed of intimate quantities of tenderness and love. We had no feeling of shame or embarrassment with respect to the illness he was suffering. We were appalled to know he was suffering from an incurable illness about which we could do nothing. Our daily life was upset, yes, but not our relationship with him. We never loved him more or less. We simply loved him to the end.'

After Berry threw him a surprise sixtieth birthday party in April 1992 in New York, many of the guests remarked that Tony looked more emaciated than ever. Berry pleaded with him to confide in his devoted friends.

'I said to him, Look, I'm going to share this with a few close friends that I trust otherwise I'm going to go crazy. I'm not that good an actress. I can't play this charade . . . Finally, when he went into the hospital, we made a very conscious decision, the boys and I, that we could either go through it completely alone in this house – just the four of us – and be really sad, or we could invite our close friends in to share this grief with us.'

Berry then called each of their intimate friends, who immediately responded with great swathes of affection. The house, which had been tomblike for two years, echoed with the sounds of bustling people, sobbing and laughing in equal measure.

'For two weeks before he died we had this liveathon of people who would come and sleep on the floor in his room and curl up on couches and bring food, and he finally got how much people cared about him,' recalled Berry. 'It was a really nice thing for Tony to realize that people were willing to have a pajama party at his bedside. He was not a big pajama-party kind of person – he didn't grow up with groups of people who had fun together.'

'He had fun watching other people have fun,' remarked Osgood. 'He liked to have a vicarious fun experience.'

Richard Benjamin recalled how Tony tried to distance himself from death, even though he was face to face with it. It was the last game he was to play.

'He would say to me, "This is very, very interesting." He was not shying away from it. He was looking right at it as it happened – right directly at it. And because he was looking into the eye of this, it gave us the courage to be there also.'

Noel Black, who saw Tony two or three weeks before his death, remembered his interest in what his visitors were doing, what their plans were for a future he would not see. He even found time to congratulate a woman friend on her perfume as she sat at his bedside.

Towards the end, when he was very tired, and could not stand up any longer, he would say, 'I'm ready to go.'

'It's okay, why don't you?' his friends would say. But he clung to life for as long as he could.

On the morning of 12 September 1992, Berry, conscious that the end could not be far away, called several friends to come over to the house, including her sister and mother. They arrived to find Tony unconscious and gasping for breath, with Berry and two nurses in attendance. The little group assembled just outside the bedroom with Osgood and Elvis, hugging each other and weeping. A few hours later, the sound of Tony's gasping stopped. With Berry clutching her husband's hand, he was pronounced dead.

Not long after the news was out, reporters and photographers with telephoto lens descended on the Perkins home like vultures, attempting to pick up any morsel they could find, following the housekeeper to the supermarket, hounding the doctor, and eventually chasing the hearse.

The memorial service, held at the house in Beverly Hills, was attended by, among others, friends, colleagues and co-stars such as Sue Mengers, Mike Nichols, Janet Leigh, Sophia Loren, David Geffen, Dan Aykroyd and Paula Prentiss. At the end of the service, relayed by loudspeaker to the hundreds of people cramming the road outside, the gardens and the deck, everybody sang the song that Tony had crooned to his sons when putting them to bed – 'Don't Fence Me In.'

As Chapter 1 of this book began with the first words of Kafka's novel, *The Trial*, (with one significant name substitution), it could have ended with the last words: 'With failing eyes P. could still see the two of them, cheek leaning against cheek, immediately before his face, watching the final act. "Like a dog!" he said: it was as if he meant the shame of it to outlive him.'

However, like the actor Brad Davis, Tony issued a posthumous statement about his condition that contradicted the above: 'I chose not to go public because, to misquote *Casablanca*, I'm not much at being noble but it doesn't take much to see that the problems of an old actor don't amount to a hill of beans in this crazy world. There are many who believe this disease is God's vengeance. But I believe it was sent to teach people how to love and understand and have compassion for each other. I have learned more about love, selflessness and human understanding from people I have met in this great adventure in the world of AIDS, than

I ever did in the cut-throat, competitive world in which I spent my life.'

Osgood remarked: 'You know, twenty or thirty years from now it will always be known who Anthony Perkins was because his movies will still exist – those masterpieces by John Huston, George Cukor, William Wyler, Alfred Hitchcock, Orson Welles and so many others from whom he was inseparable. And who will remember how or why he died?'

Frank Rose summed up Tony's life in a few sentences: 'The story of Tony Perkins is the story of Freudianism run amok in theme park America. It's the story of Hollywood abandoning its talent to the pop-culture miasma it creates. Ultimately, however, it's the story of one man's attempt to repair his damaged life – damaged as all our lives are damaged – and to seek meaning and redemption through every means at his disposal: acting, fame, psychotherapy, spiritual gurus, home and family.'

'We had a very satisfying life together,' Berry mused. 'It was a wonderful love affair. If anything else was going down, I certainly didn't know about it, and I don't think he intended to hurt me in any way.'

There is always a tragic feeling of loss when someone close to you dies. When a film star dies, the number of people feeling this loss is multiplied, because of the intimacy that is generated between the image on the screen and audiences in the darkened auditorium. What Roland Barthes called (referring to Garbo): 'The moment in cinema when capturing the human face still plunged audiences into the deepest ecstasy, when one literally lost oneself in a human image as one would in a philtre, when the face represented a kind of absolute state of the flesh, which could be neither reached nor renounced.'

Although we may suffer pain at the passing of a well-loved

writer, composer or painter, our relationship with movie actors, in all their manifestations, is more intense for being physical. (By using the first person plural from here on, I make the presumption of shared perceptions.) Like our life-long friends and relatives, we observe them age over the years, and even if we are not contemporaries of the star, films act as a moving picture album in which we are able to observe the idols at different stages of their lives. If we watch films unsequentially, as one dips into an album at random, we catch a glimpse of the actor or actress in middle age, then in youth, then in old age. In this way, truly, the child is father of the man.

In contrast to life, in which the future is uncertain, we need no crystal ball to see what will become of the star we see on screen in their younger days. Taking what could be termed a future historic perspective, we know what the young Clark Gable, James Stewart, Mickey Rooney, Judy Garland, Errol Flynn, Henry Fonda and Katharine Hepburn will look like in later years. There are exceptions – we have only one image of Jean Harlow or Marilyn Monroe, both of whom existed, like butterflies, for one brief period; we will never know how James Dean or River Phoenix would have aged.

Anthony Perkins did not have to die young to be indelibly remembered as young. When we see the aging and lined face, in contrast to the last image in *Psycho*, we superimpose the unlined smooth and youthful one upon it. We ignore the skull beneath the skin. When we watch Tony in *Friendly Persuasion* or in *Fear Strikes Out*, we see a young man of beauty and talent. And while we watch, we forget what was in store for him, because if we remember, we will be reminded of the worms ingesting our own lost youth.

Despite the fact that Tony continued to work until he died at the age of sixty, when his name is mentioned, most people think of a man in his early twenties; perhaps under a Quaker hat trying to reconcile his pacifist upbringing with the brutal realities around him; or looking at his dad for approval before pitching a ball; as a green sheriff – a boy doing a man's job – his adam's apple a-leaping as he approaches an outlaw, and saying softly, 'I just want your guns, that's all'; his eyes gleaming as he excitedly decides to leave Yonkers for an adventurous day in New York; trying to explain to his young wife why she and her baby must take a suicide pill to avoid death by radiation; having been made to stand all day in the hot sun by an Indian tribe in the jungles of Venezuela, mumbling through cracked lips, 'I'm still on my feet. I'm still talking. Never give up, never give up'; defiantly addressing a court, where he is accused of an unnamed crime; and telling the older woman he loves, 'Since I've known you I've played the brilliant young lawyer, the bashful lover, the spoiled child – God knows what else. But it's all been for you, only for you. Don't you think that's love?'; his long neck craning over a motel desk, and the disarming smile he flashes at his intended victim, when he gets her to call him by his first name – 'Thank you, "Norman".'

In a strange way, the clock of Tony's career seemed to have stopped in 1960 with *Psycho*, no matter what came after. It is his portrait of Dorian Gray. Such is the bitter irony, but also a consolation devoutly to be wished. He will always be that lonely and insecure young man, unsure and afraid of his sexuality, confused by the cruelty and chaos of the world and yet wanting to make sense of it. Perhaps, when we look at the life of Anthony Perkins, for all its substantive differences, it is possible to see our own. After all, as Norman Bates said, 'We're all in our private traps – clamped in them,' and 'We all go a little mad sometimes. Haven't you?'

APPENDIX

Films

The Actress

USA 1953. MGM. *Director*: George Cukor. *Producer*: Lawrence Weintraub. *Screenplay*: Ruth Gordon (from her play *Years Ago*). *Director of Photography*: Harold Rosson. *Music*: Bronislau Kaper. *Cast*: Spencer Tracy (Clinton Jones), Jean Simmons (Ruth Gordon Jones), Teresa Wright (Annie Jones), **Anthony Perkins** (Fred Whitmarsh), Ian Wolfe (Mr Bagley), Mary Wickes (Emma Glavey). 89 mins.

Friendly Persuasion

USA 1956. Allied Artists. *Director*: William Wyler. *Producer*: Wyler. *Screenplay*: (uncredited) Michael Wilson, Jessamyn West, Robert Wyler. *Director of Photography*: Ellsworth Fredericks. *Music*: Dimitri Tiomkin. *Cast*: Gary Cooper (Jess Birdwell), Dorothy McGuire (Eliza Birdwell), Marjorie Main (Widow Hudspeth), **Anthony Perkins** (Josh Birdwell), Richard Eyer (Little Jess), Phyllis Love (Mattie Birdwell), Robert Middleton (Sam Jordan), Mark Richman (Gard Jordan). 137 mins.

The Lonely Man

USA 1957. Paramount. *Director*: Henry Levin. *Producer*: Pat Duggan. *Screenplay*: Harry Essex, Robert Smith. *Director of Photography*: Lionel Lindon. *Music*: Van Cleave. *Cast*: Jack Palance (Jacob Wade), **Anthony Perkins** (Riley Wade), Neville Brand (King Fisher), Robert Middleton (Ben Ryerson), Elaine Aikin (Ada Marshall), Elisha Cook (Willie). 87 mins.

Fear Strikes Out

USA 1957. Paramount. *Director*: Robert Mulligan. *Producer*: Alan Pakula. *Screenplay*: Ted Berkman, Raphael Blau. *Director of Photography*: Haskell Boggs. *Music*: Elmer Bernstein. *Cast*: **Anthony Perkins** (Jim Piersall), Karl Malden (John Piersall), Norma Moore (Mary Teevan), Adam Williams (Dr Brown), Perry Wilson (Mrs Piersall). 100 mins.

The Tin Star

USA 1957. Paramount. *Director*: Anthony Mann. *Producer*: William Perlberg, George Seaton. *Screenplay*: Dudley Nichols. *Director of Photography*: Loyal Griggs. *Music*: Elmer Bernstein. *Cast*: Henry Fonda (Morg Hickman), **Anthony Perkins** (Ben Owens), Betsy Palmer (Nora Mayfield), Michael Ray (Kip Mayfield), Neville Brand (Bogardus), John McIntire (Dr McCord), Mary Webster (Millie). 92 mins.

Desire Under The Elms

USA 1958. Paramount. *Director*: Delbert Mann. *Producer*: Don Hartman. *Screenplay*: Irwin Shaw (from the play by Eugene O'Neill). *Director of Photography*: Daniel L. Fapp. *Music*: Elmer Bernstein. *Cast*: Sophia Loren (Anna Cabot), **Anthony Perkins** (Eben Cabot), Burl Ives (Ephraim Cabot), Frank Overton (Simeon Cabot), Pernell Roberts (Peter Cabot). 111 mins.

The Matchmaker

USA 1958. Paramount. *Director*: Joseph Anthony. *Producer*: Don Hartman. *Screenplay*: John Michael Hayes (from the play by Thornton Wilder). *Director of Photography*: Charles Lang. *Music*: Adolph Deutsch. *Cast*: Shirley Booth (Dolly Levi), **Anthony Perkins** (Cornelius Hackel), Shirley MacLaine (Irene Molloy), Paul Ford (Horace Vandergelder), Robert Morse (Barnaby Tucker), Perry Wilson (Minnie Fay), Wallace Ford (Malachi Stack). 100 mins.

This Angry Age (aka The Sea Wall)

USA 1958. Columbia. *Director*: René Clément. *Producer*: Dino De Laurentiis. *Screenplay*: Irwin Shaw, René Clément (from the novel *Barrage contre le Pacifique* by Marguerite Duras). *Director of Photography*: Otello Martelli. *Music*: Nino Rota. *Cast*: **Anthony Perkins** (Joseph Dufresne), Silvana Mangano (Suzanne Dufresne), Richard Conte (Michael), Jo Van Fleet (Madame Dufresne), Nehemiah Persoff (Albert Legros), Alida Valli (Claude). 111 mins.

Green Mansions

USA 1959. MGM. *Director*: Mel Ferrer. *Producer*: Edmund Grainger. *Screenplay*: Dorothy Kingsley (from the novel by W. H. Hudson). *Director of Photography*: John Ruttenberg. *Music*: Bronislau Kaper. (*Special music*: Heitor Villa-Lobos.) *Cast*: Audrey Hepburn (Rima), **Anthony Perkins** (Abel), Lee J. Cobb (Nuflo), Sessue Hayakawa (Runi), Henry Silva (Kua-Ko), Nehemiah Persoff (Don Panta). 104 mins.

On The Beach

USA 1959. United Artists. *Director*: Stanley Kramer. *Producer*: Kramer. *Screenplay*: John Paxton (from the novel by Nevil Shute). *Directors of Photography*: Giuseppe Rotunno, Daniel Fapp. *Music*: Ernest Gold. *Cast*: Gregory Peck (Dwight Towers), Ava Gardner (Moira Davidson), Fred Astaire (Julian Osborn), **Anthony Perkins** (Peter Holmes), Donna Anderson (Mary Holmes), John Tate (Admiral Bridie). 134 mins.

Tall Story

USA 1960. Warner Bros. *Director*: Joshua Logan. *Producer*: Logan. *Screenplay*: Julius J. Epstein (based on a play by Howard Lindsay and Russel Crouse). *Director of Photography*: Ellsworth Fredericks. *Music*: Cyril. J. Mockridge. *Cast*: **Anthony Perkins** (Ray Blent), Jane Fonda (June Ryder), Ray Walston (Professor Leo Sullivan), Marc Connelly (Professor Charles Osman), Anne Jackson (Myra Sullivan), Murray Hamilton (Coach Hardy). 89 mins.

Psycho

USA 1960. Paramount. *Director*: Alfred Hitchcock. *Producer*: Hitchcock. *Screenplay*: Joseph Stefano (from the novel by Robert Bloch). *Director of Photography*: John L. Russell. *Music*: Bernard Herrmann. *Cast*: **Anthony Perkins** (Norman Bates), Janet Leigh (Marion Crane), Vera Miles (Lila Crane), John Gavin (Sam Loomis), Martin Balsam (Milton Arbogast), John McIntire (Sheriff Chambers), Simon Oakland (Dr Richman), Patricia Hitchcock (Caroline), Frank Albertson (Tom Cassidy), Lurene Tuttle (Mrs Chambers). 109 mins.

Goodbye Again

USA 1961. United Artists. *Director*: Anatole Litvak. *Producer*: Litvak. *Screenplay*: Samuel Taylor (from the novel *Aimez-Vous Brahms?* by Françoise Sagan). *Director of Photography*: Armand Thirard. *Music*: Georges Auric. *Cast*: Ingrid Bergman (Paula Tessler), Yves Montand (Roger Demarest), **Anthony Perkins** (Philip Van der Besh), Jessie Royce Landis (Mrs Van der Besh), Jackie Lane (Maisie I), Pierre Dux (Maître Fleury), Jean Clarke (Maisie II), Michèle Mercier (Maisie III), Diahann Carroll (Singer). 120 mins.

Phaedra

Greece-USA 1961. United Artists. *Director*: Jules Dassin. *Producer*: Dassin. *Screenplay*: Margarita Liberaki. *Director of Photography*: Jacques Natteau. *Music*: Mikis Theodorakis. *Cast*: Melina Mercouri (Phaedra Kyrilis), **Anthony Perkins** (Alexis Kyrilis), Raf Vallone (Thanos Kyrilis), Elisabeth Ercy (Ercy), Olympia Papadoukas (Anna). 115 mins.

Five Miles to Midnight

France-Italy-USA 1962. United Artists. *Director*: Anatole Litvak. *Producer*: Litvak. *Screenplay*: Peter Viertel, Hugh Wheeler. *Director of Photography*: Henri Alekan. *Music*: Mikis Theodorakis. *Cast*: Sophia Loren (Lisa Macklin), **Anthony Perkins** (Robert Macklin), Gig Young (David Barnes), Jean-Pierre Aumont (Alan Stewart), Yolande Turner (Barbara Ford). 110 mins.

The Trial

France-Italy-Germany 1962. Paris Europa/FICIT/Hisa Films. *Director*: Orson Welles. *Producers*: Alexander and Michael Salkind. *Screenplay*: Welles (from the novel by Franz Kafka). *Director of Photography*: Edmond Richard. *Music*: Jean Ledrut. *Cast*: **Anthony Perkins** (Joseph K.), Orson Welles (Hastler), Jeanne Moreau (Miss Burstner), Romy Schneider (Leni), Elsa Martinelli (Hilda), Akim Tamiroff (Bloch), Suzanne Flon (Miss Pittl), Madeleine Robinson (Mrs Grubach), William Chappell (Titorelli). 120 mins.

The Fool Killer

USA 1963. Allied Artists. *Director*: Servando Gonzales. *Producer*: David Friedkin. *Screenplay*: Friedkin, Morton Fine (from the novel by Helen Eustis). *Director of Photography*: Alex Phillips Jr. *Music*: Gustavo Cesar Carreon. *Cast*: **Anthony Perkins** (Milo Bogardus), Edward Albert (George Mellish), Dana Elcar (Mr Dodd), Henry Hull (Dirty Jim Jelliman), Salome Jens (Mrs Dodd), Charlotte Jones (Mrs Ova Fanshawe). 100 mins.

Two Are Guilty (Le Glaive et la Balance)

France 1964. Gaumont-Trianon/Ultra/MGM. *Director*: André Cayatte. *Producer*: Alain Poire. *Screenplay*: Cayatte. *Director of Photography*: Roger Fellows. *Music*: Louiguy. *Cast*: **Anthony Perkins** (Johnny), Jean-Claude Brialy (Jean-Philippe), Renato Salvatori (François), Pascal Audret (Agnès), Maria Déa (Madame Winter), Michèle Mercier (Brigitte). 131 mins.

A Ravishing Idiot (Une Ravissante Idiote)

France 1964. Belles Rives/Flora. *Director*: Edouard Molinaro. *Producer*: Michel Ardan. *Screenplay*: Molinaro, Georges and André Tabet (from the novel by Charles Exbrayat). *Director of Photography*: Andréas Winding. *Music*: Michel Legrand. *Cast*: Brigitte Bardot (Penelope Lightfeather), **Anthony Perkins** (Harry Compton), Grégoire Aslan (Bagda), Denise Provence (Lady Barbara Dumphreys), André Luguet (Sir Reginald Dumphreys). 110 mins.

Is Paris Burning? (Paris Brûle-t-il?)

France-USA 1966. Paramount. *Director*: René Clément. *Producer*: Paul Graetz. *Screenplay*: Gore Vidal, Francis Ford Coppola, Jean Aurenche, Pierre Bost, Claude Brule (from the novel by Larry Collins and Dominique Lapierre). *Director of Photography*: Marcel Grignon. *Music*: Maurice Jarre. *Cast*: Jean-Paul Belmondo (Morandot), Charles Boyer (Monod), Leslie Caron (Françoise Labé), Jean-Pierre Cassel (Henri Karcher), Alain Delon (Jacques Chaban-Delmas), Kirk Douglas (Patton), Glenn Ford (Bradley), Yves Montand (Bizien), **Anthony Perkins** (Warren), Simone Signoret (Café Owner), Robert Stack (Sibert), Orson Welles (Nordling). 165 mins.

The Champagne Murders (Le Scandale)

France 1967. Universal. *Director*: Claude Chabrol. *Producers*: Raymond Eger, Jacques Natteau. *Screenplay*: Chabrol, Claude Brule. *Director of Photography*: Jean Rabier. *Music*: Pierre Jansen. *Cast*: **Anthony Perkins** (Christopher), Maurice Ronet (Paul), Stéphane Audran (Jacqueline), Yvonne Furneaux (Christine), Suzanne Lloyd (Evelyn). 105 mins.

Pretty Poison

USA 1968. 20th Century-Fox. *Director*: Noel Black. *Producers*: Black, Marshal Backlar. *Screenplay*: Lorenzo Semple Jr. (from the novel *She Let Him Continue* by Stephen Geller). *Director of Photography*: David Quaid. *Music*: Johnny Mandel. *Cast*: **Anthony Perkins** (Dennis Pitts), Tuesday Weld (Sue Ann Stepanek), Beverly Garland (Mrs Stepanek), John Rudolph (Azenauer), Dick O'Neill (Bud Minsch). 89 mins.

Catch-22

USA 1970. Paramount. *Director*: Mike Nichols. *Producers*: John Calley, Martin Ransohoff. *Screenplay*: Buck Henry (from the novel by Joseph Heller). *Director of Photography*: David Watkin. *Music*: John Hammell. *Cast*: Alan Arkin (Captain Yossarian), Martin Balsam (Colonel Cathcart), Richard Benjamin (Major Danby), Art Garfunkel (Captain Nately), Bob Newhart (Major Major), **Anthony Perkins** (Chaplain Tappman), Paula Prentiss (Nurse Duckett), Martin Sheen (Lieutenant Dobbs), Jon Voight (Milo Minderbinder), Orson Welles (General Dreedle). 121 mins.

WUSA

USA 1970. Paramount. *Director*: Stuart Rosenberg. *Producers*: Paul Newman, John Foreman. *Screenplay*: Robert Stone (from his novel *A Hall of Mirrors*). *Director of Photography*: Richard Moore. *Music*: Lalo Schifrin. *Cast*: Paul Newman (Rheinhardt), Joanne Woodward (Geraldine), **Anthony Perkins** (Rainey), Laurence Harvey (Farley), Pat Hingle (Bingamon), Cloris Leachman (Philomene). 115 mins.

Ten Days' Wonder (La Décade Prodigieuse)

France 1971. Boetie/Euro International. *Director*: Claude Chabrol. *Producer*: André Génovès. *Screenplay*: Paul Gardner, Eugène Archer (from the novel by Ellery Queen). *Director of Photography*: Jean Rabier. *Music*: Pierre Jansen. *Cast*: Orson Welles (Théo), Marlène Jobert (Hélène), **Anthony Perkins** (Charles), Michel Piccoli (Paul), Guido Alberti (Ludovic). 105 mins.

Someone Behind the Door (Quelq'un Derrière la Porte)

France 1971. Lira/GSF. *Director*: Nicolas Gessner. *Producer*: Raymond Danon. *Screenplay*: Gessner, Jacques Robert, Marc Boehm, Lorenzo Ventavoli (from the novel by Robert). *Director of Photography*: Pierre Lhomme. *Music*: Georges Garvarentz. *Cast*: Charles Bronson (The Stranger), **Anthony Perkins** (Laurence Jeffries), Jill Ireland (Frances Jeffries), Henri Garcin (Paul Damien), Adriano Magestretti (Andrew). 90 mins.

Play It As It Lays

USA 1972. Universal. *Director*: Frank Perry. *Producers*: Perry, Dominick Dunne. *Screenplay*: Joan Didion, John Gregory Dunne (from the novel by Didion). *Director of Photography*: Jordan Croneweth. *Music*: Don Fendley. *Cast*: Tuesday Weld (Maria Wyeth), **Anthony Perkins** (B. Z.), Tammy Grimes (Helene), Adam Roarke (Carter Lang), Ruth Ford (Carlotta), Eddie Firestone (Benny Austin). 101 mins.

The Life and Times of Judge Roy Bean

USA 1972. First Artists. *Director*: John Huston. *Producer*: John Foreman. *Screenplay*: John Milius. *Director of Photography*: Richard Moore. *Music*: Maurice Jarre. *Cast*: Paul Newman (Judge Roy Bean), Victoria Principal (Maria Elena), **Anthony Perkins** (Reverend LaSalle), Tab Hunter (Sam Dodd), John Huston (Grizzly Adams), Stacy Keach (Bad Bob), Roddy McDowall (Frank Gass), Jacqueline Bisset (Rose Bean), Ava Gardner (Lily Langtry). 120 mins.

Lovin' Molly

USA 1974. Columbia. *Director*: Sidney Lumet. *Producer*: Stephen Friedman. *Screenplay*: Friedman (from the novel *Leaving Cheyenne* by Larry McMurtry). *Director of Photography*: Edward Brown. *Music*: Fred Hellerman. *Cast*: **Anthony Perkins** (Gid), Beau Bridges (Johnny), Blythe Danner (Molly), Edward Binns (Mr Fry), Susan Sarandon (Sarah), Conrad Fowkes (Eddie). 98 mins.

Murder on the Orient Express

USA 1974. Paramount. *Director*: Sidney Lumet. *Producers*: John Brabourne, Richard Goodwin. *Screenplay*: Paul Dehn (from the novel by Agatha Christie). *Director of Photography*: Geoffrey Unsworth. *Music*: Richard Rodney Bennett. *Cast*: Albert Finney (Hercule Poirot), Lauren Bacall (Mrs Hubbard), Ingrid Bergman (Greta), Jacqueline Bisset (Countess Andrenyi), Jean-Pierre Cassel (Pierre), Sean Connery (Colonel Arbuthnot), John Gielgud (Beddoes), Wendy Hiller (Princess Dragomiroff), **Anthony Perkins** (McQueen), Vanessa

Redgrave (Mary Devenham), Richard Widmark (Ratchett), Michael York (Count Andrenyi). 127 mins.

Mahogany

USA 1975. *Director*: Berry Gordy. *Producers*: Rob Cohen, Jack Ballard. *Screenplay*: John Byrum. *Director of Photography*: David Watkin. *Music*: Lee Holdridge. *Cast*: Diana Ross (Tracy), Billy Dee Williams (Brian), **Anthony Perkins** (Sean), Jean-Pierre Aumont (Christian Rosetti), Beah Richards (Florence), Nina Foch (Miss Evans), Marisa Mell (Carlotta Gavina). 109 mins.

Remember My Name

USA 1978. Columbia. *Director*: Alan Rudolph. *Producer*: Robert Altman. *Screenplay*: Rudolph. *Director of Photography*: Tak Fujimoto. *Music*: Alberta Hunter. *Cast*: Geraldine Chaplin (Emily), **Anthony Perkins** (Neil Curry), Berry Berenson (Barbara Curry), Jeff Goldblum (Mr Nudd), Timothy Thomerson (Jeff). 95 mins.

Winter Kills

USA 1979 (made in 1976). Avco Embassy. *Director*: William Richert. *Producer*: Fred Caruso. *Screenplay*: Richert (from the novel by Richard Condon). *Director of Photography*: Vilmos Zsigmond. *Music*: Maurice Jarre. *Cast*: Jeff Bridges (Nick Kegan), John Huston (Pa Kegan), **Anthony Perkins** (John Cerutti), Sterling Hayden (Z. K. Dawson), Eli Wallach (Joe Diamond), Dorothy Malone (Emma Kegan), Toshiro Mifune (Keith). 97 mins.

The Black Hole

USA 1979. Walt Disney. *Director*: Gary Nelson. *Producer*: Ron Miller. *Screenplay*: Jeb Rosebrook, Gerry Day. *Director of Photography*: Frank Phillips. *Music*: John Barry. *Cast*: Maximilian Schell (Dr Hans Reinhardt), **Anthony Perkins** (Dr Alex Durant), Robert Forster (Captain Dan Holland), Joseph Bottoms (Lieutenant Charles Pizer), Yvette Mimieux (Dr Kat McCraw), Ernest Borgnine (Harry Booth). 97mins.

Twice a Woman (Twee Vrouwen)

Holland 1979. Actueel Film. *Director*: George Sluizer. *Producers*: William Howerd, Anne Lorden. *Screenplay*: Sluizer, Jurrien Rood (from the novel by Harry Mulisch). *Director of Photography*: Mat van Hensbergen. *Music*: Willem Breuker. *Cast*: Bibi Andersson (Laura), **Anthony Perkins** (Alfred), Sandra Dumas (Sylvia), Tilly Perin Bouwmeester (Laura's mother), Kitty Courbeois (Sylvia's mother). 113 mins.

ffolkes

UK-USA 1980. Universal. *Director*: Andrew V. McLaglen. *Producer*: Elliott Kastner. *Screenplay*: Jack Davies (from his novel *Esther, Ruth and Jennifer*). *Director of Photography*: Tony Imi. *Music*: Michael J. Lewis. *Cast*: Roger Moore (ffolkes), James Mason (Admiral Brinsden), **Anthony Perkins** (Kramer), Michael Parks (Shulman), David Hedison (King), George Baker (Fletcher), Faith Brook (Prime Minister). 99 mins.

Double Negative

Canada 1980. Quadrant. *Director*: George Bloomfield. *Producers*: Jerome Simon, David Main. *Screenplay*: Thomas Hedley Jr, Charles Dennis, Janis Allen (from the novel *The Three Roads* by Ross Macdonald). *Director of Photography*: René Verzier. *Music*: Paul Hoffert. *Cast*: Michael Sarrazin (Michael Taylor), Susan Clark (Paula West), **Anthony Perkins** (Lawrence Miles), Howard Duff (Lester Harlen), Kate Reid (Mrs Swanscott). 96 mins.

Psycho II

USA 1983. Universal. *Director*: Richard Franklin. *Producer*: Hilton A. Green. *Screenplay*: Tom Holland. *Director of Photography*: Dean Cundey. *Music*: Jerry Goldsmith. *Cast*: **Anthony Perkins**, Vera Miles (Lila Loomis), Meg Tilly (Mary), Robert Loggia (Dr Raymond), Dennis Franz (Toomey), Hugh Gillin (Sheriff Hunt). 113 mins.

Crimes of Passion

USA 1984. New World Pictures. *Director*: Ken Russell. *Producers*: Barry Sandler, Donald P. Borchers. *Screenplay*: Sandler. *Director of Photography*: Dick Bush. *Music*: Rick Wakeman. *Cast*: Kathleen Turner (China Blue), **Anthony Perkins** (Reverend Peter Shayne), John Laughlin (Bobby Grady), Annie Potts (Amy Grady), Bruce Davison (Donny Hopper). 101 mins.

Psycho III

USA 1986. Universal. *Director*: **Anthony Perkins**. *Producer*: Hilton A. Green. *Screenplay*: Charles Edward Pogue. *Director of Photography*: Bruce Surtees. *Music*: Carter Burwell. *Cast*: **Anthony Perkins** (Norman Bates), Diana Scarwid (Maureen), Jeff Fahey (Duane), Roberta Maxwell (Tracy), Hugh Gillin (Sheriff Hunt), Lee Garlington (Myrna). 96 mins.

Destroyer

USA 1988. *Director*: Robert Kirk. *Producers*: Peter Garrity, Rex Hauck. *Screenplay*: Garrity, Hauck. *Director of Photography*: Chuy Elizondo. *Music*: Patrick O'Hearn. *Cast*: Deborah Foreman (Susan Malone), Clayton Rohner (David Harris), Lyle Alzado (Ivan Moser), **Anthony Perkins** (Edwards), Tobias Anderson (Russell). 94 mins.

Lucky Stiff

USA 1988. New Line Cinema. *Director*: **Anthony Perkins**. *Producer*: Gerald T. Olson. *Screenplay*: Pat Proft. *Director of Photography*: Jacques Haitkin. *Music*: Tom Jenkins, Mike Taverna. *Cast*: Donna Dixon (Cynthia Mitchell), Joe Alaskey (Ron Douglas), Jeff Kober (Ike), Barbara Howard (Frances), Fran Ryan (Ma). 82 mins.

Edge of Sanity

GB 1989. Allied Vision. *Director*: Gerard Kikoine. *Producers*: Edward Simons, Harry Alan Towers. *Screenplay*: J. P. Felix, Ron Raley. *Director of Photography*: Tony Spratling. *Music*: Frederic Talgorn. *Cast*: **Anthony Perkins**

(Dr Jekyll/Mr Hyde), Glynis Barber (Elizabeth Jekyll), Sarah Maur-Thorp (Susannah), Ben Cole (Johnny), David Lodge (Underwood), Harry Landis (Coroner). 90 mins.

A Demon In My View

Germany 1991. Pro-ject Filmverlag-Vidmark Entertainments. *Director*: Petra Haffter. *Producer*: Theo Hinz. *Screenplay*: Petra Haffter. *Director of Photography*: Frank Bruhne. *Cast*: **Anthony Perkins** (Arthur Johnson), Uwe Bohm (Anthony Johnson), Sophie Ward (Helen Schweizer), Stratford Johns (Stanley Caspian), Brian Bovell (Winston Mervin).

Television Plays (as comprehensive as research has allowed)

The Missing Years (1954)

Kraft Theatre. NBC. *Cast*: Mary Astor, Ted Brenner, **Anthony Perkins**.

The Fugitive (1954)

Armstrong Circle Theatre. NBC. *Cast*: Dolly Haas, **Anthony Perkins**, Marcel Hillaire.

The Case of the Narcotics Rackets (1954)

Man Behind the Badge. CBS. *Cast*: **Anthony Perkins**, Vinton Hayworth Jr, Mimi Kelly.

Mr Blue Ocean (1955)

General Electric Theatre. CBS. *Cast*: Boris Karloff, Susan Strasberg, Eli Wallach, Bramwell Fletcher, **Anthony Perkins**.

The World Out There (1955)

Windows. CBS. *Cast*: Mary Perry, **Anthony Perkins**, Joseph Sweeney.

Home is the Hero (1956)

Kraft Theatre. NBC. *Cast*: Brian Donlevy, Glenda Farrell, **Anthony Perkins**, Dennis Patrick.

The Silent Gun (1956)

Studio One. CBS. *Cast*: Lloyd Bridges, **Anthony Perkins**, Frank McHugh, Paul Stevens.

Winter Dreams (1956)

Front Row Centre. CBS. *Cast*: **Anthony Perkins**, Piper Laurie, Gloria Talbott.

Joey (1956)

Goodyear TV Playhouse. NBC. *Cast*: **Anthony Perkins**, Kim Stanley, Peggy McCoy, Ruth White.

Evening Primrose (1966)

ABC Stage 67. ABC. *Cast*: **Anthony Perkins**, Charmian Carr, Dorothy Stickney, Larry Gates.

The Male Animal (1968)

Play of the Month. BBC. *Cast*: Anthony Perkins, Toby Robbins, Alan Clifford, Lee Montague.

The Ghost Writer (1989)

Cast: **Anthony Perkins**, Leigh Taylor-Young, Juliet Sorcey, Joshua Miller.

Television Films

How Awful About Allan (1970)

Director: Curtis Harrington. *Cast*: **Anthony Perkins**, Julie Harris, Joan Hackett, Kent Smith.

First You Cry (1978)

Director: George Schaefer. *Cast*: Mary Tyler Moore, **Anthony Perkins**, Richard Crenna, Jennifer Warren, Richard Dysart.

Les Misérables (1978)

Director: Glenn Jordan. *Cast*: Richard Jordan, **Anthony Perkins**, Cyril Cusack, Claude Dauphin, John Gielgud, Ian Holm, Celia Johnson, Joyce Redman, Flora Robson.

For the Term of His Natural Life (1983)

Director: Rob Stewart. *Cast*: **Anthony Perkins**, Samantha Eggar, Patrick MacNee, Diane Cilento.

The Sins of Dorian Gray (1983)

Director: Tony Maylam. *Cast*: **Anthony Perkins**, Belinda Bauer, Joseph Bottoms, Olga Karlotos.

The Glory Boys (1984)

Director: Michael Ferguson. *Cast*: Rod Steiger, **Anthony Perkins**, Joanna Lumley, Alfred Burke, Gary Brown.

Napoleon and Josephine: A Love Story (1987)

Director: Richard Heffron. *Cast*: Armand Assante, Jacqueline Bisset, Stephanie Beacham, **Anthony Perkins**, Anthony Higgins, Nickolas Grace.

Daughter of Darkness (1990)

Director: Stuart Gordon. *Cast*: Mia Sara, **Anthony Perkins**, Jack Coleman, Robert Reynolds.

I'm Dangerous Tonight (1990)

Director: Tobe Hooper. *Cast*: Madchen Amick, Corey Parker, Daisy Hall, Dee Wallace Stone, **Anthony Perkins.**

Psycho IV: The Beginning (1990)

Director: Mick Garris. *Cast*: **Anthony Perkins**, Henry Thomas, Olivia Hussey, C.C.H. Pounder, Donna Mitchell, Warren Frost.

In the Deep Woods (1992)

Director: Charles Connell. *Cast*: Rosanna Arquette, **Anthony Perkins**, Will Patton, D.W. Moffett, Chris Rydell, Amy Ryan, Beth Broderick.

Theatre (excluding college productions)

Junior Miss (summer stock 1947)

by Jerome Chodorov and Joseph Fields. A. P. as Haskell Cummings.

Kiss and Tell (summer stock 1947)

by F. Hugh Herbert. A. P. as Raymond Pringle.

George Washington Slept Here (summer stock 1947)

by Moss Hart and George S. Kaufman. A. P. as Raymond.

Sarah Simple (summer stock 1948)

by A. A. Milne. A. P. as Amyas.

But Not Goodbye (summer stock 1948)

by George Seaton. A. P. as Jimmie Griggs.

Charm (summer stock 1950)

by John Kirkpatrick. A. P. as Claude

My Sister Eileen (summer stock 1950)

by Joseph Fields and Jerome Chodorov. A. P. as a Sailor

Years Ago (summer stock 1950)

by Ruth Gordon. A. P. as Fred Whitmarsh.

George and Margaret (summer stock 1951)

by Gerald Savory. A. P. as Dudley.

Two Blind Mice (summer stock 1951)

by Samuel Spewack. A. P. as Ensign Jamison.

The Walrus and the Carpenter (summer stock 1951)

by Noel Langley. A. P. as Roland Wayne.

Theatre (summer stock 1952)

by W. Somerset Maugham. A. P. as Roger Gosselyn.

Family Portrait (summer stock 1953)

by Lenore Coffee and William Joyce Cowen. A. P. as Judah.

Tea and Sympathy (Broadway 1954–1955)

by Robert Anderson. *Director*: Elia Kazan. *Cast*: Joan Fontaine (Laura Reynolds), **Anthony Perkins** (Tom Lee), Leif Erickson (Bill Reynolds), Dick York (Al), John McGovern (Herbert Lee).

Look Homeward, Angel (Broadway 1957)

by Ketti Frings (from the novel by Thomas Wolfe). *Director*: George Roy Hill. *Cast*: **Anthony Perkins** (Eugene Gant), Arthur Hill (Ben Gant), Jo Van Fleet (Eliza Gant), Hugh Griffith (W. O. Gant), Rosemary Murphy (Helen Gant Barton).

Greenwillow (Broadway 1960)

Music and lyrics by Frank Loesser. Book by Loesser and Lesser Samuels (from the novel by B. J. Chute). *Director*: George Roy Hill. *Cast*: **Anthony Perkins** (Gideon Briggs), Cecil Kellaway (Reverend Birdsong), Dortha Duckworth (Clara Clegg), Pert Kelton (Gramma Briggs), Elaine Swan (Maidy), Ellen McCown (Dorrie Whitbred), Grover Dale (Andrew).

Damn Yankees (summer stock 1960)

Music and lyrics by Richard Adler and Jerry Ross. Book by George Abbott and Douglass Wallop (from the novel *The Year the Yankees Lost the Pennant* by Wallop). *Director*: David Tihmar. *Cast*: **Anthony Perkins** (Joe Hardy), Murray Matheson (Applegate), Cathryn Diamond (Lola), Harry Stanton (Joe Boyd), Bob Dishy (Rocky).

Harold (Broadway 1962)

by Herman Raucher. *Director*: Larry Blyden. *Cast*: **Anthony Perkins** (Harold Selbar), Don Adams (Odee Zwick), Sudie Bond (Miss Prose), Rochelle Oliver (Iris Munger), Nathaniel Frey (Fatto Kleest), John Fielder (Lew Brindle).

Star-Spangled Girl (Broadway 1966–1967)

by Neil Simon. *Director*: George Axelrod. *Cast*: **Anthony Perkins** (Andy Hobart), Richard Benjamin (Norman Cornell), Connie Stevens (Sophie Rauschmeyer).

Star-Spangled Girl (Road Tour 1967–1968)

Director: **Anthony Perkins.** *Cast*: **Anthony Perkins** (Andy Hobart), Remak Ramsey (Norman Cornell), Sheila Wells (Sophie Rauschmeyer).

The Unknown Soldier and His Wife (summer stock 1968)

by Peter Ustinov. *Director*: **Anthony Perkins.**

The Imaginary Invalid (Milwaukee Repertory Theatre 1968)

by Molière. *Director*: **Anthony Perkins.**

The Burgomaster (Milwaukee Repertory Theatre 1969)

by Gert Hofmann. *Director*: **Anthony Perkins.**

Steambath (Off-Broadway 1970)

by Bruce Jay Friedman. *Director*: **Anthony Perkins.** *Cast*: **Anthony Perkins** (Tandy), Hector Elizondo (Attendant), Marvin Lichterman (Bieberman), Annie Rachel (Meredith), Conrad Bain (Oldtimer).

Angel Street (Playhouse in the Park, Cincinnati 1971)

by Patrick Hamilton. *Director*: **Anthony Perkins.**

The Gingerbread Lady (summer stock 1973)

by Neil Simon. *Director*: **Anthony Perkins.**

Don't Call Back (summer stock 1974)

by Russell O'Neil. *Director*: **Anthony Perkins.**

The Wager (Off-Broadway 1974)

by Mark Medoff. *Director*: **Anthony Perkins.**

Equus (Broadway 1975–1977)

by Peter Shaffer. *Director*: John Dexter. *Cast*: **Anthony Perkins** (Martin Dysart), Thomas Hulce (Alan Strang), Marion Seldes (Dora Strang), Page Johnson (Frank Strang), Laurinda Barrett (Hester Saloman).

The Voice of the Turtle (Cape Cod 1977)

by John Van Druten. *Director*: **Anthony Perkins.** *Cast*: **Anthony Perkins**, Berry Berenson.

Romantic Comedy (Broadway 1979)

by Bernard Slade. *Director*: Joseph Hardy. *Cast*: **Anthony Perkins** (Jason Carmichael), Mia Farrow (Phoebe Craddock), Carole Cook (Blanche Dailey), Holly Palance (Allison St. James).

(No records have been found of two productions A. P. had mentioned once or twice. *The Royal Family* by George S. Kaufman and Edna Ferber in Seattle, and *A Streetcar Named Desire* by Tennessee Williams in Florida.)

Screenplays (with Stephen Sondheim)

The Last of Sheila (Warner Bros. 1973)
Crime and Variations (Unproduced 1981)
The Chorus Girl Murder Case (Unproduced. Date unknown)

Recordings

1956 (Epic)

A Little Love Can Go A Long, Long Way; If You'll Be Mine;
Friendly Persuasion (Thee I Love); If You Were The Only Girl;

Melody For Lovers; Fools In Love.

1957 (Epic)

April Fool; Just Friends; Hit The Road To Dreamland; This Time The Dream's On Me; Why Shouldn't I?; I Wish I Knew; Accidents Will Happen; Gone With The Wind; How Long Has This Been Going On?; But Beautiful; Better Luck Next Time; How About You?

1957 (RCA)

First Romance; Moonlight Swim; When School Starts Again; Rocket To The Moon; Indian Giver; Just Being Your Age; The Prettiest Girl in School; No, No, No; She Used To Be My Girl; Gonna Get Some Lovin'; Treasure Island.

1958 (RCA Victor)

The Kentuckian Song; The Careless Years; Taking A Chance On Love; Saddle The Wind; The More I See You; Too Marvelous For Words; Ole Buttermilk Sky; Boy On A Dolphin; Swinging On A Star; Speak Low; You Keep Coming Back Like A Song; This Is My Lucky Day; The World Is Your Balloon; I Remember You; Why Was I Born?; Miss Otis Regrets; I've Got Sand In My Shoes; Long Ago And Far Away; You'd Be So Nice To Come Home To; Have You Met Miss Jones?; You Came Along; It Could Happen To You; Darn That Dream; Back In Your Own Back Yard.

1960 (RCA)

Greenwillow – Original Cast Album.

1964 (Columbia)

On Ne Meurt Pas Pour Ça; Il N'y a Plus D'Aprés; Ne Dis Plus Rien; Quand Tu Dors Prés de Moi.

1966 (Painted Smiles)

Ben Bagley's George Gershwin Revisited: There's More To The Kiss

Than XXX; Under a One Man Top; Tra-La-La; Drifting Along With The Tide; Virginia Don't Go Too Far; Back Bay Polka; Changing My Tune; Three Times A Day; Scandal Walk.

1970 (Painted Smiles

Ben Bagley's Vernon Duke Revisited: Now; Spring Again; Lady; Roundabout; I Cling To You.

1978 (Painted Smiles)

Ben Bagley's Rodgers and Hart Revisited: Someone Should Tell Them; Life Was Monotonous; I Can Do Wonders With You; I'm Talking To My Pal; You're The Mother Type.

1979 (Painted Smiles)

Ben Bagley Presents Rodgers and Hart's Too Many Girls: Love Never Went To College; Too Many Girls; I Didn't Know What Time It Was.

1985 (Painted Smiles)

Ben Bagley's Contemporary Broadway Revisited: All My Friends Have Gone To California.

NOTES

Chapter 1: I am Norman Bates

p.3 'You're a Mamma's Boy. . .' Robert Bloch, *Psycho* (Corgi, 1962).

p.5 'She is so undependable . . .' *Interview*, November 1990.

p.6 'Do you think there was sexual abuse? . . .' *ibid.*

p.7 'I saw women as beautiful predators . . .' *Sunday Times*, August 1983.

p.9 'No one says it . . .' Theodore Price, *Hitchcock and Homosexuality* (Scarecrow, 1992).

p.10 'By using Perkins . . .' Peter Biskind, *Seeing is Believing* (Pantheon Books, 1983).

Chapter 2: Private Traps

p.13 'We're going to be alright . . .' *Photoplay*, February 1958.

p.15 'I sometimes wonder . . .' *ibid.*

p.15 'I'm a wreck . . .' *New York Post*, January 1958.

p.16 'He was also a terrific mimic . . .' John Kerr to author.

p.17 'A very nice looking . . .' Jane Wyatt to author.

p.18 'At five, we need . . .' Mildred Newman and Bernard Berkovitch, *How To Be Your Own Best Friend* (Heinemann, 1974).

p.19 'I loathed school . . .' *New York Times*, December 1957.

p.19 'All but completely buried . . .' *Motion Picture*, April 1957.
p.19 'Taught me not to run away. . .' *New York Times*, December 1957.
p.21 'I've never really had the clout . . .' National Film Theatre interview, August 1983.
p.22 'His feelings for me . . .' *Photoplay*, February 1958.
p.22 'Whatever Tony did . . .' *Motion Picture*, December 1957.
p.22 'I remember when we were living . . .' *Photoplay*, February 1958.

Chapter 3: I am thy father's spirit

p.24 'It didn't seem that difficult . . .' *Reflections on the Silver Screen*, radio interview with Richard Brown, 1993.
p.26 'As with so many things . . .' *Photoplay*, February 1958.
p.26 'Would you like to . . .' *ibid.*
p.26 'I got into acting . . .' National Film Theatre interview, August 1983.
p.28 'He had a bit in that play. . .' Merv Griffin TV interview, October 1984.
p.29 'With the prospect of death . . .' *New York Herald Tribune*, December 1937.
p.30 'He was rather shorter . . .' *Motion Picture*, April 1957.
p.30 'He was supposed to be famous . . .' *Seventeen*, November 1953.
p.31 'My hands got . . .'quoted in Laura Kay Palmer, *Osgood and Anthony Perkins.* (McFarland & Company, Inc., 1991).
p.31 'For closeups of hands . . .' Nicolas Gessner to author.
p.31 'I was fiercely. . .' *Mail on Sunday*, August 1983.

Chapter 4: Oggie

p.34 'It was the beginning . . .' *New York Herald-Tribune*, January 1933.
p.37 'It was a grand show. . .' Jed Harris, *A Dance on the High Wire* (Crown, 1979).
p.37 'My first minister role . . .' *New York American*, September 1926.
p.38 'I read [*The Front Page*]. . .' Jed Harris, *A Dance on the High Wire* (Crown, 1979).
p.40 'I always had a theory. . .' Jerome Lawrence, *Actor: The Life and Times of Paul Muni* (G. P. Putnam's Sons, 1974).
p.40 'He and Jane . . .' Jane Wyatt to the author.
p.41 'Thank God . . .' *Baltimore Sun*, September 1937.

Chapter 5: Hello Hollywood . . . and Goodbye

p.44 'It's all right, Mother . . .' *Photoplay*, February 1958.

p.44 'When he went to college . . .' *ibid.*

p.44 'When I was in college . . .' *Motion Picture*, April 1957.

p.46 'Tony was about sixteen . . .' *Modern Screen*, January 1957.

p.47 'It was the power of self-confidence . . .' *Reflections on the Silver Screen*, radio interview with Richard Brown 1993.

p.47 'One day they were testing . . .' *New York Times*, November 1972.

p.48 'I thought someone was kidding . . .' *Films and Filming*, July 1965.

p.49 'Cukor would let me . . .' *Seventeen*, November 1953.

p.49 'Off the set . . .' Teresa Wright to the author.

p.50 'But it didn't bother me . . .' *New York Times*, November 1972.

p.50 'An everchanging list . . .' Patrick McGilligan, *George Cukor: A Double Life* (Faber & Faber, 1991).

p.50 'I wanted to get right out . . .' publicity notes for *Edge of Sanity.*

p.51 'It was an adventure . . .' National Film Theatre interview, August 1983.

Chapter 6: TV and Sympathy

p.53 'I wondered how much . . .' *Photoplay*, February 1958.

p.53 'In each letter . . .' *ibid.*

p.54 'Family plays . . .' *The New Yorker*, November 1961.

p.54 'He was the definition . . .' Elia Kazan, *Kazan: A Life* (Alfred A. Knopf, 1988).

p.55 'The very thing . . .' Robert Anderson to the author.

p.56 'Paralyzed-trying-to-be-calm . . .' *New York Journal-American*, August 1960.

p.56 'The theatre was dark . . .' *Motion Picture*, April 1957.

p.57 'My hunch was justified . . .' John Kerr to the author.

p.57 'Kerr was too sturdy . . .' Miles Kreuger to the author.

p.59 'That we must understand . . .' Vincente Minnelli, *I Remember It Well* (Doubleday, 1974).

p.59 'I can't work . . .' *McCall's*, October 1957.

p.60 'Always seemed to have a chip . . .' Robert Anderson to the author.

p.60 'I messed up the part . . .' *McCall's*, October 1957.

p.60 'During the time . . .' John Kerr to the author.

p.63 'We shared a common interest . . .' Miles Kreuger to the author.

p.64 'He cared for Helen . . .'Alan Helms to the author.

p.64 'She ruled his life . . .' *Premiere*, October 1993.

p.64 'A stern looking woman . . .' *ibid.*

p.64 'I have a small apartment . . .' *Photoplay*, February 1958.

p.66 'Oh, I can't keep . . .' Miles Kreuger to the author.

p.67 'On live TV. . .' National Film Theatre interview, August 1983.

p.68 'I'm very adaptable . . .' *New York World-Telegram*, October 1957.

p.68 'He had always sung . . .' *Photoplay*, February 1958.

Chapter 7: Thou Swell!

p.73 'It was a most ironic . . .' *Films and Filming*, July 1965.

p.75 'Oh yes, I remember . . .' *ibid.*

p.76 'I think it was the most . . .' *ibid.*

p.76 'It was in *Friendly Persuasion* . . .' *The New Yorker*, November 1961.

p.76 'He was a man to watch . . .' National Film Theatre, August 1983.

p.77 'That boy should get out . . .' *Coronet*, November 1957.

p.77 'Wyler was a practical man . . .' National Film Theatre, August 1983.

p.80 'I had previously made one film . . .' *ibid.*

p.80 'They call me another James Dean . . .' *Ranch Romances*, March 1957.

p.82 'The one thing I can never . . .' *New York Times*, March 1957.

Chapter 8: Strike The Father Dead

p.86 'An absolute slave . . .' *The New Yorker*, November 1961.

p.90 'Tony went through the scenes . . .' *Motion Picture*, February 1957.

p.91 'You're out on the field . . .' *Good Housekeeping*, November 1959.

p.91 'There's a feminized man . . .' Peter Biskind, *Seeing is Believing* (Pantheon Books, 1983).

p.92 'Get a big kick . . .' *Newsweek*, March 1958.

p.92 'He loves being important . . .' *ibid.*

p.92 'You can go to school . . .' *Mail on Sunday*, August 1983.

p.93 'It was one hour . . .' Peter Collier, *The Fondas: A Hollywood Dynasty* (HarperCollins, 1991).

Chapter 9: But When I Became A Man

p.99 'Such a sense of humour . . .' National Film Theatre, August 1983.
p.103 'I couldn't sit . . .' *Holiday*, May 1958.
p.103 'Somebody told her . . .' *Cue*, November 1957.
p.104 'I thought the other actors . . .' *Newsweek*, March 1958.
p.104 'Scram! . . .' *ibid.*
p.105 'The brat stories . . .' Jules Dassin to the author.
p.105 'It's become a bore . . .' *Newsweek*, March 1958.
p.106 'Tony represents . . .' *ibid.*
p.106 'Mr Perkins was no Garrick . . .' John Mason Brown, *Two on the Aisle* (W.W. Norton and Co., 1938).
p.107 '*The Matchmaker* was a sad story . . .' *Newsweek*, March 1958.
p.109 'Whenever Tony and I . . .' *Newsweek*, March 1958.
p.112 'I have a friend . . .' *Premiere*, October 1993.

Chapter 10: Look Abroad and Homeward, Angel

p.114 'Would have a lengthy . . .' *New York Post*, October 1957.
p.116 'When things are really . . .' *Photoplay*, February 1958.
p.118 'When I see a group . . .' *Long Island Press*, October 1957.
p.120 'I was a kid . . .' *Time*, December 1957.
p.120 'It's a character . . .' *New York Herald-Tribune*, December 1957.
p.122 'Intellectual and exploratory . . .' *New York Times*, November 1972.

Chapter 11: Tall Stories

p.127 'They sent two doubles . . .' *New York Times*, July 1970.
p.128 'Tony had the smoothest . . .'Alan Helms to the author.
p.131 'Perkins was shy . . .'*Ava: My Story*, Bantam Press, 1990.
p.132 'A loner . . .' Stanley Kramer to the author.
p.133 'He was terribly . . .' *Saturday Evening Post* (July 1960).
p.134 'I didn't want too many . . .' Stanley Kramer to the author.
p.135 'Although Tony was delightful . . .' Joshua Logan, *Movie Stars, Real People and Me* (Delacorte, 1978)
p.137 'In a way it was touching . . .' Christopher Andersen, *Citizen Jane* (Virgin, 1990).

p.138 'Jane turned pale . . .' *ibid.*

p.138 'Jane Fonda wasn't naked . . .' National Film Theatre interview, August 1983.

p.138 'Timmy was a troubled guy. . .' Peter Collier, *The Fondas: A Hollywood Dynasty* (HarperCollins, 1991).

Chapter 12: Hot and Cold Running Blood

p.144 'Well, you're not going . . .' Stephen Rebello, *Alfred Hitchcock and the Making of Psycho* (Dembner Books, 1990).

p.144 'The minute you put a star . . .' *ibid.*

p.145 'I really couldn't get involved . . .' *ibid.*

p.145 'He always cast from seeing . . .' National Film Theatre interview (August 1983).

p.147 'I asked the question . . .' Stephen Rebello, *Alfred Hitchcock and the Making of Psycho* (Dembner Books, 1990).

p.148 'Tony was surprised . . .' *ibid.*

p.148 'He let me make several . . .' National Film Theatre interview, August 1983.

p.148 'It was clear . . .' *ibid.*

p.149 'Tony was and is . . .' Stephen Rebello, *Alfred Hitchcock and the Making of Psycho* (Dembner Books, 1990).

p.149 'I think Mr Hitchcock . . .' *ibid.*

p.149 'That was sweet of him . . .' National Film Theatre interview, August 1983.

p.150 'Hitchcock had decided . . .' Stephen Rebello, *Alfred Hitchcock and the Making of Psycho* (Dembner Books, 1990).

p.151 'Margo, because of . . .' *ibid.*

p.151 'The reason she was hired . . .' *ibid.*

p.156 'You can feel your loneliness . . .' *Premiere*, October 1993.

p.156 'My screen persona . . .' *Reflections on the Silver Screen*, radio interview with Richard Brown, 1993.

p.157 'It was a stormy afternoon . . .' National Film Theatre interview, August 1983.

p.157 'I remember my surprise . . .' Stephen Rebello, *Alfred Hitchcock and the Making of Psycho* (Dembner Books, 1990).

p.157 'Look, you're living . . .' *Interview*, September 1985.

p.158 'Norman appears on request . . .' National Film Theatre interview, August 1983.

Chapter 13: 'Never Will I Marry'

p.159 'In one way. . .' *New York Times*, February 1960.

p.159 'Frank brought the book . . .' *ibid.*

p.161 'Tony wanted me . . .' *ibid.*

p.161 'They had Anthony Perkins . . .' Susan Loesser, *A Most Remarkable Fella (Donald I. Fine Inc., 1993).*

p.161 'I thought the book . . .' *New York Times*, July 1970.

p.162 'That's your cue . . .' *New York Post*, June 1967.

p.165 'I waited for seven . . .'Alan Helms to the author.

p.165 'He would have been uncomfortable . . .' *ibid.*

p.165 'I didn't realize . . .' *ibid.*

p.166 'When the lights . . .' *ibid.*

p.166 'I visited . . .' *ibid.*

p.166 'I went down . . .' *ibid.*

p.167 'The last time . . .' *ibid.*

Chapter 14: Aimez-Vous Tony?

p.169 'So, you're Tony. . .' Laurence Leamer, *As Time Goes By* (Hamish Hamilton, 1982).

p.170 'It'll take time . . .' *ibid.*

p.171 'I took Anthony. . .' Ingrid Bergman, *My Story* (Michael Joseph, 1980).

p.173 'I felt somewhat betrayed . . .' *Films and Filming*, July 1965.

p.173 'When they started making . . .' *ibid.*

p.174 'I'm not really suited . . .' *New York Post*, March 1963.

Chapter 15: Oedipus At Home

p.177 'A friend answered . . .' Jules Dassin to the author.

p.179 'I think the picture . . .' *Films and Filming*, July 1965.

p.179 'He was cleverer . . .' Jules Dassin to the author.

p.180 'The car scene . . .' *Films and Filming*, July 1965.

p.180 'Tony was the worst . . .' Jules Dassin to the author.
p.180 'Making *Phaedra* . . .' *Hollywood Reporter*, July 1979.
p.180 'I would have liked . . .' Jules Dassin to the author.
p.181 'When I play opposite . . .' *Newark Evening News*, September 1964.

Chapter 16: Anthony P. and Joseph K.

p.184 'I did *The Trial* . . .' *New York Times*, September 1964.
p.185 'We discussed . . .' *Films and Filming*, July 1965.
p.185 'When we worked . . .' National Film Theatre interview, August 1983.
p.187 'The only thing . . .' *Films and Filming*, July 1965.
p.188 'We used to call . . .' *ibid.*
p.189 'We got up in our . . .' *Reflections on the Silver Screen*, radio interview with Richard Brown, 1993.
p.189 'He's extremely good . . .' National Film Theatre interview, August 1983.
p.189 'I don't think it's a successful . . .' *ibid.*

Chapter 17: The Two Masks

p.196 'Tony cared too much . . .' Alan Helms to the author.
p.196 'It was never much . . .' Jules Dassin to the author.
p.196 'He told me he had to hide . . .' Claude Chabrol to the author.
p.197 'I think and still . . .' *Boston Herald*, February 1963.
p.198 'Although I read it . . .' *Films and Filming*, July 1965.

Chapter 18: An American In Paris

p.202 'You have to make movies . . .' *Newark Evening News*, February 1964.
p.207 'We talked a little . . .' Claude Chabrol to the author.
p.207 'I thought we'd have some fun . . .' *ibid.*
p.208 'It was something . . .' *ibid.*

Chapter 19: Star-Spangled Tony

p.213 'When I asked . . .' *New York Times*, July 1970.

Chapter 20: Curiouser and Curiouser

p.219 'Tuesday and Tony . . .' Noel Black to the author.

p.220 'While I was looking . . .' *ibid.*

p.222 'He made a lot of people . . .' *Premiere*, October 1993.

p.223 'Like an Airedale . . .' *Observer*, July 1979.

p.223 'Where's your fucking . . .' Dodson Rader to the author.

p.224 'A quack shrink . . .' *ibid.*

p.224 'Looking for a heterosexual . . .' *Premiere* (October 1993).

p.224 'If you decide . . .' Mildred Newman and Bernard Berkovitch, *How To Be Your Own Best Friend* (Heinemann 1974).

p.226 'I was impressed . . .' Laura Kay Palmer, *Osgood and Anthony Perkins* (McFarland & Company, Inc., 1991).

p.227 'He was so agreeable . . .' National Film Theatre interview, August 1983.

p.229 'We walked around . . .' Curtis Harrington to the author.

p.229 'He had to be led . . .' *ibid.*

Chapter 21: God and Mammon

p.232 'I told them that I know . . .' Craig Zadan, *Sondheim & Co.* (Macmillan Publishing Co., Inc., 1974).

p.232 'For some reason . . .' *ibid.*

p.234 'Directing and acting . . .' *Interview*, November 1972.

p.236 'When I met David . . .' *Tennessee, Cry of the Heart* (Doubleday, 1985)

p.236 'We were both lovers . . .' Dodson Rader to the author.

p.236 'Finally, Tony . . .' *ibid.*

p.237 'I was awestruck . . .' Chris Makos to the author.

p.237 'I was too young . . .' *ibid.*

p.237 'He was like everyone . . .' *ibid.*

p.238 'We were going to film . . .' Claude Chabrol to the author.

p.238 'Still a little overawed . . .' *ibid.*

p.238 'Orson always wanted . . .' National Film Theatre interview, August 1983.

p.240 'One thing I saw . . .' Claude Chabrol to the author.

p.241 'I think I did him . . .' *ibid.*

p.242 'Nicolas, why did you . . .' Nicolas Gessner to the author.

p.243 'Tony and I . . .' *ibid.*

p.244 'I never had to . . .' *ibid.*

Chapter 22: Dump The Fags

p.246 'Everybody wanted to . . .' Lawrence Grobel, *The Hustons* (Bloomsbury, (1990) 1980).

p.246 'I didn't talk . . .' *ibid.*

p.247 'The greatest thing . . .' *Interview*, October 1972.

p.248 'Analysts once thought . . .' Mildred Newman and Bernard Berkovitch, *How To Be Your Own Best Friend* (Heinemann, 1974).

p.249 'The place was filled . . .' Dodson Rader to the author.

p.249 'When I was twelve . . .' *Interview*, November 1972.

p.251 'I really didn't want . . .' *Premiere*, October 1993.

p.251 'I thought she was cute . . .' *Mail on Sunday*, August 1983.

p.253 'We were sitting there . . .' *Premiere*, October 1993.

p.253 'What have I done? . . .' *Mail on Sunday*, August 1983.

Chapter 23: The Mating Game

p.255 'Steve started work . . .' Craig Zadan, *Sondheim & Co.* ((Macmillan Publishing Co., Inc., 1974).

p.255 'The writing took . . .' National Film Theatre interview, August 1983.

p.257'One of the things . . .' Craig Zadan, *Sondheim & Co.* ((Macmillan Publishing Co., Inc., 1974).

p.258 'Tony had the Olympian . . .' *Premiere*, October 1993.

p.260 'I found a number . . .' Dodson Rader to the author.

p.260 'All actors look for . . .' Chris Makos to the author.

p.260 'Tony was very crazy . . .' *ibid.*

p.261 'Tony was always looking . . .' Ben Bagley to the author.

p.262 'Tony was undoubtedly . . .' Ben Bagley to the author.

p.262 'Tony always talked . . .' Chris Makos to the author.

p.263 'A lot of people . . .' *ibid.*

p.263 'She was very innocent . . .' *Premiere*, October 1993.

p.263 'Berry had moved with . . .' Frank Rose to the author.

p.263 'Berry and he were like . . .' Noel Black to the author.

p.264 'Berry had great compassion . . .' Dodson Rader to the author.
p.265 'Will it make me . . .' *Premiere*, October 1993.
p.265 'Tony and Berry . . .' *ibid.*

Chapter 24: High and Low

p.270 'They try to get it right . . .' *Premiere*, October 1993.
p.271 'Okay, Diana . . .' Diana Ross, *Secrets of a Sparrow* (Headline, 1993).
p.272 'The atmosphere on the set . . .' Tony Richardson, *Long Distance Runner* (Faber & Faber, 1993).

Chapter 25: Horse Feathers

p.278 'Talk about family values . . .' *Premiere*, October 1993.
p.279 'He wanted to take care . . .' *ibid.*
p.279 'My brother and I . . .' *Hello Magazine*, December 1993.
p.280 'We were watching . . .' *Chelsea Clinton News* (May 1976).

Chapter 26: Mr, Mrs and Miz

p.281 'I had an appointment . . .' National Film Theatre interview, August 1983.
p.282 'Considering Berry . . .' *ibid.*

Chapter 27: Evil Days

p.288 'Most of the acting . . .' Mervin Griffin TV interview, October 1984.
p.291 'Seemed unable to establish . . .' *Premiere*, October 1993.
p.291 'It was almost like . . .' *ibid.*
p.293 'Where the good time . . .' *ibid.*
p.293 'It was as if she . . .' Dodson Rader to the author.

Chapter 28: Light Relief

p.296 '*Romantic Comedy* was good . . .' National Film Theatre interview, August 1983.
p.297 'He was angry . . .' *New York Times*, November 1992.

Chapter 29: The Bates Motel Revisited

p.303 'I spent about ten . . .' *L'Ecran Fantastique*, August 1983.
p.304 'I wanted to return . . .' National Film Theatre interview, August 1983.
p.305 'None could excel . . .' *ibid.*
p.306 'We needed something . . .' *ibid.*

Chapter 30: Judgement Days

p.314 'Very sensitively. . .' Mervin Griffin interview, October 1984.
p.314 'I hadn't thought of the demonic . . .' Brian Sandler to the author.
p.315 'A real prince . . .', *A British Picture* Ken Russell (Heinemann, 1989).
p.317 'When Tony's name . . .' Mike Ferguson to the author.
p.317 'I hated dubbing . . .' *Films and Filming*, July 1965.
p.318 'What surprised me . . .' Mike Ferguson to the author.
p.319 'Tony was very much . . .' *ibid.*

Chapter 31: Weird Directions

p.322 'I've never seen a dime . . .' *Reflections on the Silver Screen*, radio interview with Richard Brown, 1993.
p.323 'We were discussing . . .' *Cinéfantastique*, March 1986.
p.326 'It was really an excellent . . .' *Reflections on the Silver Screen*, radio interview with Richard Brown, 1993.
p.327 'Why can't I have . . .' Patrick Duynslaegher to the author.
p.327 'He was putting on . . .' *ibid.*
p.328 'Was standing downstairs . . .' Brian Baxter to the author.
p.333 'For us, Anthony Perkins . . .' *Hello Magazine*, December 1993.
p.334 'My first attempt . . .' *Reflections on the Silver Screen*, radio interview with Richard Brown, 1993.
p.334 'Cannibalism and incest . . .' *Cinéfantastique*, January 1989.

Chapter 32: Dr Perkins and Mr Bates

p.337 'I got them to find me . . .' *Washington Times*, May 1989.
p.344 'I immediately thought . . .' *Ciné-Revue*, April 1992.
p.346 'There was a sense of sadness . . .' John Mason Brown, *Two on the Aisle*

(W. W. Norton and Co. 1938).

End Game

p.350 'I was devastated . . .' *New York Times*, November 1992.

p.351 'He simply never wanted . . .' *ibid.*

p.351 'Anthony Perkins' reticence . . .' *San Francisco Chronicle*, September 1992.

p.352 'When Tony heard . . .' *New York Times*, November 1992.

p.352 'Apparently, Tony passed . . .' *San Francisco Chronicle*, September 1992.

p.352 'Tony worked without complaining . . .' *ibid.*

p.354 'He became very depressed . . .' *Premiere*, October 1993.

p.354 'Anthony Perkins was a star . . .' *Hello Magazine*, December 1993.

p.355 'I said to him . . .' *New York Times*, November 1992.

p.356 'For two weeks before . . .' *Premiere*, October 1993.

p.356 'He had fun watching . . .' *ibid.*

p.356 'He would say to me . . .' *ibid.*

p.358 'You know, twenty or thirty . . .' *Hello Magazine*, December 1993.

p.358 'The story of Tony . . .' *Premiere*, October 1993.

p.358 'We had a very satisfying life . . .' *ibid.*

INDEX